Comptroller's Handbook

Safety and Soundness

| Capital Adequacy (C) | Asset Quality (A) | Management (M) | Earnings (E) | Liquidity (L) | Sensitivity to Market Risk (S) | Other Activities (O) |

Mortgage Banking

February 2014

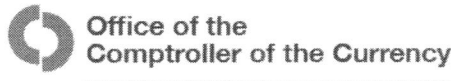

Office of the Comptroller of the Currency

Washington, DC 20219

Contents

Introduction

The Office of the Comptroller of the Currency's (OCC) *Comptroller's Handbook* booklet, "Mortgage Banking," provides guidance for bank examiners and bankers on various mortgage banking activities, such as the purchase or sale of mortgages in the secondary mortgage market. Throughout this booklet, national banks and federal savings associations (FSA) are referred to collectively as banks, except when it is necessary to distinguish between the two.

Background

Mortgage banking generally involves loan originations as well as purchases and sales of loans through the secondary mortgage market. A bank engaged in mortgage banking may retain or sell loans it originates or purchases from affiliates, brokers, or correspondents. The bank may also retain or sell the servicing on the loans. Through mortgage banking, banks can participate in any combination of these activities.

Banks have traditionally originated residential mortgage loans to hold in their loan portfolios. Examiners should refer to the "Retail Lending Examination Procedures" and the to-be-published "Residential Real Estate Lending" booklets of the *Comptroller's Handbook* for guidance on banks that primarily originate mortgage loans to be retained in their loan portfolios. More expansive mortgage banking activities are a natural extension of the traditional origination process. This booklet and the examination procedures it outlines are intended for banks that engage in purchases or sales of mortgages in the secondary market.

Mortgage banking is affected by changing economic conditions and new legislation, regulations, accounting principles, regulatory guidance, examination efforts, and legal actions. Numerous changes have addressed systemic issues revealed in the recent financial crisis, including deficiencies related to the origination and servicing of residential mortgage loans.

In 2010, Congress passed the Dodd–Frank Wall Street Reform and Consumer Protection Act (Dodd–Frank), which included a number of changes to consumer protection laws and created the Consumer Financial Protection Bureau (CFPB). The CFPB has undertaken various rulemakings to implement Dodd–Frank changes, including amending Regulation Z to implement changes to the Truth in Lending Act (TILA) and Regulation X to implement changes to the Real Estate Settlement Procedures Act (RESPA). For instance, in January 2013, the CFPB issued final rules amending Regulation X and Regulation Z to introduce new servicing-related standards and requirements. Other final rules further amend Regulation Z, including to require that creditors make a reasonable, good faith determination of a consumer's ability to repay any consumer credit transaction secured by a dwelling, to establish certain protections from liability for "qualified mortgages," and to implement changes to the requirements for certain home-secured loans. Many of these rules are expected to become effective in January 2014.[1]

The CFPB's rulemaking efforts, however, are ongoing. Bankers and examiners should ensure that the standards they follow are current. Examiners should contact the OCC's Credit and Market Risk Division to obtain information on recent developments that are not reflected in this booklet. In particular, the booklet does not attempt to address the specific requirements of the various rules issued by the CFPB implementing requirements of Dodd–Frank, including amendments to Regulation Z (implementing TILA), Regulation X (implementing RESPA), and servicing standards, which are effective January 2014. The safety and soundness principals discussed in this booklet are consistent with those rules. Compliance with these and other finalized rules, such as the Qualified Residential Mortgage Rule, is a basic tenet of a safe and sound mortgage operation.

The mortgage banking industry is highly competitive and involves many types of firms, including brokers, correspondents, mortgage banks, commercial banks, investment banks, and savings associations. Some of these firms are small and local, while others are large and national. Banks and their subsidiaries and affiliates make up a large and growing proportion of the mortgage banking industry. Banks that originate or purchase residential loans need to have sound third-party risk management practices.

Mortgage banking activities generate fee income and may provide cross-selling opportunities that can enhance a bank's retail banking franchise. The expansion of traditional lending to encompass other mortgage banking activities has taken place in the context of a general shift by commercial banks from activities that produce interest income to ones that produce noninterest income and fees.

Information technology (IT), including business processes, has evolved into an increasingly important support function that facilitates mortgage banking operations. Sophisticated origination and servicing systems, Web-based applications, the use of third parties to perform business processes, and complex valuation models are notable examples. The increased reliance on technology and its dependency on data and telecommunication infrastructures have led to an increased number of risks that must be managed appropriately.

Primary and Secondary Mortgage Markets

A mortgage lender's key function is to provide funds for the purchase or refinancing of residential properties. This function is carried out in the primary mortgage market, in which lenders originate mortgages by lending to homeowners and purchasers. In the secondary mortgage market, lenders and investors buy and sell loans that were originated in the primary mortgage market. Lenders and investors also buy and sell securities in the secondary market that are collateralized by pooled mortgage loans.

---

[1] More comprehensive information regarding Regulation X and Regulation Z, including recent amendments to those rules, is provided in other *Comptroller's Handbook* booklets, including "Truth in Lending Act" and "Real Estate Settlement Procedures Act" in the *Consumer Compliance* series.

Banks participate in the secondary market to gain flexibility in managing their long-term interest rate exposures, to increase liquidity, manage credit risk, and expand opportunities to earn fee income.

The secondary mortgage market is a result of various public policy measures and programs to promote homeownership that date back to the 1930s. Several government agencies and government-sponsored enterprises (GSE) have played important parts in fostering homeownership. The Federal Housing Administration (FHA), for example, encourages private mortgage lending by providing insurance against default. The Federal National Mortgage Association (Fannie Mae), the Federal Home Loan Mortgage Corporation (Freddie Mac), and the Federal Housing Agency provide market liquidity for conventional, FHA, and U.S. Department of Veterans Affairs (VA) mortgages by operating programs to purchase loans and convert them into securities to sell to investors. In addition, beginning in 1997, several Federal Home Loan Banks (FHLB) entered the mortgage loan purchase business.

Banks can sell loans directly to GSEs and private investors or they can convert loans into mortgage-backed securities (MBS). MBSs include pass-through securities, an arrangement in which undivided interests or participations in the pool are sold and the security holders receive pro rata shares of the resultant cash flows. Collateralized mortgage obligations (CMO) are another form of MBS. CMOs stratify credit and prepayment risk into tranches with various levels of risk and return for investors.

The mortgage industry continues to evolve, with new mortgage products being developed in both the conforming (eligible for sale to the GSEs) and nonconforming markets.

Fundamentals of Mortgage Banking

When a bank originates a mortgage loan, it creates two commodities: a loan and the right to service the loan. Banks can sell loans in the secondary market with servicing retained or released. Servicing is inherent in most lending assets; it becomes a distinct asset or liability only when contractually separated from the underlying lending assets or loans. A mortgage bank can separate servicing from a loan in two ways: (1) by selling a loan and retaining the servicing or (2) by separately purchasing or assuming the servicing of a loan from a third party.

Successful mortgage banking operations require effective management information systems (MIS) to accurately identify the value created and costs incurred to produce and service different mortgage products. The largest mortgage servicing firms invest heavily in technology to manage and process large volumes of individual mortgage loans with a variety of payment structures, escrow requirements, and investor disbursement schedules. These firms also operate sophisticated call centers to handle customer service, collections, default management, and foreclosure referrals. A highly developed technology infrastructure is a requisite for banks to effectively handle large and rapidly growing portfolios.

The benefits of economies of scale in loan production and servicing activities have led to greater industry consolidation. Given the cyclical nature of mortgage banking activities and industry consolidation trends, banks need to maximize efficiencies to compete effectively. Well-defined business processes combined with continuous improvements enable management to enhance operational effectiveness.

Common Mortgage Banking Structures

While a mortgage banking business is rather simple in theory, the combination of different types of operations and the various levels of risk make the review of each bank unique. Management can structure a bank to participate in one or several parts of the mortgage banking process. Examiners should expect management to have appropriately evaluated the bank's operation and risk profile to determine the relevant measurement criteria for its income and expenses.

Banks with similar operational profiles may have different goals. In all cases, management and the board should outline the strategies and goals of their mortgage banking operation. At the outset of a review, examiners should determine the type of mortgage banking operation in place and obtain management reports for monitoring mortgage banking activities.

Management's strategic planning process and business plan should address the activity, risk, and goals of the bank's operation. Management and the board should set reasonable limits, guidelines, and measurement standards for the bank's operation. This planning also should address strategies to deal with changes as the mortgage banking operation goes through business cycles. See appendix D for more details on mortgage banking structures.

Mortgage Banking Profitability

Overview

Mortgage banking is a cyclical business, and earnings can be volatile. Without proper management, a profitable mortgage banking operation can quickly generate substantial losses. Consistent profitability in mortgage banking requires a significant level of oversight by the board and senior management, and careful management of all mortgage banking activities. This section provides guidance for reviewing the earnings of a mortgage banking operation, and offers an overview of the components of mortgage banking profitability and how each component relates to the value of mortgage servicing rights (MSR).[2]

Mortgage Banking Earnings

Mortgage banking earnings can be volatile, and management must closely monitor the operation's performance. Unlike the revenue from many banks' operations, mortgage banking revenue consists primarily of gain on sale and mortgage servicing revenue.

---

[2] As defined in the "Glossary," mortgage servicing right (MSR) and mortgage servicing asset (MSA) are often used interchangeably. For purposes of this booklet, the tern MSR is used in the context of trading, profitability, hedging, and other general matters. MSA is applied to those discussions associated with the functional overview, examination procedures, and accounting practices.

A mortgage banking operation's income and expense components can change at significantly different rates and in different directions over time, resulting in substantial shifts in profitability. Each segment of a mortgage banking operation (originations, sales, and servicing) contributes to the operation's net earnings.

The potential for rapid changes in interest rates and mortgage volume creates a need for flexible, cost-efficient funding arrangements. The financing structure is largely dependent on the nature of the mortgage banking operation, typically balancing the need for flexibility with protection against interest rate changes. A bank can pay off short-term funding as origination volumes decline but remains highly susceptible to interest rate changes. Conversely, longer-term funding arrangements offer a fixed interest rate but create costs if volumes decline.

A bank's interest income and interest expense generally move in the same direction as rates change over time, depending on the repricing characteristics of the bank's assets and liabilities. By contrast, a mortgage bank's noninterest income and expense components can change at significantly different rates and directions. As a result, substantial shifts in profitability can occur very quickly.

The success of a mortgage banker's operations often depends on how effective the banker is at creating or acquiring the MSR and how the bank disposes of it (through sale or the operation of a servicing department). If the MSR is sold, the value is reflected in the gain on sale. If retained, the benefit to the bank is the value of the MSR relative to the cost of servicing it. The value of the MSR depends on the size and timing of the various costs and income streams associated with the entire servicing operation. To create the MSR, a mortgage bank

- originates or purchases a volume of loans at the smallest net cost possible, keeping production expenses in line with fee income received. Some mortgage bankers are willing to produce the loans slightly below targeted profitability levels to create the MSR value.
- elects to sell the loans servicing released or retained. If the loans are sold servicing released, the MSR value is reflected in the servicing release premium and in the increased gain on sale. If sold servicing retained, the MSR is recorded at fair value and affects the gain on sale.
- elects to acquire MSR directly from third parties. Some banks purchase bulk servicing pools or servicing through flow operations.
- develops a servicing operation that can economically execute the servicing operation.

Scalable Cost Structure

A bank generates small net gains or losses on numerous origination, sales, and servicing transactions. A bank's income fluctuates with production volume, and that volume generally changes with interest rates. Management should structure a mortgage banking operation so that expenses move in scale with volume. The scalable cost structure should work in both directions. To generate larger earnings when volumes surge, management must efficiently increase personnel, systems, funding, and facilities. Inefficient expansion of these cost centers reduces the profitability of the added volume. Conversely, management must be able to quickly reduce personnel, systems, funding, and facilities in response to declining volumes. When volumes decline, an inflexible mortgage banking operation can quickly shift from generating profits to producing losses.

Production Costs

Many mortgage bankers use wholesale production channels to expand their volume and keep their production costs scalable. By outsourcing some or all production, a substantial portion of the production costs per loan shifts from a fixed expense to a variable expense. While many of the costs are embedded in the prices paid for the loans, these costs are not incurred until the loans are purchased.

While this wholesale production strategy enables scalability for many of the production costs, there are several areas of production that are infrequently outsourced and less scalable. A core group of high-quality underwriting, closing, quality control, compliance, and other back-office personnel is essential to the viability of a mortgage banking operation. Management often retains these key production-based personnel, making their costs nearly fixed in nature. Outside the core group there is some scalability, though not as much as with the origination staff or in the servicing operation. A growing trend is the use of contract underwriters to respond to increased volumes and to manage expenses.

Many retail mortgage banking operations have large fixed costs in their branches, loan production offices, and MIS. When volumes decline, many of these costs remain the same. Excessive fixed costs, as volume slows, result in an increase in the cost per loan as production volumes decline. This can lead to significant declines in profitability or, in some cases, operating losses. Without scalability and careful management, retail mortgage banking production expenses can easily cause the entire mortgage banking operation to incur losses. Such a structure can put pressure on a bank to lower its underwriting standards as a way of maintaining volume.

Secondary Marketing

Secondary marketing expenses fall into two categories: (1) general and administrative (G&A) operating expenses and (2) hedging gains and losses. Most secondary marketing G&A costs are not scalable, but they can vary with the type of mortgage banking operation. Generally, larger operations carry higher fixed costs, because of expenses associated with the highly skilled personnel, advanced technology infrastructure (i.e., databases and reporting systems for document, warehouse, and pipeline management, and pricing, valuation, and hedging models), and professional service fees, such as legal and accounting. Conversely, smaller operations often use multifunctional secondary marketing staff, whose fixed G&A cost spreads over several areas. Some mortgage bankers also categorize these G&A expenses with production costs, leaving the other secondary marketing expenses free of personnel- and overhead-related cost distortions. See appendix B, "Hedging," and appendix C, "Mortgage Banking Accounting."

Another key secondary marketing expense is the hedging impact on the gain or loss on sale. Break-even secondary marketing transactions have become more common with the advent of available secondary marketing trading software. Unintended secondary marketing losses are usually the result of poor policies or procedures, speculation, inadequate MIS, or weak internal controls. Significant gains can be indicative of interest rate speculation, which may lead to comparable losses if rates move unfavorably.

Mortgage Loan Servicing

When a bank sells a loan to an investor, the bank may retain or sell the servicing of that loan. Servicing, or loan administration, consists of collecting the monthly payments from the borrower, forwarding the proceeds to the investors who purchased the loans, maintaining escrow accounts for the payment of taxes and insurance, and acting as the investor's representative for other issues and problems.

The loans serviced for others (LSFO) operation is one area where mortgage bankers leverage fixed cost structures to achieve economies of scale and greater efficiencies. Smaller servicing operations, however, often can achieve efficiencies similar to those of larger operations because of geographic advantages that allow them to incur lower personnel and facilities costs. A bank may also outsource servicing to another entity with a subservicing arrangement. The major drawbacks to outsourcing are that the MSR owner remains liable for the terms of the servicing contract but does not have direct control over the operation, and the bank loses direct contact with the customer. Strong oversight programs are required where critical business processes and technology are outsourced.

Historically, the direct expenses associated with the MSR have been minimal, while the operational function of servicing loans owned by other investors has been one of the most scalable management expenses in mortgage banking. Going forward, there should be some expectation of increased costs due to the need for servicers to have more robust foreclosure policies and procedures, staffing, management of third-party service providers, compliance with applicable laws (including new regulations related to loan servicing), loss mitigation strategies, document control processes, and quality control. Because the volume of loans in a servicing portfolio can be large, the resulting staff, servicing facilities, and MIS required to process the LSFO can be substantial.

Business-Line Profitability Reporting

As indicated above, a mortgage banker strives to generate small returns on a very large number of loan transactions. Each transaction takes several steps to complete. The amounts of fee income and other noninterest income received in the different segments of a mortgage banking operation are predominately set by the marketplace and competition, so profitable operations depend on controlling expenses. To effectively monitor and manage the profitability of a mortgage banking operation, management should develop a cost center reporting system that aggregates the individual components of the mortgage banking operation. A mortgage banker's income and expense change at different rates over time and through volume fluctuations. Because of this variation, the only way to accurately identify if costs are in line with production is by implementing a cost accounting reporting system.

An effective system breaks out information for key income and expense metrics in a particular segment of a mortgage banking operation, while also maintaining a perspective on the whole operation. A common name for this type of cost center reporting is business-line profitability reporting. Though the specifics vary, each cost center or segment report should include line items for all major income sources, funding costs, personnel, G&A, facilities, and MIS expenses, plus any provisions for reserves.

A business-line profitability reporting system can separate the mortgage banking operation's results from those of the rest of the bank to facilitate transparency. The bank may already be divided along other key business lines (e.g., retail banking, commercial lending, or wholesale investment and funding). In addition to reporting the financial results of the entire mortgage banking operation as a whole, these types of reporting systems provide management with

- the income and expense components for each operating segment.
- key income and expense amounts on a per-loan or per-full-time-equivalent basis, not just on a total-dollar basis per line item.
- comparisons of the bank's results with industry metrics appropriate for each segment.

In the past, standard operating segment breakouts in a business-line profitability reporting system only included production, secondary marketing, and servicing. Given the complexity and competitiveness of mortgage banking, however, a more detailed stratification of the segment subcomponents is common. Production can be stratified by source into retail, wholesale (broker or correspondent), Internet, or other categories. Similarly, risk management reporting should be stratified by segment.

Likewise, stratification by subcomponents within secondary marketing is useful. Management may separate such areas as derivative recognition, the impact of hedging, the impact of recourse and indemnification, and different timings of gain- and loss-on-sale recognition. For servicing, any MSR valuation changes and any associated hedging activities should be reported separately. The servicing operation can be stratified into the major portfolio types. Expense-sharing reports between a parent company and a subsidiary or holding company affiliate are a different monitoring tool and should not be confused with a business-line profitability reporting system. Similarly, quarterly MSR valuation reports are not a business-line profitability reporting system.

Statutory and Regulatory Authority

12 USC 371 provides the statutory authority for a national bank to engage in mortgage banking activities and permits national banks to make, arrange, purchase, or sell loans or extensions of credit secured by liens or interests in real estate. 12 CFR 34 clarifies the types of collateral that qualify as real estate and sets forth other real estate lending standards.

12 USC 1464 provides the statutory authority for an FSA to engage in mortgage banking activities and permits FSAs to invest in, sell, or otherwise deal in residential real property loans and loans secured by nonresidential real property. 12 CFR 160 clarifies the types of collateral that qualify as real estate and sets forth other real estate lending standards.

Preemption and Visitorial Powers

In 2004, the OCC issued two final rules concerning preemption and visitorial powers. These new regulations were intended to clarify the authority of national banks to operate under uniform federal standards and federal supervision.[3] The visitorial powers rules implemented the visitorial powers statute, 12 USC 484.

In 2011, the OCC revised these rules[4] to implement the preemption and visitorial powers provisions of Dodd–Frank. These revisions

- eliminate preemption for national bank operating subsidiaries.
- apply national bank and national bank subsidiary preemption standards, as well as the visitorial powers standards applicable to national banks, FSAs, and each of their subsidiaries.
- revise the OCC's visitorial powers rule to conform to the holding of the Supreme Court's decision in *Cuomo* v. *Clearing House Association, LLC*, recognizing the ability of state attorneys general to bring enforcement actions in court to enforce non-preempted state laws against national banks.
- remove language from OCC rules that provides that state laws that "obstruct, impair, or condition" a national bank's powers are preempted.

The revised preemption rules are codified at 12 CFR 7.4007, 7.4008, 34.3, 34.4, and 34.6. The revised visitorial powers rules are codified at 12 CFR 7.4000.

---

[3] See 69 *Fed. Reg.* 1904 (January 13, 2004) (final preemption rule) and 69 *Fed. Reg.* 1895 (January 13, 2004) (final visitorial powers amendments).

[4] 76 *Fed. Reg.* 43549 (July 21, 2011).

Capital Requirements

Banks that engage in mortgage banking activities must comply with the OCC's risk-based capital and leverage ratio requirements that apply to those activities. (For a more complete discussion of OCC capital requirements, see the call report instructions for risk-based capital.)

In addition to the OCC's requirements, Freddie Mac, Fannie Mae, the Government National Mortgage Association (Ginnie Mae), and FHLBs require banks, nonbanks, and individuals conducting business with them to maintain a minimum level of capital. Failure to satisfy any agency's minimum capital requirement may result in the bank losing the right to securitize, sell, and service mortgages for that agency. Because the capital requirements are different for each agency, examiners should determine whether the bank or its mortgage banking subsidiary meets the capital requirements of each agency with which it has a relationship.

Risks Associated With Mortgage Banking

From a supervisory perspective, risk is the potential that events, expected or unexpected, will have an adverse effect on a bank's earnings, capital, or franchise or enterprise value. The OCC has defined eight categories of risk for bank supervision purposes: credit, interest rate, liquidity, price, operational, compliance, strategic, and reputation. These categories are not mutually exclusive. Any product or service may expose a bank to multiple risks. Risks also may be interdependent and may be positively or negatively correlated. Examiners should be aware of this interdependence and assess the effect in a consistent and inclusive manner. Refer to the "Bank Supervision Process" booklet of the *Comptroller's Handbook* for an expanded discussion of banking risks and their definitions.

All eight risks are associated with mortgage banking. These risks are discussed more fully in the following paragraphs.

Credit Risk

In mortgage banking, credit risk arises in a number of ways. For example, if the quality of loans originated or serviced deteriorates, the bank is not able to sell the loans at prevailing market prices. Purchasers of these assets discount their bid prices or avoid acquisition if credit problems exist. Poor credit quality can also result in the loss of favorable terms or the possible cancellation of contracts with secondary market agencies or private investors.

For banks that service loans for others, credit risk directly affects the market value and profitability of a bank's mortgage servicing portfolio. Most servicing agreements require servicers to remit principal and interest payments to investors and keep property taxes and hazard insurance premiums current even when the servicer has not received payments from past-due borrowers. These agreements also require the bank to undertake costly collection efforts, which may not be fully reimbursable to the servicing bank. Servicing costs may rise on lower-quality loans due to the increased collection and administrative activities required.

A bank is also exposed to credit risk when it services loans for investors on a contractual recourse basis and retains risk of loss arising from borrower default. When a customer defaults on a loan under a recourse arrangement, the bank is typically responsible for all credit loss because it must repurchase the loan serviced.

A related form of credit risk involves concentration risk. This risk can arise if exposures are concentrated within a geographic region, borrower segment, or product type. For example, concentration risk can occur if a servicing portfolio is composed of loans in a geographic area that is experiencing an economic downturn, or if a portfolio is composed of nontraditional or subprime product types.

Credit risk can exist even if the loan and servicing have been sold. For example, loans sold on a servicing-released basis can be subject to repurchase or put-back provisions under early payment default provisions. If a bank repurchases a loan, the bank most likely has to reimburse the purchaser for the remaining par value of the loan as well as for the value of the servicing asset.

A bank can be exposed to counterparty credit risk if a counterparty fails to meet its obligation. Counterparties associated with mortgage banking activities include broker-dealers, correspondent lenders, private mortgage insurers, vendors, sub-servicers, and loan closing agents. If a counterparty becomes financially unstable or experiences operational difficulties, the bank may be unable to collect receivables owed, or may be forced to seek services elsewhere. Therefore, a bank should regularly monitor counterparties' actions and perform appropriate analysis of financial stability.

Interest Rate Risk

The assessment of interest rate risk should consider the impact of complex, illiquid hedging strategies or products, and also the potential impact on fee income that is sensitive to changes in interest rates. Accordingly, effective risk management practices and oversight by an asset and liability committee or similar panel are essential elements of a well-managed mortgage banking operation. These practices are described in this booklet's "Management and Supervision" section.

Rising interest rates can reduce homebuyers' willingness or ability to finance a real estate loan. Higher rates may adversely affect the volume of loan originations and can negatively affect profitability. Rising interest rates, however, and the accompanying lower prepayments can increase servicing income and the value of the mortgage servicing assets (MSA) portfolio.

MSAs exhibit what is referred to as negative convexity, meaning that the value of an MSA does not move in a linear relationship with interest rate changes. When interest rates fall, prepayment speeds increase, causing a decline in MSA values. When rates rise, MSA values do not increase as much as they decline when rates fall (asymmetrical effect). The effect of changes in interest rates on the fair value and market price of MSAs depends on both the severity of rate movements and the asymmetrical nature of MSA value changes.

Falling interest rates and mortgage refinancing can subject the selling bank to premium recapture. The selling bank may have to forfeit premiums received from the sale of loans that refinance within a defined period (as described in the investor agreement).

Liquidity Risk

In mortgage banking, credit and operational risk weaknesses can cause liquidity problems if the bank fails to underwrite or service loans in accordance with investors' or insurers' requirements. As a result, the bank may not be able to sell mortgage inventory or servicing rights. Additionally, the investor may require the bank to indemnify or repurchase loans that were inappropriately underwritten or serviced. Servicers face increased liquidity risk from elevated levels of defaulted loans that require continued remittance of principal and interest to investors during the liquidation process of properties where the loan has gone into default.

Failure to appropriately manage the liquidation process can result in delayed or denied reimbursement from the insuring agency.

Price Risk

Price risk focuses on the changes in market factors (e.g., interest rates, market liquidity, and volatility) that affect the value of traded instruments. Changes in interest rates can affect the value of warehouse loans and pipeline commitments and cause market losses if not adequately hedged. The risk that changes in interest rates will lower the fair value of MSAs is normally considered interest rate risk. It could be considered price risk, however, if the bank is actively buying and selling its MSAs.

Falling interest rates may cause borrowers to seek more favorable terms and withdraw loan applications before the loans close. If customers do not close on their loan applications, commonly known as fallout, a bank may be unable to originate enough loans to meet its mandatory forward sales commitments. Because of "fallout," a bank may have to purchase additional loans in the secondary market at higher prices. Alternatively, a bank may choose to terminate its sales commitment to deliver mortgages by paying a fee to the counterparty, commonly known as a pair-off arrangement. Rising rates may result in more loans closing at a below-market rate without sufficient pipeline hedge protection. These loans typically are sold at a loss. Rate volatility can produce significant risk when pipeline managers take inappropriate risk positions based on their biased view of future rates. For definitions of pair-off arrangements and pair-off fees, see the "Glossary" and appendix B, "Hedging."

Operational Risk

The volume, cyclical nature, and complexity of the mortgage banking business can strain the capacity of operating systems, processes, and personnel. Operational risk is a function of the internal controls, information systems, employee capability and integrity, and operating processes involved in the mortgage banking operation.

To be successful, a mortgage banking operation should be able to originate, sell, service, and process payments on large volumes of loans efficiently. Any of the functions of a successful mortgage banking operation may be performed internally or contracted out to a third party.[5] Management should be diligent in its oversight of third-party providers through initial due diligence, appropriate counterparty risk reviews, comprehensive contract requirements, customer complaint reviews, and sufficient business continuity planning for third-party replacement. Operational risks that are not controlled can cause the bank substantial losses.

If reviews by investors indicate that a loan was not properly underwritten, a bank may have to repurchase the loan or indemnify the investors against losses. To manage operational risk, a mortgage banking company should employ competent management and staff, maintain effective operating systems and internal controls, and use comprehensive MIS. Back-office

---

[5] See OCC Bulletin 2013-29, "Third-Party Relationships: Risk Management Guidance."

processing functions are vulnerable to inadequate or poorly trained staff and ineffective processes or workflows.

Excessive levels of missing collateral documents are another source of operational risk that can impair asset quality, collectability, and marketability. Management should establish and maintain control systems that properly identify and manage this risk. If the bank has a large number of loans with missing documents, these loans may have to be sold at a discount.

Mortgage servicers are exposed to considerable operational risk when they manage escrow accounts, reset payments, process payments, and perform document custodian activities. As the escrow account administrator, the servicer must collect and protect borrowers' funds and make timely payments on their behalf to taxing authorities, various insurance providers, and other parties. The servicer also must ensure that escrow accounts are administered within legal constraints and investor guidelines. Nontraditional mortgage products can present unique payment processing challenges. The bank must ensure that payments and payment adjustments are properly recorded, especially with varying monthly payment options on nontraditional mortgages. As document custodian, the bank must obtain, track, and provide safekeeping of original loan documents for investors.

To limit operational risk, a bank's information and record-keeping systems must be able to accurately and efficiently process large volumes of data. IT can affect both the quantity and quality of operational risk. Because of the large number of documents involved and the high volume of transactions, detailed subsidiary ledgers must support all general ledger accounts. Similarly, management should ensure that accounts are reconciled at least monthly and are supported by effective supervisory controls.

The best reconcilement processes are automated and performed at the transaction level rather than by aggregate totals. Automated reconcilement processes can facilitate increased volumes and provide detailed management information. Reconciliations are a key control to effectively manage origination, secondary marketing, and servicing operations. High-volume periods can give rise to reconcilement difficulties, untimely reconcilements, unreconciled accounts, and a high volume of aged items that require writeoff. Mortgage banking operations are especially vulnerable to these problems when manually intensive processes cannot easily cope with increased volume.

Institutional operational inflexibility arises when resources devoted to mortgage origination or servicing cannot be easily changed during cyclical up- or downturns in those operations. It also arises when banks have long-term fixed-rate cost commitments in facilities and personnel that cannot be reduced in periods of lower production volume. Changes in laws and regulations often cause needed adjustments to processes and procedures. As such, banks may experience difficulties institutionalizing regulatory modifications in an efficient and cost-effective manner.

Compliance Risk

Banks should ensure that consumers have clear and balanced information about mortgages, including nontraditional and subprime mortgage products, before making a mortgage product choice. The bank must also ensure that its representatives or agencies do not improperly steer the consumer to any particular mortgage product. Promotional materials, sales representations, and other product descriptions should provide consumers with information about the cost, terms, features, and risks of mortgage products that can assist consumers in their product selection decisions. Where applicable, these materials should include information about potential payment shock, negative amortization, prepayment penalties, and balloon payments.

A bank or bank operating subsidiary that originates or services mortgages is responsible for complying with applicable federal and state laws. There are a number of federal consumer protection laws and associated regulations that apply to the real estate lending activities of banks and their operating subsidiaries or service corporations, including, but not limited to, the following:[6]

- Bank Secrecy Act (BSA)
- Community Reinvestment Act
- Dodd–Frank (Title IX, Subtitle D)
- Equal Credit Opportunity Act (ECOA)
- Fair Credit Reporting Act (FCRA), as amended by the Fair and Accurate Transactions Act
- Fair Debt Collection Practices Act
- Fair Housing Act
- Fair Housing Home Loan Data System
- Federal privacy laws, including provision of Gramm–Leach–Bliley Act
- Federal Trade Commission Act (FTC Act), section 5
- Flood Disaster Protection Act[7]
- Home Mortgage Disclosure Act (HMDA)
- Home Ownership and Equity Protection Act (HOEPA)
- Homeowners Protection Act of 1998 (HPA)
- Homeownership counseling requirements under the Housing and Urban Development Act of 1968, as amended
- Protecting Tenants in Foreclosure Act of 2009
- RESPA
- Servicemembers Civil Relief Act (SCRA)
- TILA

---

[6] Other *Comptroller Handbook* booklets address these laws and regulations more fully. Please refer to the relevant *Consumer Compliance* booklet for each of these laws and regulations, which include updated information and complete examination procedures.

[7] And amendments created by the Biggert Waters Flood Insurance Reform Act of 2012.

- OCC rules, including the anti-predatory-lending rules in 12 CFR 7, 12 CFR 34, and 12 CFR 160.110
- Standards for national banks' residential mortgage lending practices in appendix C to 12 CFR 30 and 12 CFR 160
- Rules for the sale of debt cancellation and suspension agreements, 12 CFR 37 and 12 USC 1461 et seq
- SAFE Mortgage Licensing Act

Dodd–Frank[8] amended several of these statutes, including RESPA and TILA, and the CFPB has issued significant amendments to the implementing regulations, Regulation X and Z, respectively. In particular, these new amendments to Regulation X and Regulation Z include new requirements relevant to the loan production and servicing functions, some of which are discussed below.

Additionally, banks should be aware of applicable OCC guidance, including but not limited to guidance on nontraditional mortgage product risks, subprime mortgage lending, and working with mortgage borrowers.

Failure to comply with these consumer protection laws can have far-reaching effects, including possible losses from litigation and administrative actions. For instance, failure to comply with disclosure requirements, such as those imposed under TILA, could subject the bank to civil money penalties or make it a target of class-action litigation.

Fair Lending

Mortgage banking operation managers must be aware of fair lending requirements and implement effective procedures and controls to help them identify practices that could result in discriminatory treatment of any class of borrowers. For example, discretionary pricing that is not properly controlled may increase fair lending risk. For a more complete discussion of fair lending, see the "Fair Lending" booklet of the *Comptroller's Handbook*.

Predatory and Abusive Lending

The concept of predatory lending has gained much publicity in recent years, although there is no single, generally accepted legal definition of a "predatory loan." HOEPA covers mortgage loans with relatively high interest rates and fees, as specified in the implementing regulation, Regulation Z (12 CFR 1026), and imposes on them a range of additional consumer protections. Additionally, Regulation Z imposes specific rules and restrictions on "higher-priced" mortgage loans, which have interest rates and fees that are above the prime rate but are not as high as the HOEPA-related rates and fees. More generally, the CFPB's 2012 rulemakings amending Regulation X and Regulation Z to implement various Dodd–Frank amendments to TILA and HOEPA include additional consumer protections. The term

---

[8] Dodd–Frank also specifies that the banking agencies develop rules requiring securitizers to retain an economic interest in loans that do not meet qualified residential mortgage standards.

"predatory" in its general use, however, refers to a wide range of practices. Banks must have systems in place to monitor and prevent predatory lending.

The OCC has issued specific guidance relating to preventing predatory and abusive lending practices, including the following:

- OCC guidelines establishing standards for national banks' residential mortgage lending practices in 12 CFR 30, appendix C[9]
- Standards on unfair and deceptive practices on preventing predatory and abusive practices in direct lending, brokered, and purchased loan transactions (Advisory Letter 2003-2, "Guidelines for National Banks to Guard Against Predatory and Abusive Lending Practices")
- Guidance on nontraditional mortgage product risks (OCC Bulletin 2006-41, "Guidance on Nontraditional Mortgage Product Risks")
- Guidance on subprime mortgage lending (OCC Bulletin 2007-26, "Subprime Mortgage Lending: Statement on Subprime Mortgage Lending")
- OCC rules, including the anti-predatory lending rules for national banks in 12 CFR 7 and 12 CFR 34 (national banks)
- Rules for the sale of debt cancellation and suspension agreements by national banks, 12 CFR 37[10]

Strategic Risk

In mortgage banking, inadequate strategic risk management practices can expose the bank to financial losses caused by changes in the quantity or quality of products, management supervision, hedging decisions, acquisitions, competition, and technology. If these risks are not adequately understood, measured, monitored, and controlled, they may result in high earnings volatility.

Management should understand the economic dynamics and market conditions of the industry in order to limit strategic risk. This includes understanding the cost structure and profitability of each major segment of mortgage banking operations to ensure that initiatives are based on sound information. Management should consider this information before offering new products and services, such as nontraditional mortgage products; altering pricing strategies; undertaking growth initiatives; or pursuing acquisitions. Management should ensure a proper balance between the mortgage bank's risk appetite and its supporting resources and controls. The management structure and talent of the organization should adequately support the bank's strategies and degree of innovation.

---

[9] For FSAs, the parameters set forth in 12 CFR 30 should be considered.

[10] Although there is no corresponding regulation for FSAs, the parameters set forth in 12 CFR 37 should be considered.

Reputation Risk

An operational breakdown or general weakness in any part of a bank's mortgage banking activities can harm the bank's reputation. For example, a mortgage bank that services loans for third-party investors bears operational and administrative responsibilities to act prudently on behalf of investors and borrowers. Without appropriate controls and monitoring systems, misrepresentations, breaches of duty, administrative lapses, errors in payment collection and processing, disclosure of confidential customer information, and conflicts of interest may occur. Any of these operational breakdowns can result in loss of business, lawsuits, financial loss, or damage to the bank's reputation.

Banks that engage in discriminatory or predatory practices, or that otherwise fail to comply with applicable consumer laws and regulations, expose themselves to significant reputation risk. Claims of unfair or deceptive lending practices may attract unwanted publicity, customer complaints, or litigation, even if third parties absorb the credit exposure. Loan sales and securitization of nontraditional or subprime mortgage loans may increase reputation risk if borrowers or investors do not understand the risks of these loans.

Banks that originate and sell loans into the secondary market must follow effective underwriting and documentation standards to protect their reputations in the market and to support future loan sales. When a significant number of loans in an investment pool go into default, the secondary market can develop concerns about all loans originated by that bank. These defaults can negatively affect the bank's ability to sell new loans on the secondary market.

Similarly, improperly executed foreclosures can be a violation of state and federal laws and ultimately have an adverse effect on a bank's reputation. Banks typically face negative publicity over foreclosure actions regardless of whether the bank made the loan or is currently servicing the loan. A large number of foreclosures, even if properly executed, can also adversely affect a bank's reputation and servicing rating by a rating agency.

Risk Management

The OCC expects each bank to identify, measure, monitor, and control risk by implementing an effective risk management system appropriate for its size and the complexity of its operations. When examiners assess the effectiveness of a bank's risk management system, they consider the bank's policies, processes, personnel, and control systems. Refer to the "Bank Supervision Process" booklet of the *Comptroller's Handbook* for an expanded discussion of risk management.

Management and Supervision

The success of a mortgage banking enterprise depends on a clearly articulated risk appetite and effective risk management systems, including proper corporate governance, effective policies, strong internal controls, effective compliance management processes, relevant strategic plans, and comprehensive MIS. Management of mortgage banking risks should be integrated into the bank's overall risk management framework. Weaknesses in any of these critical areas could diminish the bank's ability to respond quickly to changing market conditions and could jeopardize the bank's financial condition.

Proper corporate governance is critical to the safety and soundness of a bank's mortgage banking and mortgage servicing business. Appropriate organizational structure, communication, and reporting are key aspects that determine the effectiveness of a bank's corporate governance. Segregation of duties is an important feature of both corporate governance and internal control.

Effective policies are needed in mortgage banking to govern numerous and interdependent activities that pose significant risks. Effective policies help ensure that the bank benefits through efficiencies gained from standard operating procedures. Policies should ensure that appropriate accounting procedures for the bank's mortgage banking activities are followed and that associated interest rate risk and price risk exposures are monitored and controlled.

Policies should provide mortgage banking personnel with a consistent message that appropriate underwriting standards, compliance with all applicable laws and regulations, including fair lending and anti-predatory laws and regulations, and complete and accurate documentation are necessary to ensure that loans meet investor requirements for sale into the secondary market. Similarly, policies should provide clear guidance on loss mitigation and foreclosure activities to ensure compliance with all applicable federal and state laws, regulations, and documentation requirements. Compensation programs and practices must comply with applicable laws, regulations, and internal standards designed to mitigate risk, and should reward qualitative factors, not just the quantity of loans originated.

Strong internal controls are essential to effective management supervision. For a more complete discussion of internal controls, see the "Internal Control" booklet of the *Comptroller's Handbook*. The board of directors and senior management should define the mortgage banking operation's permissible activities, lines of authority, operational responsibilities, and acceptable risk levels.

Strategic plans should be based on management's assessment of current and prospective market conditions and industry competition. Management should ensure that sufficient long-term resource commitments exist to endure the cyclical downturns normal to this industry. In the strategic plan, outsourcing should be anticipated and clearly enumerated, with definitive policies documented by management. If the company intends to be a niche player, management should clearly delineate its targeted market segment and develop appropriate business strategies. Additionally, detailed contingency plans should be in place to manage increases in originations and servicing activity.

A mortgage banking operation's business plan should include specific financial objectives. The plan should be consistent with the bank's overall strategic plan and should describe strategies that management intends to pursue when acquiring, selling, and servicing mortgage banking assets. The plan should also provide for adequate financial, human, technological, and physical resources to support the operation's activities.

The strategic planning process should include an assessment of the servicing time necessary to recapture production costs and achieve required returns. An understanding of this basic information is also critical to decisions to purchase servicing rights, and should be incorporated into servicing asset hedging strategies.

Comprehensive MIS is essential to a successful mortgage banking operation. MIS should provide accurate, up-to-date information on all functional areas and support the preparation of accurate financial statements. MIS reports should facilitate identification and evaluation of operating results and monitoring of primary sources of risk. Management also should establish and maintain systems for monitoring compliance with laws, regulations, other legal obligations, and investor requirements.

Internal and External Audits

Because of the variety of risks inherent in mortgage banking activities, internal audit coverage should include an evaluation of all the risks and controls in the bank's mortgage banking operations. The scope and frequency of these audits should be based on the risk of associated controls and activities for the bank. Audits should assess strategic business risks and the overall risk management framework, including compliance with bank policies or approved practices, limits, investor criteria, federal and state laws, and regulatory issuances and guidelines. Internal audit staff should be independent and knowledgeable about mortgage banking activities. Staff should report audit findings, including identified control weaknesses, directly to the board or the audit committee. See the "Internal and External Audits" booklet of the *Comptroller's Handbook*.

The board and management should ensure that the internal audit staff has the necessary qualifications and expertise to review mortgage banking activities, including all related IT environments, or should mitigate voids with qualified external sources.

Corporate failures resulted in Congress enacting the Public Company Accounting Reform and Investor Protection Act of 2002 (the Sarbanes–Oxley Act of 2002). This law, along with its implementing rules issued by the U.S. Securities and Exchange Commission (SEC), renewed the emphasis on sound corporate governance. The OCC and the Federal Reserve Board conveyed their expectations for sound corporate governance in an interagency advisory issued May 6, 2003 (OCC Bulletin 2003-21, "Application of Recent Corporate Governance Initiatives to Non-Public Banking Organizations"), and the Federal Deposit Insurance Corporation (FDIC) issued separate guidance in FIL-17-2003. Examiners should refer to these issuances for general guidance on corporate governance.

Information Technology

Mortgage banking is highly technology dependent. From the time of the loan application through the remaining life of the loan, technology plays a key role in operations, risk management, and regulatory reporting. IT and the IT infrastructure allow bankers to leverage resources and increase both operational and financial efficiency. Additionally, a strong IT culture is needed for high-volume banks and for banks that sell to the secondary and private markets, because of the high level of MIS and reporting for both investor and regulatory requirements.

Assessment of IT systems within mortgage banks should include an assessment of the capability of the IT systems to support operational, risk management, and risk control functions within a mortgage banking operation. The assessment also should consider continuity planning for IT as well as overall resiliency of business processes. IT systems should be compatible and able to process the high volume of data generated during the life of a mortgage loan.

Mortgage Banking Functional Areas

Mortgage banking involves four major activities. The bank or mortgage banking company may perform one or more of the following activities in separate departments:

- **Loan production:** This unit originates, processes, underwrites, and closes mortgage loans.
- **Secondary marketing:** This unit develops, prices, and sells loan products and delivers loans to investors. The unit also manages price risk from loan commitments in the pipeline and loans held-for-sale in the warehouse.
- **Servicing (sometimes referred to as loan administration):** This unit collects monthly payments from borrowers; remits payments to the investor or security holder; handles contacts with borrowers about delinquencies, assumptions, escrow accounts, loss mitigation activities, and other customer service activities; and pays real estate taxes and insurance premiums. Foreclosure and liquidation processes may also reside within this unit.
- **MSA:** This unit manages servicing assets' valuation and hedging. MSAs are complex, interest-sensitive assets that arise from owning the right to service mortgage loans that have been sold or securitized in the secondary market.

Loan Production

Loan production activities should be governed by policies and procedures to ensure effective practices and processes. These policies should address

- types of mortgage loans the bank originates or purchases.
- risk layering.
- sources from which the loans are acquired.
- banks acting as broker or agent.
- appraisal and evaluation functions.
- production processes (origination, processing, underwriting, closing).
- portfolio management.
- production quality control.

Types of Mortgage Loans

Mortgage banking operations deal primarily with two types of mortgage loans: government loans and conventional loans.

Government loans are insured by the FHA for credit losses, and the respective servicers' activities are guaranteed by Ginnie Mae. These loans are bound by maximum mortgage amounts and strict underwriting standards. These mortgages are commonly sold into pools that back Ginnie Mae securities.

Conventional loans are not insured or guaranteed by the U.S. government. Conventional loans are further divided into conforming and nonconforming mortgages. Conforming loans may be sold to Freddie Mac, Fannie Mae, or GSEs. Many of these loans are then securitized, packaged, and sold to investors in the secondary market. Conforming loans must comply with GSE loan size limits, terms, amortization periods, and underwriting guidelines.

Nonconforming mortgages do not meet the standards of eligibility for purchase or securitization by the GSEs. Nonconforming loans may include jumbo, Alt-A, A-minus, or subprime loans. Jumbo loans exceed the GSE maximum loan purchase amount. Unlike A loans, Alt-A loans may have limited or reduced income or asset documentation, or may be secured by alternate property types (e.g., investor property or a second home). A-minus loans generally have a credit profile between A and subprime loans. Subprime[11] (or nonprime) loans are loans whose borrowers exhibit weakened credit histories, reduced repayment capacity, or incomplete credit histories. Many banks differentiate the quality of loans by credit scoring models.

Effective in January 2014, the CFPB's 2012 Regulation Z rules generally require mortgage lenders to consider and verify a consumer's ability to repay a mortgage before extending

---

[11] In addition to other requirements, including new Regulation Z rules requiring consideration of consumers' ability to repay the mortgage, banks are expected to comply with the interagency "Statement on Subprime Mortgage Lending" for certain ARM products offered to subprime borrowers (OCC Bulletin 2007-26).

credit. A component of these rules is a category of residential mortgages called qualified mortgages. The requirements for a qualified mortgage include prohibitions on certain product features (e.g., negative amortization and interest-only payments) and limitations on points and fees paid by consumers as well as prepayment penalties. The rules also set forth certain presumptions that qualified mortgages satisfy the ability-to-repay requirements.

Conventional (conforming and nonconforming) loans can include traditional and nontraditional mortgage products.

Traditional Mortgage Products

Traditional mortgage loans are commonly considered to include amortizing fixed-rate mortgages, adjustable rate mortgages (ARM), hybrid ARMs, and balloon mortgages. These products do not normally allow borrowers to contractually defer payment of principal and interest.
Fixed-rate mortgages allow borrowers to amortize payments over a predetermined number of years, usually 15, 20, or 30, and sometimes 40. The principal and interest payment is fixed throughout the term of the loan.

ARMs have interest rates that change over the life of the loan, based on market conditions. Conventional ARMs have interest rates that adjust periodically based on a published index rate, e.g., prime rate, London interbank offered rate (LIBOR), monthly Treasury average, or a cost of funds index. Annual and periodic caps limit the maximum interest rate change per year and over the life of the loan. The interest rate is determined by adding a margin to the index mandated by the loan documents. Some ARMs have conversion features that give the borrower the option to fix the rate at specified times.

Hybrid ARMs set a fixed interest rate for a specific period of time, e.g., three years, and then convert to an adjustable rate. Hybrids commonly offer periods of two, three, five, seven, or 10 years at a fixed rate. The industry refers to a loan with a fixed interest rate for 10 years, commonly followed by a 20-year period of annually adjusted rate resets, as a 10/1 ARM. Annual and periodic caps may limit the maximum interest rate change each year and over the life of the loan.

Balloon mortgages set payments for a specific period of time, followed by one large payment for the remaining amount of the principal. For example, a seven-year balloon loan may require payments based on a 30-year amortization schedule but require full payment of the entire remaining balance at the end of the seventh year. For balloon mortgages that contain a borrower option for an extended amortization period, the balloon mortgages are considered traditional mortgage products. If there is no borrower option for an extended amortization period, however, the balloon mortgage is considered a nontraditional mortgage product, because there is a deferral of principal, as the payments do not fully amortize during the loan term. The 2012 Regulation Z ability-to-repay rules impose significant limitations on balloon payment terms.

Nontraditional Mortgage Products

Nontraditional mortgage products allow borrowers to defer payment of principal and sometimes interest. The CFPB 2012 rules amending Regulation Z, in particular the ability-to-repay requirements, impose significant limitations on nontraditional mortgage products. Previously, the federal financial regulators issued "Guidance on Nontraditional Mortgage Product Risks" (OCC Bulletin 2006-41) in recognition that these products could cause consumers confusion and harm. Examples include interest-only loans, payment option ARMs, and certain balloon mortgages.

Interest-only loans: For a specified number of years (e.g., three, five, or 10 years) the borrower is required to pay only the interest due on the loan, during which time the rate may fluctuate or be fixed. Interest-only loans can be fixed-rate mortgages, hybrid mortgages, or ARMs. After the interest-only period, the rate may be fixed or fluctuate based on the prescribed index, and payments include both principal and interest. The primary risk of an interest-only mortgage to a borrower is the payment shock resulting from potentially higher mortgage payments once the interest-only period ends. Generally, an interest-only loan cannot be a "qualified mortgage" under the 2012 Regulation Z ability-to-repay rule.

Payment-option ARM: This ARM product allows the borrower to choose from a number of different payment options. For example, each month, the borrower may choose a minimum payment option based on a "start" or introductory interest rate, an interest-only payment option based on the fully indexed interest rate, or a fully amortizing principal and interest payment option based on a 15-year or 30-year loan term, plus any required escrow payments. The minimum payment option can be less than the interest accruing on the loan, resulting in negative amortization. The interest-only option avoids negative amortization but does not provide for principal amortization. After a specified number of years, or if the loan reaches a certain negative amortization cap, the required monthly payment amount is recast to require payments that will fully amortize the outstanding balance over the remaining loan term.

Borrowers may not fully understand the risks associated with this product. If they choose from various payment options and solely focus on minimum payment amounts, they may not realize that payment shock is possible or that their loan amount may increase due to negative amortization, creating an obligation greater than the value of the home. The level of the obligation relative to the value of the home will worsen if a home declines in value during interest-only or negative amortization periods. The risks resulting from payment shock and negative amortization, if not properly managed, could produce higher defaults and losses as well as significant reputation risk, and could prove inappropriate for a borrower. Generally, loans with negative amortization or interest-only payment cannot be a qualified mortgage under the 2012 Regulation Z ability-to-repay rule.

While the OCC encourages banks to respond to customers' credit needs, banks should be aware that nontraditional mortgage products can pose a variety of safety and soundness, compliance, consumer protection, and other risks. Banks must comply with the Regulation Z requirements, including the 2012 Regulation Z ability-to-repay rule, and other applicable laws. Additionally, banks are expected to comply with the "Guidance on Nontraditional

Mortgage Product Risks" (OCC Bulletin 2006-41) and other guidance. The "Nontraditional Mortgage" guidance directs banks to recognize and mitigate the risks inherent in these products. Risk mitigation includes ensuring that loan terms and underwriting standards are consistent with prudent lending practices, including credible consideration of a borrower's repayment capacity. The guidance also mandates ensuring that consumers are provided with clear and balanced information about the relative benefits and risks at a time that allows them to make informed decisions.

Risk Layering

Risk layering is the cumulative effect of risk factors that pose increased credit risk. The OCC has significant concerns that exercising such a practice places the borrower in a position of unaffordable payments and eventual default. An example of risk layering is combining payment deferral with other risk factors, such as simultaneous second-lien loans, reduced documentation loans, and non-owner-occupied investor loans. If risks are layered, loan terms should reflect this increased risk by including strong mitigating factors that support the underwriting decision and the borrower's repayment capacity. Mitigating factors can include lower loan-to-value (LTV) and debt-to-income (DTI) ratios, credit enhancements, and mortgage insurance. Risk layering can be present in both traditional and nontraditional mortgage products.

Simultaneous second-lien loans are lending arrangements in which either a closed-end second lien or a home equity line of credit (HELOC) is originated simultaneously with the first-lien mortgage loan, typically in lieu of a higher down payment. The first mortgage is sized to meet loan limit and LTV requirements for sale in the secondary mortgage market without private mortgage insurance (PMI), while the simultaneous second enables the borrower to receive a larger loan with a smaller down payment. The first and second mortgages used in simultaneous second-lien loans often are originated by the same lender, but they also can be simultaneous loans issued by different lenders. Simultaneous second-lien loans typically are referred to as "piggyback" mortgages.

Simultaneous second-lien loans result in reduced owner equity and potentially higher credit risk. Historically, as combined loan-to-value (CLTV) ratios rise, defaults rise as well. A delinquent borrower with little or no equity in a property may have little incentive to work with the lender to bring the loan current to avoid foreclosure. In addition, second-lien HELOCs increase borrower exposure to increasing interest rates and monthly payment burdens because HELOCs typically do not include interest rate caps. For additional guidance on HELOCs, see OCC Bulletin 2005-22, "Home Equity Lending: Credit Risk Management Guidance," and OCC Bulletin 2006-43, "Home Equity Lending: Addendum to OCC Bulletin 2005-22."

Reduced documentation loans are commonly referred to as "low doc/no doc," "no income/no asset," "stated income," or "stated asset" loans. Little or no documentation is provided with these loans to verify the borrower's income and assets. The lack of key financial information makes it difficult to assess the borrower's repayment ability.

The OCC strongly discourages the practice of reduced documentation lending, given that it relies on assumptions and unverified information instead of an analysis of a borrower's repayment capacity and creditworthiness. As the level of credit risk increases, banks should be more diligent in verifying and documenting borrowers' income and debt reduction capacity. Clear policies should govern the use of reduced documentation loans. For example, a borrower's stated income should be accepted only if there are mitigating factors that clearly minimize the need for direct verification of repayment capacity.

For many borrowers, banks should be able to readily document income using recent W-2 statements, pay stubs, or tax returns. When reduced documentation, such as stated income, is used, compensating factors such as lower LTV and other more conservative underwriting standards are necessary. Banks should allow reduced income documentation in accordance with applicable laws and regulations only after considering the borrower's occupation, verification of employment, asset levels, credit score, cash reserves, fraud potential, credit report, job history, and other similar characteristics. A critical evaluation of the reasonableness of the applicant's stated income and credit bureau information is essential to underwriting these loans, as is the need for effective collateral valuations and property appraisals.

The cost of reduced documentation loans should be properly disclosed to consumers. If a bank offers both reduced and full documentation loan programs and there is a pricing premium attached to the reduced documentation program, consumers should be informed.

Sources of Mortgage Loans

Banks commonly create mortgage production through both retail (internal) and wholesale (external) sources.

Retail sources for mortgage loans include bank-generated loan applications, contacts with real estate agents, and home builders. Retail origination channels include the branch network, direct mail, telemarketing, and the Internet. Subject to RESPA requirements, retail originations may also be generated through affiliated business arrangements between a bank and partnered builders or real estate agents.

Although originating retail loans allows a bank to maintain tighter controls over its products and affords the opportunity to cross-sell other bank products, the volume of loans generated in this manner may not consistently support a bank's related fixed overhead costs. A bank that engages in mortgage banking, therefore, may supplement its retail loan production volume with additional mortgages purchased from or acquired through wholesale sources.

Wholesale sources for loans include loans originated through third-party originators (TPO), including brokers and correspondents.

Mortgage brokers typically perform loan processing functions, such as taking loan applications and ordering credit reports and appraisals. Unless they have delegated underwriting authority, mortgage brokers do not generally underwrite loans or close loans in their name. Instead, the acquiring bank underwrites the loan and provides funds for closing in the bank's name. Some loans are table-funded. Table-funded loans are closed in the name of a TPO, but the bank simultaneously provides the funds and acquires the loans.

Management should have effective systems to oversee delegated underwriting arrangements. Management should ensure that the TPO is appropriately managed, financially sound, providing high-quality mortgages that meet prescribed underwriting guidelines, and complying with applicable laws and regulations.

Correspondents generally perform most or all loan processing functions, such as taking loan applications, ordering credit reports and appraisals, and verifying income and employment. Mortgages produced by a correspondent are closed in the correspondent's name and are subsequently sold to the bank. Correspondents sell mortgages to purchasing banks under either a flow or a bulk loan sale agreement. A flow sale encompasses new loans sold one at a time or in small groups. A bulk loan sale involves the sale of a portfolio or pool of mortgages to an investor, usually in one transaction.

The quality of loans originated through the wholesale production channel should be closely monitored through underwriting reviews, evaluation by quality control and appraisal units, testing for compliance, and ongoing portfolio performance management activities. Monitoring the quality and documentation of loans originated by a bank's wholesale channel enables bank management to determine whether individual brokers or correspondents are meeting the bank's expectations. If credit, compliance, or documentation problems are discovered, the bank should take appropriate action, which could include terminating its relationship with the broker or correspondent.

There is an unfounded expectation that wholesale production of mortgage loans allows banks to expand volume without significantly increasing related fixed costs. The wholesale business is highly competitive. As a result, there may be periods during the business cycle when it is difficult for a bank to obtain required loan volume at an attractive price. In addition, wholesale production has increased the potential for fraud if proper control systems are not in place.

Before entering into TPO agreements, banks should establish a framework for the initial approval and ongoing monitoring of brokers, correspondents, and service providers. This framework should outline contractual requirements specifying underwriting and consumer compliance criteria, periodic site visits, warranties, and recourse and indemnification provisions. The bank should establish minimum acceptable performance standards in the contractual sales agreement with brokers and correspondents. The bank should establish appropriate procedures for ongoing monitoring of TPO activities.

Bank Acting as Broker or Agent

In some cases, a bank's loan officers may act solely as brokers or agents, taking mortgage applications and forwarding the applications and supporting documentation to a third party. The resulting applications are typically processed, underwritten, closed, and funded by another institution. This activity usually involves mortgage products that the bank does not offer and is provided as a customer service. The practice of loan officers acting solely as brokers or agents is also referred to as "brokering out."

Although these loans are not considered originations or purchases by the bank, this activity subjects the bank to reputation, compliance, and operational risks. In this broker or agent role, bank loan officers are permitted to make contact with and advise mortgage applicants. Thus, the bank should have policies, procedures, and MIS that govern and track this activity. These policies and procedures should address permissible products, counterparties, and fees, as well as compliance with applicable consumer laws and regulations. The bank's quality control and audit functions should also monitor this activity to ensure adherence to the bank's policies and risk controls.

Appraisal and Evaluation Functions

There must be an effective, independent real estate appraisal and evaluation process that covers all residential real estate lending. A key element in this process is the independent selection of qualified and experienced persons to appraise or evaluate real estate. Appraisal processes should be monitored for ongoing effectiveness and accuracy. The appraiser selection and engagement process is the most important part of a lender's appraisal and evaluation program. This function must be independent from influence by anyone in a loan production function. Appraisers are to be selected based on competency for a particular assignment. State licensure or certification is a necessary prerequisite; any appraiser engaged to perform an appraisal for a federally related transaction must be certified or licensed, but an appraiser cannot be considered competent solely because he or she holds that credential. Engaged appraisers must not be subject to coercion and must be free from prohibited conflicts of interest. Examiners must carefully examine a bank's appraisal program to determine how the competency requirement is documented in policies and procedures, and how the selection and engagement process works in practice.

In addition to the appraisal ordering function, the appraisal review functions must be independent of the loan production process. Qualified staff must appropriately review the appraisal before loan approval. Additionally, banks must obtain appraisals and provide applicants with copies of an appraisal or other valuation as required by applicable law, including Regulation B and Regulation Z.

For additional guidance on real estate appraisals, see 12 CFR 1026 (Regulation Z); 12 CFR 1002 (Regulation B); OCC Bulletin 2010-42, "Sound Practices for Appraisals and Evaluations: Interagency Appraisal and Evaluation Guidelines"; and OCC Bulletin 2005-6, "Appraisal Regulations and the Interagency Statement on Independent Appraisal and Evaluation Functions: Frequently Asked Questions." For banks, see 12 CFR 34, "Real Estate Lending and Appraisals," and for FSAs, see 12 CFR 164, "Appraisals," and 12 CFR 160.101, "Real Estate Lending Standards."

Production Process

Mortgage loan production normally consists of four phases: origination, processing, underwriting, and closing. Management is responsible for supervising each of these areas and ensuring adherence to internal and external requirements, including complying with applicable law.

Origination

Originators are the sales staff of the mortgage banking units. Their primary role is the solicitation of applications from prospective borrowers. Banks originate loans in many ways besides face-to-face customer contacts. These methods could include telemarketing, Web sites, direct mailing, origination through brokers or affiliated business arrangements, or purchases from correspondents. Regardless of the source, mortgage originators must be appropriately knowledgeable regarding investor loan requirements, company loan products, origination technology, and consumer law. Loan originators must be appropriately registered or licensed, including as required by the Secure and Fair Enforcement for Mortgage Licensing Act of 2008 (SAFE Act) and its implementing regulations, Regulation G and Regulation H. Additionally, beginning in January 2014, Regulation Z will require loan originator organizations to verify that their individual loan originators are appropriately licensed or registered (including pursuant to the SAFE Act) and, for loan originator employees not required to be licensed, to undertake certain duties to help make sure such employees are qualified, trustworthy, and properly trained.

Loan origination functions, including the taking and processing of loan applications, have become increasingly automated. Most originators use automated underwriting engines, laptop origination systems, and Web-based loan application processes. Concurrently, many investors require the use of automated underwriting programs and the electronic submission of data to create a more cost-efficient production process.

Management may compensate mortgage loan originators only as permitted by law, including the material limitations on such compensation set forth in Regulation Z, as amended by the recent CFPB amendments effective in January 2014. A significant portion of originator compensation takes the form of commissions, which generally cannot be based on specified terms or conditions of the transaction (e.g., interest rate or product type). Originators should not have the authority to set or dominate loan pricing decisions, as this potential conflict can create unacceptable reputation, market, compliance, and credit risks. Originators should not be compensated solely on volume without regard for the quality of loans originated. Specific pricing guidance and origination practices should be established to prevent abusive pricing and origination practices.

Originators must be aware of and comply with the regulations implementing consumer protection laws and requiring various disclosures, which may change over time. These laws and regulations include the following:

- Regulation B, implementing ECOA
- Fair Housing Act
- Regulation V, implementing FCRA
- Flood Disaster Protection Act
- Regulation Z, implementing HOEPA and TILA
- HMDA
- Regulation X, implementing RESPA

Management should ensure that timely and accurate disclosures are provided to mortgage applicants and that all other applicable requirements are met. Such efforts should take into account multiple changes to mortgage origination-related disclosures that have been implemented over the last several years, including 2012 amendments to Regulation X and Regulation Z that are effective in January 2014.

Management must have processes to prevent loan originators from improperly steering customers to accept a mortgage loan that is not in the consumer's interest in order to increase the originator's compensation.

In addition to providing the required disclosures, banks offering mortgage banking services should provide information to applicants that enables them to understand material terms, costs, and risks of loan products at a time that helps the applicant select a product. Communication with consumers, including advertisements, oral statements, and promotional materials, should provide clear and balanced information about the relative benefits and risks of mortgage products.

Banks offering mortgage banking services should not become involved, directly or indirectly, in abusive, predatory, unfair, or deceptive lending practices. Banks must comply with regulatory and investor requirements relative to predatory lending. Investor requirements often include compliance with state laws that define and restrict predatory lending practices, in addition to compliance with any applicable federal law.

The OCC believes that a fundamental characteristic of predatory lending is the provision of credit to borrowers who cannot afford the credit on the terms being offered. In addition to the new Regulation Z ability-to-repay standards, OCC regulations prohibit banks from making a consumer loan based predominantly on the foreclosure or liquidation value of the collateral, without regard to the borrower's ability to service and repay the loan according to its terms.

Prohibited predatory lending practices include, but are not limited to, the following:

- **Equity stripping and fee packing:** Repeat financings where a borrower's equity is depleted as a result of financing excessive fees for the loan or ancillary products.
- **Loan flipping:** Repeat refinancings in which the relative terms and the cost of the newly refinanced loan do not provide a tangible economic benefit to the borrower.
- **Refinancing of special mortgages:** Refinancing of a special subsidized mortgage that contains terms favorable to the borrower with a loan that does not provide a tangible economic benefit to the borrower relative to the refinanced loan.

- **Encouragement of default:** Encouraging a borrower to breach a contract and default on an existing loan before and in connection with the consummation of a loan that refinances all or part of the existing loan.

In some circumstances, certain loan terms, conditions, and features may be susceptible to abusive, predatory, unfair, or deceptive practices. To the extent permitted after January 2014, when new Regulation Z rules take effect, banks should prudently consider the circumstances in which they engage directly or indirectly in making mortgage loans with the following terms, conditions, and features:

- Financing single-premium credit life, disability, or unemployment insurance.
- Negative amortization involving a payment schedule in which regular periodic payments are not sufficient to cover interest, causing the principal to increase.
- Balloon payments in short-term transactions.
- Prepayment penalties that are not limited to the early years of the loan, particularly in subprime loans.
- Interest rate increases upon default at a level not commensurate with risk mitigation.
- Call provisions permitting the bank to accelerate payment of the loan under circumstances other than the borrower's default under the credit agreement, or to mitigate the bank's exposure to loss.
- Absence of an appropriate assessment and documentation of the consumer's ability to repay the loan in accordance with its terms, commensurate with applicable laws and loan type.
- Mandatory arbitration clauses or agreements, particularly if the eligibility of the loan for purchase in the secondary market is thereby impaired.
- Pricing terms that result in the loan's being subject to the provisions of HOEPA or being a higher-priced loan.
- Original principal balance in excess of appraised value.
- Payment schedules that consolidate more than two periodic payments and that call for them to be paid in advance from the loan proceeds.
- Payments to home improvement contractors under a home improvement contract from the proceeds of a mortgage loan other than by an instrument payable to the consumer, jointly to the consumer and the contractor, or through an independent third-party escrow agent.

Processing

Loan processing consists of document verification and data gathering. The processor must ensure that the loan file contains all of the supporting documents for credit analysis, e.g., income and employment verification, collateral valuation, down-payment sources, and any other required information. The loan processor must ensure that all necessary steps are performed in accordance with investor requirements and applicable law. This should include ensuring that all property taxes are paid current and that appropriate hazard and flood insurance, as applicable, is in effect with accurate loss payee instructions. Nonautomated processing includes preparing the loan application, obtaining supporting documents, verifying all information included in the mortgage loan application, and submitting information to the underwriting department. With the advent of automated underwriting, much of the processing often occurs after the loan is submitted to automated underwriting systems (AUS). These systems indicate what additional documentation requirements and data validations must be performed.

The amount of documentation required may be reduced for applicants that qualify for streamlined documentation under GSE or private investor underwriting standards. Other types of loans, such as Alt-A, also have reduced documentation requirements. The processing unit should use an automated processing system or a system of checklists to ensure that all required steps are completed.

Processors must also ensure that files are adequately documented. Incomplete loan files can cause unnecessary processing delays and expense to the consumer and the company.

Underwriting

The underwriting unit's primary function is to approve or deny loan applications. Underwriters determine whether a prospective borrower qualifies for the requested mortgage loan program, and whether income and collateral coverage meet bank and investor requirements. To ensure that loans are eligible for sale in the secondary market, most lenders apply underwriting and documentation standards that conform to those specified by the GSEs or private investors.

Beginning in January 2014, Regulation Z requires that in connection with consumer credit transactions secured by a dwelling, creditors generally must make a reasonable, good faith determination of a consumer's ability to repay the loan according to its terms, including considering and verifying certain consumer-specific information.

Banks increasingly use AUSs in the underwriting process. Both Fannie Mae and Freddie Mac have developed AUSs for conventional conforming loans: Fannie Mae Desktop Underwriter and Freddie Mac Loan Prospector. (See www.efanniemae.com and www.freddiemac.com/singlefamily for additional information on their respective seller and servicer guides.) Additionally, proprietary underwriting engines for nonconforming products have been developed by some of the more significant mortgage companies and investors.

Banks should establish proper model validation procedures for the information and assumptions entered into the models, the logic and processing of the information within proprietary models, and the accuracy of the reports generated. OCC Bulletin 2011-12, "Sound Practices for Model Risk Management," provides detailed guidance regarding model validation, and OCC Bulletin 1997-24, "Credit Scoring Models: Examination Guidance," provides guidance on the use of credit scoring models.

AUSs are designed to help lenders perform an assessment of the credit risk of borrowers and determine the "salability" of a mortgage loan. AUSs do not approve or deny loans. Rather, they indicate whether a loan would likely qualify for sale into a particular program. The lender is responsible for the integrity of the data entered into the model and the final underwriting decision. AUS recommendations do not relieve the lender of underwriting responsibilities or liability from standard sales representations and warranties.

AUSs provide a quick risk assessment that assists the lender in making the final underwriting decision. They often identify specific documents and information that must be obtained or validated, and outline specific conditions that must be cleared by an underwriter. They also assist in the appropriate pricing of a mortgage loan.

Underwriting engines typically have four components: a credit assessment of the borrower based on a credit score; an evaluation of the borrower's ability to service debt based on financial ratios; a collateral assessment using a statistical appraisal of the property generated by an automated valuation model; and property type.

The value generated by an automated valuation model may allow a streamlined appraisal or no appraisal at all. Typically, it provides a recommendation on whether an interior or drive-by-only appraisal is needed. Ultimately, it is incumbent on the bank to ensure that its appraisal practices are safe and sound and fully comply with the appraisal regulations (12 CFR 34, subpart C, for national banks, and 12 CFR 164 for FSAs).

When permitted, reduced documentation mortgages (such as stated income, stated assets, no ratio, and no documentation) require highly diligent underwriting. Underwriting should focus on conformance to loan program standards, the reasonableness of stated income and assets, credit bureau reports, application declarations, and collateral valuation.

Banks are strongly cautioned against ceding underwriting standards to third parties (e.g., investors, competitors) that have different business objectives, risk appetites, and core competencies. Loan terms should be based on a disciplined analysis of potential exposures and compensating factors to ensure risk levels remain manageable.

Closing

After the underwriting unit approves a loan, the closing unit ensures that the loan is properly closed and settled, including providing consumers with all required disclosures, and that the bank has all required documentation. Closings may be performed by an internal loan closing unit or by title companies or attorneys acting as agents for the bank. Whether a bank employee or agent performs the closing, all required documents should be obtained before disbursing any loan proceeds. Obtaining all front-end documents (e.g., note, preliminary title insurance, mortgage assignment(s), and guarantee certificate) is the responsibility of the closing function. The loan closer should maintain control over the closing package and submit it to the mortgage company within three business days of closing.

Management should ensure that adequate internal controls exist over loan closings, including third-party settlement services. The controls should promote the integrity of settlement documents, fraud prevention, and compliance with all applicable laws and regulations, including RESPA and TILA. The post-closing unit should review each loan within 10 days of closing. This review should determine whether the bank or its agent closed each loan according to the underwriter's instructions and that all documents were properly executed. Missing or inaccurate documents identified in post-closing reviews should be formally tracked, both by reason and by responsible closing individual, and promptly remedied. The post-closing unit should monitor trailing documents (e.g., the recorded mortgage, assignments, and final title insurance policy) to ensure they are received in a timely fashion. Management's tracking and reporting systems should list and age all missing documents, with pertinent commentary on collection efforts. The list should be prioritized based on specific investor requirements.

Mortgage Electronic Registration Systems

Mortgage Electronic Registration Systems (MERS) is a subsidiary of MERSCORP Holdings, which is owned by Fannie Mae, Freddie Mac, and other leading mortgage industry participants. MERS is a national, central database of mortgage loan information. MERS was created by the mortgage industry to streamline the mortgage process and to make mortgage-loan-related transactions more efficient. MERS as original mortgagee (or MOM) loans are approved by Fannie Mae, Freddie Mac, Ginnie Mae, the FHA, the VA, the California and Utah housing finance agencies, and all of the major Wall Street rating agencies.

MERS serves as a mortgagee in land records for the lenders and servicers. For loans registered on MERS, MERS acting as the mortgagee eliminates the need for future assignments when notes are sold or servicing is traded, because MERS remains the mortgagee regardless of the number of subsequent transactions. Beneficiaries of MERS include mortgage originators, servicers, warehouse lenders, wholesale lenders, retail lenders, document custodians, settlement agents, title companies, insurers, and investors.

Portfolio Management

It is essential that a bank effectively monitor the quality of mortgage loans it originates. The credit quality of loans that a bank originates affects the overall value of the MSAs and the bank's cost of servicing those loans. Poor credit quality lowers the value of servicing assets, increases underlying servicing costs, and raises the risk of repurchases or indemnifications from investors. A bank's reputation can be negatively affected if it originates poor-quality loans. Banks with poor credit quality may also receive lower prices for loans sold.

Banks typically monitor mortgage loan quality through vintage analysis, which tracks delinquency, foreclosure, loss, and prepayment ratios of similar products over comparable time periods. For example, vintage analysis can compare the 60-day delinquency rate of conventional, 30-year mortgages originated in the first quarter of one year with similar products originated in different quarters with the same seasoning (e.g., 12 months from origination). The objective of vintage analysis is to identify the sources of credit quality problems early so that corrective measures can be taken.

Mortgages generally reach peak delinquency levels after they have seasoned (been held by the borrower) for 30 to 48 months. Tracking the payment performance of seasoned loans over their entire term provides important historical information. It allows the bank to evaluate the quality of its nonseasoned mortgages over comparable time periods and to forecast the impact that aging will have on credit quality.

Management should track key financial information and credit characteristics and perform statistical analysis of performance over time. This information can be used to monitor trends and provide insights into delinquency, loss, prepayment, and foreclosure by product type, documentation type, and channel. Original and updated scores, LTV and DTI ratios, housing and debt coverage ratios, concentrations, and owner occupancy are relevant financial statistics that warrant monitoring.

For lenders originating or servicing traditional and nontraditional mortgage products, MIS tracking reports and vintage analysis should provide early warning to changes in the portfolio's risk profile. Reporting and tracking systems should allow management to isolate key products, layered risks, loan features, and borrower characteristics. These systems should help identify and isolate the causes of performance deterioration. Portfolio volume and performance results should be tracked against expectations, internal lending standards, and policy limits. The impact of changing markets and market conditions also should be assessed. Banks should perform stress tests on key portfolio segments to help identify and quantify events that can increase risks within a segment of the entire portfolio.

The impact of changing markets and economic conditions also should be assessed. Banks should perform stress tests on key portfolio segments to help identify and quantify macroeconomic factors that can increase risks within a portfolio segment as well as the entire portfolio in aggregate. Special attention should be given to the impact of unemployment and interest rate changes on delinquencies, foreclosures, and losses for each key segment of the entire portfolio.

Mortgage Fraud

Ensuring data integrity during the mortgage loan application, approval, and closing and settlement process is vital to managing and preventing fraudulent activity. Banks with significant origination volumes or significant reliance on third-party originations should have robust, comprehensive policies and procedures to manage mortgage fraud risk. Policies, procedures, and testing for mortgage fraud should be consistent with investor requirements. Key components of sound fraud risk management processes include the following:

- Comprehensive fraud training programs for employees.
- Controls to ensure accurate and complete application information.
- Effective use of automated fraud detection tools.
- Prudent underwriting, including appropriate documentation,[12] credit analysis, and verification of key data.
- Use of caution in reduced-documentation lending programs, including testing for the reasonableness of stated income or assets.

---

[12] Documentation includes, but is not limited to, the Customer Identification Program data collection and verification requirements under the BSA.

- Proper oversight of third-party and vendor relationships, including initial approval and ongoing monitoring.
- Independent appraisal ordering process and effective review programs.
- Sound loan settlement processes promoting the integrity of settlement documents and compliance with RESPA.
- Sound quality control programs, including appropriate testing programs for loans with a higher potential for fraudulent activity. Compensation programs and practices must comply with applicable laws, regulations, and internal standards designed to mitigate risk and should reward qualitative factors, not just the quantity of loans originated.
- Ongoing reviews of loan performance data and repurchase requests to help identify fraud and isolate problem origination sources.
- Thorough analysis of fraud cases, identifying root causes and all participants and strengthening internal controls, as needed.
- Adequate internal audit programs for mortgage fraud risk management.
- Appropriate accounting procedures and monitoring and reporting procedures to quantify fraud losses and related operating losses.

Banks should ensure that they have the systems in place to properly report mortgage fraud to regulatory and law enforcement authorities, insurers, and investors. Banks are required by OCC regulation (12 CFR 21.11 and 163.180, as applicable) to file Suspicious Activity Reports (SAR) for known or suspected instances of mortgage loan fraud. Processes should be in place to report the fraud to title insurers and the bank's insurer in a timely manner, because these policies often have time limits. Banks are also typically required to report suspected fraudulent activity to investors. Management should assess its investor agreements to determine exact responsibilities for fraud reporting. In addition, when a bank files a SAR because of suspected fraud involving a state-licensed appraiser, the bank should make a referral to the appropriate state appraiser board. For additional information pertaining to various fraud schemes and likely participants, visit the Federal Financial Institutions Examination Council (FFIEC) Web site for an interagency paper titled "The Detection and Deterrence of Mortgage Fraud Against Financial Institutions: A White Paper."

Production Quality Control

The U.S. Department of Housing and Urban Development (HUD), Freddie Mac, Fannie Mae, Ginnie Mae, and most private investors require that mortgage companies selling them loans have a quality control (QC) unit that independently assesses the quality of loan production. QC reviews may be performed internally or outsourced to a private vendor. These reviews often are supplemented by pre-funding QC reviews, which are beneficial because, in many cases, problems can be resolved before funding.

If QC is contracted to an outside vendor, the lender is still responsible for maintaining quality assurance procedures that monitor and measure the quality of the vendor's work. Sufficient resources should be devoted to monitoring the quality of vendor relationships.

The QC unit should sample ongoing production and ensure that investor requirements are met. The sample should include closed loans from all product types and origination channels to verify that origination, processing, underwriting, and closing processes comply with bank policies, regulations, and the requirements of investors and private mortgage insurers. Lenders often supplement investor-required sampling with discretionary sampling. Such discretionary sampling is targeted to the lender's specific needs and may include certain offices, staff, and appraisers. It may also focus on new, rapidly growing, or higher-risk loans with low credit scores, high LTV and DTI ratios, reduced documentation, early payment defaults, or potential fraud characteristics.

QC should be independent of the production function and should not report to any individual involved in the origination of loans. The unit may report to the audit committee of the board, the mortgage company president, or the chief financial officer.

QC reports should be distributed to appropriate levels of management. The reports should summarize work performed, provide overall conclusions regarding loan production quality and processes, and provide loan-specific and systemic findings. The QC reports should distinguish findings in terms of significance or materiality (e.g., issues that affect salability or allow put-back or issues resulting in legal or reputation risk or reduced valuation) or less-significant issues. Risk-based limits should be established for significant findings. QC reports should be issued within 90 days of loan closing to help ensure that the underlying causes of deficiencies are resolved in a timely manner. The QC unit should require management responses to significant deficiencies.

Secondary Marketing

Many banks engaged in mortgage banking activities originate loans and sell them into the secondary market. A bank's secondary marketing department, working with production management, should be responsible for

- developing new products.
- pricing mortgage loans.
- managing and hedging the pipeline and warehouse.
- selling mortgage loans and effecting best execution.
- contributing to mortgage banking profitability.
- documenting and delivering mortgage products to investors.
- managing repurchases, indemnifications, and recourse obligations.

For mortgage banking to be profitable, pipeline and warehouse management must be efficient. A bank must consistently demonstrate reliable performance in underwriting, documenting, packaging, and delivering quality mortgage products to remain in good standing with secondary market participants. Poor performance could lead to unfavorable prices for future sales or to terminated relationships.

Profitability targets for secondary marketing personnel must be formulated with a good understanding of the risks that would be assumed to achieve such goals. Secondary marketing is usually not considered a profit center for a mortgage bank. Consideration should be given to compensating secondary marketing personnel on overall mortgage company profitability rather than secondary marketing department profitability. If unrealistic targets are set for secondary marketing profitability, unacceptable risks may be taken. For example, if secondary marketing personnel leave significant portions of the bank's pipeline or warehouse unhedged to save on hedge costs and improve departmental profitability, the bank could be subject to unacceptable losses in the event of an adverse movement in interest rates.

A bank's relationship with an investor is usually governed by a master agreement. Agreements can be structured as mandatory or "best efforts" delivery. These agreements call for the bank to deliver a specific dollar volume or percentage of loans to an investor over a specified time period. In addition, these agreements describe investor-mandated underwriting standards, delivery requirements, and servicing requirements.

Product Development

The secondary marketing department should ensure that loan products the bank intends to sell meet investor guidelines. As discussed earlier, mortgage loans sold to the GSEs (Fannie Mae, Freddie Mac, and the FHLBs) must meet each agency's specific underwriting and eligibility guidelines. FHA and VA loans are eligible to be pooled for sale as Ginnie Mae securities. Conforming conventional loans and certain FHA and VA loans may be sold to Fannie Mae, Freddie Mac, and the FHLBs. Nonconforming mortgages (e.g., jumbo products) and mortgages that do not meet GSE underwriting guidelines may be sold through private label securities, through other financial institutions, or to private investors. The agencies' and private investors' product parameters may require outside servicer providers, such as private mortgage insurers. Past events have demonstrated that banks need to exercise a high degree of due diligence of third parties where deterioration of the third party's capital and reserves can have an adverse impact on the investor and, ultimately, the bank. Banks should establish and maintain prudent policies and procedures for identifying, selecting, and monitoring third parties, such as private mortgage insurers.

Before offering a new loan product, the secondary marketing department should determine its marketability and consider the bank's ability to price, deliver, and service the product. Moreover, a bank should have a new product review and approval process to ensure compliance with the bank's policies and applicable laws and regulations.

Banks that offer nontraditional mortgage products should have formal policies that detail acceptable structures, terms, risks, pricing, borrower qualification, and accounting standards. The unique risk characteristics of these products, such as the potential for payment shock and negative amortization, should be addressed during product development. During product development, the bank should evaluate possible target markets to ensure that the product's terms, features, marketing materials, disclosures, and documentation standards are appropriate. Particular attention should be given to meeting investor requirements and regulatory guidance, given the unique features of these products. OCC Bulletin 2006-41, "Guidance on Nontraditional Mortgage Product Risks," provides detailed guidance regarding nontraditional mortgages.

Mortgage Pricing

Mortgage pricing is closely tied to the MBS market. The servicing option and remittance cycle also influence mortgage pricing.

Price quotes for Fannie Mae, Freddie Mac, and Ginnie Mae MBSs are readily available on automated security screens at most secondary marketing departments. Because of guarantee fees and normal servicing fees, mortgages are typically sold into securities with pass-through rates 0.50 percent below the mortgage note rate. For example, if the security price for a 60-day forward, 6 percent, 30-year Fannie Mae loan is 99, the bank must charge its customer one discount point for a 6.50 percent, 30-year mortgage, to be priced at the market. This basic example assumes standard guarantee fees. GSE guarantee fees may be individually negotiated, however, and vary by bank. As a result, a loan sold into a security by one bank may generate a higher excess servicing gain on sale than a similar one sold by another bank. Therefore, a bank's pricing can be favorably affected by lower guarantee fees.

During periods of aggressive competition, banks occasionally offer their mortgage products below applicable security prices at a marketing loss (e.g., a 6.50 percent mortgage noted above with no discount points). Alternatively, banks sometimes price their mortgage products at a premium to the market (e.g., a 6.50 percent mortgage with two discount points).

Management should closely supervise mortgage pricing to ensure consistency with the company's strategic plan and earnings objectives. Secondary marketing personnel should be knowledgeable of competition, the bond markets, and investor activity, making the secondary marketing unit a logical choice for establishing loan pricing. Mortgage security prices change throughout the day. The volatility of these securities requires banks to maintain adequate controls to ensure that timely price changes are made and communicated throughout wholesale and retail origination channels. Secondary marketing personnel should establish prices with input from other key decision makers, such as finance and accounting departments. Originators should not overly influence or dominate pricing decisions. Pricing decisions should take into account other organizational strategies and goals such as servicing volume, market share, and cross-selling opportunities.

Some banks incorporate a risk-based approach in their pricing, based on their ability to analyze loan level characteristics and risk rank the quality of loan applicants. For example, banks may charge a higher interest rate for loans with high LTVs, low credit scores, or reduced documentation. Management should ensure that risk-based pricing does not cause unlawful disparate treatment or impact.

The Fair and Accurate Credit Transactions Act of 2003 amended the FCRA to require any person who makes or arranges loans, and who uses a consumer credit score in connection with an application by a consumer for a closed-end loan (or an open-end consumer purpose loan) secured by one- to four-unit residential real property, to provide to the consumer as soon as reasonably practicable and free of charge (1) the same credit scoring information it obtained from a credit reporting agency that the agency otherwise would be required to disclose to the consumer on request (with special provisions for AUSs); and (2) a notice specified in the regulation that explains the bank's use of credit scores, how credit scores generally are calculated, and how the consumer may contact the consumer reporting agency or lender with questions.

Banks should perform a profitability analysis when pricing mortgage loans. Factors to consider include the loan's size (conventional or jumbo), type (GSE or private investor), and source (wholesale or retail). Additional factors include the cost of hedging price risk through the date of sale, the value of related servicing assets created, capital allocation charges for credit risk, funding costs, and internal rate of return hurdles. Consideration should be given to the fallout and delinquency history by geographic area, product type, and origination source. In addition, marketing considerations, such as promotional pricing, should be explicitly acknowledged and included in the profitability analysis.

Pricing Methodologies, Pricing Concessions, and Overages

Banks sometimes allow retail and third-party originators to price mortgage loans above the standard rate (overage) or below it (rate concession, subsidy, or underage). Overages occur when originators are allowed to selectively increase the price or cost (interest rate, fees, or points) of a mortgage loan above the bank's standard rate and fees or points schedule. Rate concessions involve selectively reducing the mortgage price or cost.

In some cases, higher-rate overages, also referred to as yield spread premiums, permit homebuyers to pay some or all of the up-front settlement costs over the life of the mortgage through a higher interest rate. Because the mortgage carries a higher interest rate, the lender is able to sell it to an investor at a higher price. In turn, these increased proceeds, or premiums, are used to cover the borrower's up-front costs.

The yield spread premium can be a legitimate tool to assist the borrower when the increased proceeds or premium when selling the loan is used to pay the borrowers' up-front fees and costs. In consumer credit transactions, however, an overage or yield spread premium is permitted only to the extent it reduces the up-front costs of the transaction (including permissible loan originator compensation). Thus, management should monitor the use of higher rates and yield spread premiums and ensure that yield spread premiums are not permitted other than those that lower the up-front cash requirements for the borrower. Where yield spread premiums are not prohibited, management must ensure that use of such premiums is in full compliance with applicable federal rules and regulations.

Banks also may allow retail and third-party originators to make concessions in the course of negotiating a loan with a consumer; however, once a creditor has offered specified terms and conditions (e.g., rate and points) to a consumer in connection with a consumer credit transaction, it may not reduce a loan originator's compensation based on whether different loan terms are negotiated by the consumer.

Banks that allow overages or rate concessions must have effective policies and monitoring procedures to limit and control such activity and to prevent violations of TILA, the ECOA, the Fair Housing Act, HOEPA, and RESPA. To the extent that overage or rate concessions are legally permissible, before allowing such overages or rate concessions, banks should analyze the potential impact on profitability and reputation, outlining acceptable practices and limits. MIS, controls, and customer complaint tracking systems should be in place to monitor and supervise pricing concessions and overages.

Banks should ensure that they do not engage in pricing practices that are unfair and deceptive within the meaning of Section 5 of the FTC Act, which prohibits "unfair or deceptive acts or practices" in or affecting interstate commerce.

Home Mortgage Disclosure Act Reporting on Higher-Priced Loans

In 2005, lenders began publicly reporting pricing information for certain loans with higher annual percentage rates under the HMDA. Reporting for higher-priced loans is required for home purchase originations, secured home improvements, and refinancings. A loan is considered high priced and triggers the expanded reporting requirements when the spread between its APR and the "average prime offer rate" published by the CFPB is greater than 1.5 percentage points for first-lien loans, or 3.5 percentage points or more for subordinate-lien loans.

Management should thoroughly analyze its HMDA data and ensure that there is no discriminatory lending based on race, gender, or ethnicity. HMDA data or other information that suggests a bank may be violating fair lending laws will result in the bank's being scheduled for an in-depth fair lending examination.

Pipeline, Warehouse Management, and Hedging

Managing the risk in the pipeline and warehouse is a key component of a successful mortgage banking operation. Changes in interest rates can affect the value of pipeline commitments and warehouse loans and cause market losses if not adequately hedged.

The bank's pipeline and warehouse include loan applications, mortgage commitments, and closed loans being processed for ultimate sale and delivery to a third-party investor. When the loan is closed, it is placed on the bank's books in a warehouse account where it remains until sold and delivered to an investor. Loans may be sold to GSEs (Fannie Mae, Freddie Mac, FHLBs) or private investors.

A mortgage enters the pipeline when a loan application is taken from a prospective borrower. Pipeline commitments with locked rates pose unique risks and uncertainty because they are not closed loans. Mortgage lenders generally allow an applicant to "lock" the loan terms at application or during the underwriting process. While locked commitments give customers the right to receive the stated loan terms if they otherwise qualify for the loan, they are not obligated to close on the loan. Commitments remain in the pipeline throughout the processing and underwriting stages. Changes in interest rates can significantly influence the customer's desire to execute the option to close the loan. By locking an application, the lender is exposed to price risk until the loan is sold.

Warehouse loans are closed mortgages awaiting sale to a secondary market investor. Closed loans purchased from correspondents with the intent to sell are also booked in the warehouse. Loans that the bank plans to retain should be transferred to the loan portfolio after closing. The bank often holds loans in the warehouse pending receipt of critical documents and aggregation of a sufficient volume to economically sell and deliver. The ability to sell and deliver a warehouse loan to an investor depends on whether the loan meets investor underwriting, documentation, and operational guidelines.

The overall objective of hedging the pipeline and warehouse is to manage the operation's price risk and minimize market losses, not to speculate on the direction of interest rate movements. While some market risk positions are inevitable, they should always comply with board-approved risk limits. The board and management should develop prudent risk management policies and procedures, including earnings-at-risk (EaR) or value-at-risk (VaR) parameters, to guard against adverse financial results. Results of the bank's hedging practices should be quantified and regularly reported to senior management (see appendix B).

Pipeline Management

Pipeline management involves managing the price risk of loan commitments during processing, underwriting, and closing. When a consumer submits a loan application, a bank normally grants the consumer the option of "locking in" the interest rate at which the loan will close in the future. The lock-in period typically runs for up to 60 days without a fee. If the consumer decides not to lock in at the current established rate, the loan is said to be "floating." Floating rate commitments do not present price risk because the lender has not committed to providing a particular interest rate to the loan applicant.

Locked-in pipeline commitments subject the bank to price risk because the bank must make the loan at the locked rate and terms, regardless of market rate changes. To the extent the bank has hedged the loan through a forward sale to an investor, not closing the loan during the rate-lock period could expose the bank to price risk if it is unable to deliver the loan to an investor as contracted. It also exposes the bank to reputation risk with the investor and the customer.

Effective supervision of the pipeline depends on accurate, detailed MIS. Systems and pipeline modeling weaknesses, poor data quality, or inaccurate analysis could adversely affect business decisions and operating results. Reports should provide management with information needed to determine an appropriate strategy for hedging the bank's risk.

Most banks use sophisticated loan origination, pipeline management, and secondary marketing data information systems to monitor and manage pipeline applications through processing and underwriting. The bank identifies various critical points during the processing period to ensure that the application is being processed as intended. The bank's pipeline or secondary marketing manager uses data information systems to forecast the volume of anticipated loan closings in order to effectively hedge the pipeline's price risk.

Interest rate fluctuations affect mortgage pipeline activities. Changes in rates influence the volume of loan applications that must be processed and the percentage of applications that eventually close, as well as the value of pipeline commitments, commitments to sell mortgages in the secondary market, and other hedges used to manage risk.

If interest rates decline while a prospective borrower's application is being processed, the applicant may decide to renegotiate the rate or obtain a lower-rate loan elsewhere before the committed loan can be closed. For this reason, interest rate declines result in an increased number of loans that do not close as originally expected. Commitments in the pipeline that do not close are known as "fallout." The proportion of commitments that do not make it to closing is known as the "fallout percentage." Conversely, some mortgage bankers refer to the proportion of commitments that do close as the "pull-through percentage." If interest rates rise, more loans will close, as customers have greater financial incentive to close the loans.

Warehouse Management

A bank normally holds a loan in the warehouse for no more than 90 days to complete documentation, processing, and sale. Some types of loans are held longer, such as lower-volume products that take longer to amass for effective economic delivery and loans being accumulated under special investor delivery programs.

Overall warehouse turn rates (average days in the warehouse) normally range from 35 to 45 days. While in the warehouse, the bank earns net interest income on the spread between the coupon rates on the loans and the cost of funding the warehouse. If the loan is maintained in the warehouse longer than originally expected at the time the rate lock was granted, some of the net interest income will be offset by the cost of maintaining a hedge on the loan.

Banks must have adequate systems to value their warehouse loans. Management must support its estimate of the value of these loans with objective evidence and adequate documentation. See appendix C for additional discussion of warehouse valuation.

Loans remaining in the warehouse for longer time frames may reflect documentation or other salability problems, such as underwriting deficiencies, delinquency, or significantly below-market interest rates. The valuation of such loans should take into account these salability problems. Management should take appropriate action to ensure that the level of longer-term warehouse holdings is kept to a minimum and accounted for in accordance with generally accepted accounting principles (GAAP). Bank reports should quantify and track the number, dollar volume, aging, and reasons for longer-term warehouse holdings.

If the bank no longer intends to sell a loan in the warehouse, the loan should be transferred to the bank's permanent loan portfolio. Bank management should employ a formal, disciplined method for transferring such loans out of the warehouse. This transfer must be recorded according to GAAP, with consideration given to any salability problems.

The warehouse's subsidiary ledgers should be reconciled regularly to the bank's general ledger. Normally, monthly reconcilements are sufficient and provide a means of detecting funding or delivery errors.

Hedging the Pipeline and Warehouse

The bank's secondary marketing information systems are critical to effectively hedging the pipeline and warehouse. To make informed sales decisions, secondary marketing personnel must have access to current, accurate data and be able to assess whether risk levels in the pipeline or warehouse are within policy guidelines. Management should not speculate by delaying appropriate risk decisions based on directional interest rate forecasts. Reporting systems should detail the volume and status of loan applications as they move through the origination process, become marketable loans, and are delivered to investors. The reports also should monitor the status of delivery commitments to investors, historical and anticipated fallout rates by loan category (e.g., product type and coupon), salability, and effectiveness of pipeline and warehouse hedges.

Effectively hedging the pipeline depends on accurately predicting and measuring the fallout and pull-through percentages. If interest rates drop and fallout is greater than expected, the bank may not be able to meet its forward sales commitments to investors. As a result, the bank may be forced to purchase needed loans in the secondary market at unfavorable prices or pay a pair-off fee, which equals the price impact the adverse market movement had on the shortfall under the forward sale commitment.

Some banks use a pipeline hedge model to estimate fallout under various interest rate scenarios. Information systems should accurately detail loans allowed to relock at a lower rate and identify loans with float-down-only features.

If interest rates rise and pull-through is greater than expected, the bank's forward sale commitments may not be sufficient to adequately cover its increased volume of closed loans. Also, the note rates on these unhedged mortgages would be below market interest rates, causing the bank to incur a loss when it sells the loans.

There are several strategies to protect, or hedge, the bank from fallout or unforeseen problems in the pipeline. The most common technique is to sell forward the amount of mortgage loans the bank expects to close on either a mandatory or "best efforts" basis. On a best efforts basis, the bank locks in an individual loan commitment and simultaneously contracts to sell it for future delivery at the time the rate lock is granted to an applicant. The terms of this forward sale are identical to those of the rate lock, but the selling bank only agrees to deliver the loan on a best efforts basis—that is, only if the loan closes. The price risk in this arrangement is borne solely by the purchasing institution. Best efforts contracts normally yield a lower selling price than mandatory contracts, which contain more uncertainty and risk.

Under mandatory contracts, the bank is obligated to deliver a specific dollar volume of mortgages to the investor. If the bank is unable to deliver the required volume within the specified commitment period, it may be required to either purchase loans from other sources or pay the investor a pair-off fee.

The basic pipeline hedge used by banks is to sell forward the percentage of the pipeline that the bank expects to close. For example, if a bank anticipates that 30 percent of its applications will fall out, it sells forward an amount equal to 70 percent of the applications in the pipeline. If the bank estimated correctly and closed 70 percent of the loans, the pipeline was completely hedged. If the bank closed more or less than the 70 percent, it was exposed to price risk equal to the amount of the over-hedged or under-hedged position times the amount of the market price change since the lock date. A forward sale may consist of individual or multiple loans, or a to-be-issued MBS consisting of loans similar to those being sold. Some banks use futures and traded options to hedge the pipeline. The advantages of these instruments are the depth and liquidity of the market, reduced counterparty credit risk, and greater flexibility in constructing positions. There are also several disadvantages, including potential complexity in maintaining appropriate hedge ratios, the need for constant monitoring of the hedge position, higher transaction costs and up-front fees, margin requirements, and basis risk between the underlying mortgages and the hedge instruments.

Many banks use a combination of forward sales and options to offset price risk. For example, a bank might anticipate closing 70 percent of the loans in the pipeline under a most likely scenario, 80 percent if rates rise significantly, but only 65 per cent if rates decline. To hedge this risk profile the bank could sell forward an amount equal to 70 percent of the pipeline, purchase call options to provide coverage on 5 percent of the pipeline if rates fall, and sell futures or purchase put options to cover the other 10 percent of the pipeline if rates rise. This method hedges the pipeline so long as 65 percent to 80 percent of the loans close. Using options to hedge pipeline risk can be effective, but is also more expensive than using forward sale contracts alone.

Warehouse loans are typically 100 percent committed (forward sold) for delivery to an investor. If pipeline fallout is less than expected (i.e., more loans close than expected), additional loans may need to be sold forward to hedge the warehouse. If warehouse loans are not adequately hedged and interest rates rise, the bank may have to sell the loans at a loss. Banks with a material volume of unhedged warehouse loans should be able to clearly articulate how they are measuring and managing the price and interest rate risk in these mortgage holdings.

Guaranteed Mortgage Securitizations

For liquidity risk management purposes and potentially more favorable regulatory capital treatment, some banks may participate in guaranteed mortgage securitizations. In these programs, loans may be "swapped" for pass-through certificates issued by GSEs. The pass-through certificates are retained on the bank's balance sheet. The bank gives up a portion of the interest income on the loan (generally 0.25 percent or less for the guarantee fee) in return for the greater liquidity and potentially more favorable regulatory capital treatment. The bank typically retains servicing of the loans that back the certificate. See also appendix C,

"Mortgage Banking Accounting," for additional discussion of guaranteed mortgage securitizations.

Best Execution

Policies should require that best execution analyses of alternative delivery options be periodically performed and documented. Best execution is the secondary marketing practice of selling mortgages at the best available net price while giving consideration to effective trade execution and potential impact on investor relationships. Best execution involves not only getting the best price today but also obtaining the optimal set of cash flows from the loans over their servicing life. Best execution is considered when a hedge is initiated and again when the loans are sold.

Various factors must be considered in best execution analysis, including guarantee fees, published buy-up and buy-down grids, excess servicing valuations, market prices for securities, and the market price for cash-settled whole-loan transactions. Most banks use purchased or internally developed applications to automate the mathematical part of the decision process. The overall effectiveness of executing the trades and the ongoing business relationship with the individual investor must also be subjectively factored into the best execution analysis.

Guarantee Fee, Float, and Remittance Cycle

Lower guarantee fees can improve mortgage banking profitability. The amount of guarantee fees the bank pays agency and private guarantors may be negotiable and is based on volume, credit risk, and the timing of cash flows (remittance cycle) paid to the guarantor. The longer the guarantor holds the mortgage payments, the smaller the guarantee fee necessary to compensate the guarantor.

Fannie Mae and Freddie Mac allow the seller (bank) to either "buy up" or "buy down" the guarantee fee. These options provide the bank flexibility to increase or decrease the amount of excess servicing. If the bank buys up the guarantee fee (i.e., pays a higher ongoing fee to Fannie Mae or Freddie Mac), it increases the amount of cash it receives up-front in exchange for a smaller excess servicing fee when the mortgages are sold. When the bank buys down the guarantee fee, it receives less cash from the sale in exchange for a larger excess servicing fee over the life of the underlying loans.

Loan Documentation and Delivery

To fulfill its delivery responsibilities, the bank must obtain all mortgage documents for its investors. Front-end documents, such as loan applications, verification documents, credit reports, and disclosure statements, are obtained at or before closing. Post-closing documents, such as mortgages, assignments, and title policies, must be recorded by local authorities or issued by the title company. Post-closing documents may be received up to 120 days after closing.

An appropriate tracking system for monitoring document collection activities is necessary to ensure an effective process. The system should identify the customer by name, the document missing, status of collection efforts, and the number of days since loan closing. Documentation exceptions should be tracked by source of origination to identify underwriter performance issues. The bank should diligently follow up on and obtain these documents. Failure to obtain mortgage documents in a timely manner can result in unnecessary financial and legal exposure for a bank.

A bank that sells mortgages into Ginnie Mae securities must obtain a third-party certification that all loan documents are on file. A bank's affiliate or subsidiary is eligible to certify the pools; in this arrangement, however, Ginnie Mae requires the bank to have a separate trust department. The file custodian issues the final pool certification after verification that all documentation is complete. If one loan in the pool is missing a single document, the entire pool may not receive final certification.

Ginnie Mae has established tolerance levels for the final certification, transfer, and recertification of mortgage pools. Examiners should reference the most current Ginnie Mae MBS Guide for Ginnie Mae pool certification requirements. If the seller exceeds the established limit, Ginnie Mae can require the seller to post a letter of credit to protect Ginnie Mae against potential loss. Fannie Mae and Freddie Mac do not have a specific monetary penalty in place but do require an appropriate document collection process.

Sales contracts with private investors or purchasers of servicing normally require all documents to be obtained. Common contract provisions require the seller to repurchase defective mortgages, allow the buyer to hold back sales proceeds, and indemnify the buyer against losses resulting from missing documents.

Repurchases and Recourse

A bank selling loans into the secondary market should follow effective underwriting and documentation standards to protect its reputation in the market to support future loan sales.

High or increasing levels of repurchases and indemnifications can negatively affect investors' appetite for future loan purchases. Management should monitor the level of repurchase requests and determine the underlying reasons (e.g., fraud, documentation, credit, or regulatory compliance) for the loan repurchase requests.

A bank may choose to sell loans to investors on either a recourse[13] or nonrecourse basis. Selling with recourse allows the bank to increase the price at which it sells loans. Management should ensure that the bank is adequately compensated for the credit risk retained. As described more fully below, selling loans with recourse, or taking subsequent actions that result in implied recourse, has accounting and regulatory capital consequences.

Generally, recourse arises when a bank retains more than a pro rata share of credit risk when mortgage assets are sold to an investor. One common source of recourse is credit-enhancing

---

[13] For accounting treatment, see appendix C, "Mortgage Banking Accounting."

representations and warranties that obligate a bank to cover credit losses for mortgages sold. Representations and warranties are usually detailed in the purchasing agreement.

Some of these representations and warranties are credit enhancing—for example, provisions requiring repurchase for early default or premium refund clauses. Representations and warranties that are not credit enhancing do not trigger recourse, such as the return of assets for fraud, misrepresentation, or incomplete documentation.

A seller's representations and warranties that survive the date of closing on loans sold to third parties are considered guarantees and thus subject to the provisions of Accounting Standards Codification (ASC) 860 and ASC 460.[14] A guarantor is required to recognize at the inception of a guarantee a liability (a reserve) for the fair value of the obligation undertaken in issuing the guarantee. Examples of these guarantees include representations and warranties by the seller to repurchase loans because of incomplete documentation or noncompliance with underwriting standards. See appendix C, "Mortgage Banking Accounting," for additional detail.

Recourse also occurs when a bank sells mortgages and retains a first dollar loss position (a residual, including credit-enhancing interest-only strips) or agrees to reimburse an investor for credit-related losses on mortgages sold to that investor. Furthermore, implicit recourse may also occur if a bank provides a credit enhancement beyond that required by the sale agreement. For regulatory capital treatment of credit-enhancing representations and warranties (and related exemptions), disallowed credit-enhancing interest-only strips, and the appropriate risk-weighting calculations for assets sold with recourse, refer to the applicable regulations and call report instructions.[15] See also the "Asset Securitization" booklet in the *Comptroller's Handbook*, which discusses recourse, residuals, and direct credit substitutes, and appendix C, "Mortgage Banking Accounting," for a discussion of accounting issues related to sales with recourse.

Recourse has implications for calculating the limit on high-LTV mortgages. The amount of high-LTV mortgage lending is limited to an amount equal to 100 percent of total regulatory capital.[16] If banks do not correctly assess their recourse positions, they may violate this limit.

Recourse Issues Related to Federal Home Loan Bank Mortgage Programs

In 1997 the Federal Home Loan Bank of Chicago offered to purchase mortgages from its members under a pilot program, the Mortgage Partnership Finance (MPF) Program. The Federal Home Loan Bank of Seattle followed with its Mortgage Partnership Program (MPP). These programs are subject to ongoing review by the FHLBs' regulator. Under these

---

[14] See ASC 860, "Transfers and Servicing."

[15] As of January 1, 2014, advanced-approaches banks should follow the new capital rules at 12 CFR 3, subparts C, E, and F. All other banks should follow the new capital rules as of January 1, 2015, at 12 CFR 3, subparts C and D. See 12 CFR 3, subpart G, for transition rules, as appropriate.

[16] Calculate the total capital under the applicable capital rules. Note that the calculation of total capital will change as of the effective date of the new capital rules and any applicable transition periods.

programs, certain FHLBs purchase single-family loans from their member financial institutions through the MPF or MPP program. Many of these mortgages meet the same requirements as mortgages that Fannie Mae and Freddie Mac are permitted to purchase (single-family, one- to four-family conforming loans within the size limit established by Congress).

When the FHLBs buy a single-family mortgage from a participating member financial institution (participating bank), the FHLBs acquire the interest rate risk. Under all but one of the mortgage purchase programs, the FHLBs buy closed loans from participating banks. The FHLBs set up a first loss account that is usually funded at the time of the sale of the loans to the FHLBs or on a flow basis by fees due to the participating banks. The participating banks either provide supplemental primary mortgage insurance or guarantee the second loss position, and the FHLBs provide the third or catastrophic loss position. This assumption of loss by the FHLB in the event of failure of the supplemental mortgage insurer eliminates any recourse to participating banks on the second loss position protected by supplemental mortgage insurance.

For a more detailed discussion on the accounting and risk-based capital treatment of these types of programs, see the call report instructions for purchased loans originated by others. See also the call report's March 31, 2013, supplementary instructions, "Purchased Loans Originated by Others," as well as the applicable regulatory capital rules for risk weighting the program's exposures.

Examiners should ensure that the bank's credit risk management system adequately addresses the credit risk exposure arising from any second loss credit enhancement and from any performance-based credit enhancement fees receivable from the FHLB programs. The second loss credit enhancement guarantee and the related credit enhancement fees receivable are subject to the guidance for retained interests that is outlined in OCC Bulletin 1999-46, "Interagency Guidance on Asset Securitization Activities."

The appropriate accounting for and measurement of second loss credit enhancements depend on the program features. Banks should consider the guidance in ASC 860, "Transfers and Servicing," as well as ASC 460, "Guarantees," to determine the appropriate accounting for MPP second loss credit enhancements. See appendix C, "Mortgage Banking Accounting," for further guidance on these topics.

Servicing

Originating loans and selling them to the secondary market are not the only mortgage banking activities. For banks that engage in mortgage banking, loan servicing is a primary source of income. To be successful, a servicer must comply with investor requirements and applicable laws,[17] have efficient processes and strong internal controls, invest in and closely

---

[17] This handbook does not attempt to detail the requirements set forth in each of the federal laws applicable to mortgage servicing. Various other *Comptroller Handbook* booklets, however, address these laws and regulations more fully, including, among others, the "Real Estate Settlement Procedures Act," "Truth in

manage technology infrastructure, and manage costs. A servicing agreement between the bank and each investor describes the investor's requirements for servicing its assets and the manner in which the servicer will be compensated. Ultimately, if a bank fails to appropriately service an investor's portfolio, the servicing rights could be revoked.

Banks must implement policies and procedures and make other changes necessary to comply with the servicing-related requirements set forth in Regulation X and Regulation Z, which are effective January 2014. The new Regulation X requirements include those that address (1) error resolution and information requests, (2) force-placed insurance, (3) general servicing policies and procedures designed to achieve specified objectives, (4) early intervention and continuity of contact, and (5) loss mitigation procedures and limitations on dual tracking. The Regulation Z amendments include those that address (1) periodic statements, (2) ARM disclosures, and (3) prompt crediting of payment and provision of payoff statements.[18]

In addition to the contractual servicing fee paid by each investor, mortgage banks are compensated for their servicing activities through (1) income from borrower or investor payment float; (2) ancillary income from late fees, commissions on optional insurance policies (credit life, accidental death, disability, and PMI), and miscellaneous fees; and (3) benefits of compensating balances from custodial funds. Some banks are also interested in retaining a servicing relationship with borrowers because it offers opportunities for cross-selling of additional bank products.

Effective cost management is essential for servicers. Management should understand the bank's "all-in" cost to service, including costs associated with necessary computer hardware, software, and customer service communication equipment, for each major type of loan in order to assess specific product profitability. By understanding the bank's servicing profitability, management is better able to make informed strategic decisions regarding the portfolio. Detailed information systems capable of measuring and analyzing servicing costs are an essential part of this process.

Increasing levels of delinquent loans and product complexity typically increase the cost to service loans. As delinquency increases, servicers often make advances for taxes, insurance, property preservation, inspections, and legal costs. Depending on the remittance type, many servicers must make advances on principal and interest to investors, regardless of whether the servicer has received a payment from the borrower and may be financially responsible for other obligations (e.g., property maintenance requirements). Many, but not all, of these advances are reimbursed once a property is liquidated, but the servicer still faces the cost of funds for advancing fees, expenses, and debt service payments. In addition, servicing a loan that requires a modification or foreclosure requires the servicer to use additional staff and other resources.

Lending Act," "Fair Credit Reporting," and "Servicemembers Civil Relief Act" booklets. In particular, the TILA and RESPA handbooks will reflect the new requirements of the CFPB's recent multiple rulemakings.

[18] Small servicers, as defined in Regulation Z (12 CFR 1026.41(e)(4)), are exempt from various provisions of the regulatory amendments in Regulation X and Regulation Z or are subject to specially tailored provisions.

Banks typically have different systems in place for servicing prime and subprime loans. Overall, servicing subprime loans is more expensive because it often requires frequent calls to borrowers who may also be receiving calls from other collectors. Subprime borrowers may also be more likely to send in partial payments that require additional resources to process. Because more contact is needed with subprime borrowers, the number of cases that one employee can handle is lower.

Servicing the wide variety of nontraditional and new mortgage loan programs in the market requires specialized operating controls to ensure that loan administration functions are operating in accordance with servicer guidelines and applicable law. The bank may be exposed to potential litigation and reputation risk if interest rate changes, payment adjustments, or loan amortization are improperly performed.

For nontraditional and new mortgage products especially, banks should have specialized training for customer service and default management staff members to ensure that they know each product's features as well as how to comply with consumer protection laws and regulations and how to avoid predatory lending. Servicers should have extensive default management procedures for the increased delinquencies that can be associated with high delinquency environments. Servicers should also ensure that IT systems are able to handle complex payment processing requirements.

Loan servicing involves the following areas of responsibility:

- Cash management
- Investor accounting and reporting
- Document custodianship
- Escrow account administration
- Collection and default management
- Loss mitigation
- Other real estate owned (OREO)
- Loan setup and payoff
- Customer service
- Other servicing-related topics

Cash Management

Cash management consists of collecting mortgage payments and depositing those funds into custodial or other fiduciary capacity accounts at depository institutions insured by the FDIC. See 12 CFR 330.7(d) for the definition of "mortgage servicing accounts" (collectively, custodial accounts). The payments may arrive in a variety of forms, including automated clearing house or check. The principal and interest portion of each payment must be separated from the portion set aside for escrow items. These custodial accounts require daily balancing and monthly reconciliation, control over disbursements, segregation of administrative duties, and the deposit of funds into appropriate financial institutions.

Investor Accounting and Reporting

Investor accounting and reporting consists of performing various record-keeping functions on behalf of trustees and investors. Effective internal controls must be in place to ensure accurate accounting and reporting. The bank should reconcile each investor account at least monthly. Outstanding reconciling items generally should be resolved within 30 days. The bank should review the aging of unreconciled items regularly and charge off uncollectible balances.

Servicers process loan payments and remit principal and interest to investors according to the specified remittance schedule. Most commonly, the schedule of borrower payments (whether actually made or not) determines the remittance schedule to the investor. In other cases, investors are not paid until the servicer actually receives payments from the homeowners.

Investor accounting responsibilities vary according to the type of servicing program. As an example, with Ginnie Mae I servicing, the servicer remits principal and interest to individual security holders and is responsible for maintaining a current list of all security holders. With Ginnie Mae II, Fannie Mae, and Freddie Mac servicing programs, the servicer forwards remittances to a central paying agent who remits payments to the security holders based on a specified schedule. Investor reporting responsibilities involve preparing monthly reports to trustees and investors on principal and interest collections, delinquency rates, bankruptcy, foreclosure actions, property inspections, charge-offs, and OREO. Servicers also report information to consumer credit bureaus on a borrower's payment performance.

Document Custodianship

Document custodianship consists of adequately safekeeping loan documents. Banks should ensure that they are in compliance with either GSE or private investor guidelines and applicable laws for document custody. Original documents should be stored in a secure and protected area. Copies of critical documents (e.g., a certified copy of the note) should be maintained in a separate location. Servicers also should maintain an inventory log of documents held in safekeeping. The log should identify documents that have been removed and who removed them. Some investors require the servicer to employ a third-party custodian to safeguard loan documents. In such cases, the servicer is responsible for timely delivery of documents to the custodian. Refer to the "Custody Services" booklet of the *Comptroller's Handbook* for additional guidance on document custody.

In addition to traditional paper documents, the industry increasingly relies on electronic documents and imaging systems. Controls similar to those used in a paper environment are also required for these environments.

Escrow Account Administration

Mortgage servicers are often responsible for monitoring mortgages for payment of local property taxes and appropriate flood and hazard insurance. In many cases, the servicer is required to establish and manage escrow accounts to make these payments. Escrow account administration consists of collecting and holding borrower funds in escrow to pay such items as real estate taxes, flood and hazard insurance premiums, property tax assessments, and, in some cases, interest on escrow account balances. The escrow account administration unit (1) sets up the account, (2) credits the account for the tax and insurance funds received as part of the borrower's monthly mortgage payment, (3) makes timely payments of the borrower's obligations, (4) analyzes the account balance in relation to anticipated payments annually, and 5) reports the account balance to the borrower annually.

Servicers must closely monitor property taxing authorities and individual insurance contracts to ensure that escrow calculations are accurate and that insurance policies have not lapsed. If the annual escrow analysis shows a surplus or shortage, the escrow administration unit makes a lump-sum reimbursement or charge to the borrower, or adjusts the amount of the homeowner's monthly mortgage payment accordingly.

Servicers should have policies and procedures in place to ensure sufficient flood and hazard insurance as required by contract or applicable law. If not paid directly by the borrower or through an escrow account, bank procedures may include use of a bank-owned blanket insurance policy or forced-placement insurance (a bank-purchased policy covering a specific property). Any such force-placed insurance programs must comply with applicable law, including Regulation X for hazard insurance and the Flood Disaster Protection Act[19] for flood insurance, both of which impose specific timing, notice, cancellation, and other requirements. Examiners should be aware of excessively priced force-placed policies and ensure adherence to mandated compliance policies. Appropriate policies should govern accurate identification of insurance shortfalls, borrower notification, and timely cancellation of force-placed insurance once the borrower provides evidence that sufficient insurance is in place.

Servicers must comply with applicable law in connection with its management of escrow accounts, including collecting, holding, and escrowing funds on behalf of each borrower in accordance with RESPA (12 USC 2609) and Regulation X (12 CFR 1024.17 and 1024.34). RESPA allows servicers to hold up to the amount required to make expected payments over the next 12 months plus an additional one-sixth of that amount. This limit applies to funds collected at closing as well as those collected throughout the life of the loan. RESPA also requires the servicer to provide various disclosures, including the initial and annual escrow statements. Effective in January 2014, the requirement for timely escrow disbursements generally will include the payment of hazard insurance premium charges when the borrower is more than 30 days overdue, unless the servicer is unable to disburse funds from the borrower's account. Insufficient funds in a borrower's escrow account does not mean that the servicer is unable to disburse the funds.[20]

Servicers also should ensure compliance with legal requirements regarding the cessation of escrow withholding for PMI on serviced loans. According to the HPA, PMI generally may be cancelled at the borrower's written request on a mortgage balance that is 80 percent or less of

---

[19] See Biggert Waters Flood Insurance Reform Act of 2012 for additional requirements.

[20] There is a limited exemption from this restriction for "small servicers," as defined by Regulation Z.

the original appraised value, based on the initial amortization schedule (fixed-rate loans) or the then-in-effect amortization schedule (ARM loans), so long as the loan is current, the borrower has a good payment history, the property's value has not decreased, and the residence securing the mortgage is not subject to a subordinate lien. PMI is to be automatically cancelled by the servicer once principal payments reduce the LTV to 78 percent, or the loan has reached the midpoint of its term, so long as the loan is current. Separate rules govern the cancellation of FHA mortgage insurance.

Collections and Default Management

The collection unit must closely follow investor requirements, applicable law, and other legal obligations in connection with the timing and manner of collection activities. Beginning in January 2014, new requirements under Regulation X will apply to collection activities, including those related to outreach to delinquent borrowers, continuity of contact obligations, limitations on dual tracking, and information management. Additionally, FHA and VA loans have very specific requirements regarding the conditions under which certain actions may be taken. In addition to complying with specific requirements, collection personnel should document each step in the collection process, including actions taken, the date of each action, success in contacting the borrower, and the commitment received from the overdue borrower.

The servicer may use both human and computerized elements to gather information and arrive at an optimal solution to delinquency problems. For example, behavior modeling software can be used to help prioritize collection efforts by analyzing borrower payment patterns, identifying those at greatest risk of default or foreclosure, and offering the most productive communication tactics with the borrowers. Computer software can be used for updating estimates of property values and evaluating foreclosure alternatives.

Default management personnel should attempt to ascertain the cause of the delinquency, determine the borrower's ability and willingness to perform, update the borrower's financial information when it is deemed necessary, and, if necessary, make alternative payment arrangements with the borrower. To avoid unnecessary delays in execution and limit error rates, bank policies and procedures should provide for sufficient training for those personnel appointed to underwriting borrower information. These efforts and alternative payment arrangements must comply with investor guidelines, applicable law, and other legal obligations and be documented in such a way that modification volumes and trends can be tracked.

Under the HUD Act of 1968, as amended, 12 USC 1701x(c)(5), banks must inform certain borrowers who are delinquent on their mortgage loans (home loans secured by a single-family dwelling that is the borrower's principal residence) about the availability of homeownership counseling.

Collection activities must comply with applicable law. For instance, such activities should not be unfair or deceptive within the meaning of section 5 of the FTC Act, 15 USC 45, as enforced by the OCC through 12 USC 1818. In some cases, the bank may be subject to the Fair Debt Collection Practices Act, 15 USC 1692. Among other things, this law defines from whom a debt collector may gather information on a consumer, the type of information that may be collected, and the acceptable forms of communicating with the consumer and other parties.

The servicer must follow investor standards, applicable laws, and other legal obligations pertaining to collection, loss mitigation, and foreclosure actions. In some states, the bank must wait longer to foreclose on a defaulted borrower than it does in other states; borrowers in some states have more power than they do in others to redeem their property; and in some states, foreclosing or obtaining a deficiency judgment requires a judicial proceeding, while in other states it does not. Collection activities must also conform to the requirements of bankruptcy law and any bankruptcy plan into which the debtor has entered. For example, the filing of a bankruptcy petition acts as an automatic stay on any collection activities in process at the time; following such a filing, all collection efforts usually must be processed through the bankruptcy court. Banks should have policies and procedures in place to address loss mitigation efforts that are consistent with applicable law, investor or guarantor requirements, and other contractual or legal obligations.

Banks should follow prudent underwriting practices in determining whether to consider any loan modification request or other request to change the terms of the note, whether the requested changes are temporary or permanent in nature. Such arrangements can vary widely based on the borrower's financial capacity. If an acceptable payment solution cannot be implemented, the loan passes into the loss mitigation phase. The GSEs and private investors have specific guidelines for servicers that govern loss mitigation activity.

Loss Mitigation

Banks are encouraged to work constructively with residential borrowers at risk of default and to consider prudent workout arrangements that avoid unnecessary foreclosures. Prudent workout arrangements that are consistent with safe and sound lending practices are generally in the long-term best interest of borrowers and banks. There may be instances, however, when workout arrangements are not economically feasible or appropriate for a borrower to retain the home.

Prudent business practice in servicing residential mortgage loans include ensuring that, before proceeding to a foreclosure sale, the loan is in default under applicable law and investor requirements; the borrower is not subject to specific legal protections, such as those afforded under the SCRA and bankruptcy law; the bank has the appropriate legal authority to foreclose; all appropriate notices have been provided to the borrower; appropriate loss mitigation efforts have been made; the loans is not currently in an active loss mitigation program; the borrower is not currently being considered for loss mitigation action; and the bank is in compliance with applicable state and local legal requirements. Appendix E, "Standards for Handling Files With Imminent Foreclosure Sale," provides the minimum standards to be included in a mortgage servicer's ongoing collections, loss mitigation, and foreclosure-processing functions. Accordingly, the OCC requires that all banks that service residential mortgage loans incorporate the guidance into their ongoing business processes.

Beginning in January 2014, servicers must follow specified loss mitigation procedures set forth in Regulation X for a mortgage loan secured by the borrower's primary residence. For instance, there are various communication-related requirements for delinquent borrowers, including outreach and continuity of contact obligations. Generally, servicers also must adhere to specified time frames when processing an application for a loss mitigation option, which might vary depending on when the application is received; must provide a written decision that includes specified information; and must allow the borrower to appeal a servicer's denial of a loan modification. Additionally, the new Regulation X rules generally limit when a servicer may evaluate a borrower for loss mitigation options at the same time as it prepares to foreclose on the property (i.e., dual tracking).[21]

Servicers should consider the requirements of Regulation X and other applicable laws and legal obligations and review the governing documents for securitization trusts to determine the full extent of their authority to restructure loans that are delinquent, in default, or in imminent risk of default. The governing documents may allow servicers to proactively contact borrowers at risk of default, assess whether default is reasonably foreseeable, and, if so, apply loss mitigation strategies designed to achieve sustainable mortgage obligations. The SEC has provided clarification that entering into loan restructurings or modifications when default is reasonably foreseeable does not preclude a bank from continuing to treat serviced mortgages as off-balance-sheet exposures.

Additionally, servicers are encouraged to use the authority they have under the governing securitization documents to take appropriate steps when an increased risk of default is identified, including

- proactively identifying borrowers at heightened risk of delinquency or default, such as those with impending interest rate resets.
- contacting borrowers to assess their ability to repay.
- assessing whether there is a reasonable basis to conclude that default is "reasonably foreseeable."
- exploring, where appropriate, a loss mitigation strategy that avoids foreclosure or other actions that result in a loss of homeownership.

Effective foreclosure prevention relies on increasing the amount of contact between servicers and delinquent borrowers. Early contact and communication with lenders and trusted advisors to develop alternatives to foreclosures increases the likelihood that troubled borrowers will find solutions that enable them to stay in their homes.

The following are common loss mitigation strategies employed by mortgage servicers:

Reinstatement or repayment plan: A reinstatement or repayment plan might be used for borrowers who fall behind on their mortgage payments but are able to subsequently resume making monthly payments. Under this arrangement, the lender increases the regular monthly payment until the delinquency is repaid.

---

[21] "Small servicers," as defined by Regulation Z, generally are exempt from these dual-tracking requirements but will be subject to specially tailored requirements applicable to dual tracking.

Partial mortgage insurance advance claim payment: This approach might be used if a mortgage insurer is involved (either the FHA or a private mortgage insurer). Under this approach, a one-time payment is made by the mortgage insurer to the lender to cover all or a portion of the default. In these cases the borrower is required to sign an interest-free note for the amount of the advance claim payment payable to the insurer of the mortgage. The repayment of the note is scheduled to coincide with the borrower's ability to pay when the borrower recovers and structured to the individual's circumstances. The details on this program may vary among mortgage insurers.

Forbearance agreement: These agreements typically establish a repayment plan based on the borrower's financial situation and may include a temporary reduction or suspension of payments for a specific length of time. These agreements are often used when the borrower has a reduction in income or increase in expense that is not expected to be permanent.

Mortgage modification: Permanent modifications result in a refinancing of the debt or extension in the term of the mortgage loan that allows the borrower to catch up by reducing the monthly payments to a more affordable level. They are used for borrowers who have recovered from a financial problem or otherwise have demonstrated the ability to afford the new payment amount. Modifications could include lowering interest rates, adding payments to the end of the loan term, reducing the principal amount owned, paying off small amounts of arrearages each month, adding a lump-sum payment due at payoff, or simply lowering payments for a set period of time. All modifications should be evaluated to determine whether they constitute a troubled debt restructuring under ASC 310.[22]

Loan assumption: This is an arrangement where a qualified borrower agrees to assume responsibility for repayment of the mortgage.

Pre-foreclosure or short sale: This is an arrangement in which a lender can agree to accept the proceeds of a pre-foreclosure sale in satisfaction of the loan, even though the proceeds may be less than the amount owned on the mortgage.

Deed in lieu of foreclosure: This occurs when the borrower voluntarily deeds the property to the lender to avoid a lengthy foreclosure, additional accrued interest, and expenses. This action is typically used when attempts to sell the house fail before foreclosure.

As part of the loss mitigation process, the property is often inspected by outside contractors. On loans insured by HUD, property inspections must be made as early as 45 days following delinquency, if efforts to contact the borrower have been unsuccessful. In some cases a collection unit may enter into a short-term forbearance arrangement with a delinquent borrower before beginning a foreclosure action. For example, a servicer may permit the borrower to defer payments, follow an alternative repayment plan, or execute a deed in lieu of foreclosure (which grants the borrower full forgiveness of the debt).

---

[22] For loan modifications generally and modifications made under the Home Affordable Modification Program (HAMP), see the applicable regulatory capital rules.

The use of some loss mitigation techniques, such as waiving a due-on-sale clause to allow an assumption, may require the bank to repurchase the loan out of its MBS pool. Management should have adequate information systems to analyze forbearance activities. The collections or default management unit also should evaluate and thoroughly document the reason for each forbearance arrangement and obtain investor approval, if necessary.

If foreclosure is necessary, before initiating foreclosure proceedings management should ensure that any issues over disputed payments have been resolved and that all investor requirements have been met, and that any requirements of applicable law or other legal obligations have been met, including any limitations on dual tracking. Management should determine whether pursuing a deficiency judgment is legal and economically feasible. The servicer might contact any junior lien holders to determine whether they are willing to buy out the senior mortgage. Once a property is foreclosed, the servicer must decide whether to sell the property "as is" or to improve it before sale and whether to list it or offer it at auction. Any claims due from PMI in force on the property should be filed within the required time frames and with all necessary documentation.

Before the mortgage crisis, some servicers initiated foreclosures in the MERS name if MERS was acting as mortgagee. Many larger servicers, however, implemented the practices of assigning mortgages from MERS to the servicer or investor before foreclosures. MERS has published revised rules that require servicers to reassign MERS mortgages before beginning foreclosure. Banks should have appropriate controls and processes to ensure compliance with MERS rules.

A servicer advances funds and incurs costs on behalf of investors during the collection process and during the time the foreclosed property is administered as OREO. An account receivable is normally established to account for these servicer advances. The investor subsequently reimburses the servicer for much of the funds advanced and costs incurred. The servicer will likely absorb some of the costs associated with collecting a delinquent loan, even for mortgages serviced without contractual recourse.

Such cost absorption occurs in a VA "no-bid" action. If the expected loss to be recognized by the VA following a foreclosure is greater than the amount of the VA guarantee, the VA may elect to pay the full amount of its guarantee to the servicer and transfer title to the property to the servicer. The servicer is left to administer and dispose of the property, often at a substantial loss. Other noteworthy collection costs include unreimbursed interest advances on FHA loans and expenses above those considered normal and customary by investors.

The bank should establish a "foreclosure reserve" to provide for uncollectible investor advances. Using historical collection and disposal costs for each major product type as a guide, the foreclosure reserve should adequately cover expected losses. Charge-offs, recoveries, and provision expenses should be recognized through the foreclosure reserve. Processes must be in place to recognize uncollectible advances in a timely manner and to charge off rejected claims within reasonable time frames.

Vintage analysis is commonly used in the mortgage banking industry to enable lenders to compare delinquency, foreclosure, and loss rates on similar portfolio products over comparable loan origination periods. Vintage analysis assists lenders in the early identification of the underlying causes of credit quality problems and implementation of corrective measures. This analysis can also assist in the review of the adequacy of the foreclosure reserve.

Other Real Estate Owned

OREO administration consists of obtaining the title to foreclosed property and managing and disposing of such property. Some mortgage servicing agreements require the servicer to take legal title to OREO—for example, if the loan was sold with recourse or if it is a VA no-bid loan. If so, the servicer obtains title to the property following the completion of the foreclosure action. If the bank has or will obtain legal title to the property, management must follow the terms and conditions under which a national bank or FSA may hold real estate and OREO, as specified in 12 USC 29 and 12 CFR 34 for national banks, and 12 USC 1464(v), 12 CFR 160.172, 161.2(b)(2), 162.2, 163.170, and 167.5(c)(ii) for FSAs. When the bank acquires OREO, management must adhere to applicable law and policy guidance and follow call report instructions regarding loan loss recognition and OREO reporting. For further information, see the *Comptroller's Handbook* booklet "Other Real Estate Owned".

Servicing agreements may require the servicer to perform administrative duties as an agent for the investor when administering OREO. For example, the servicer may be required to secure and protect the property, conduct inspections regularly, obtain a current appraisal, and market the property.

Loan Setup and Payment Processing

Loan setup and payoff consists of inputting information into the automated servicing system and processing loan payoffs. The loan setup unit inputs information regarding the borrower and borrower's loan, such as the investor, the type of loan and repayment terms, tax and insurance information, and escrow requirements, as applicable. Appropriate servicing of the loan requires the setup unit to input data accurately and in a timely manner (usually within 15 days of loan closing or moderately longer for acquired loans). The setup unit, or a related unit, typically sends the borrower a letter that introduces the company's services and includes the first payment coupon, which provides the address for mailing payments. This "welcome letter" helps to establish positive customer relations and to reduce the volume of loans with "first payment default" (which may cause an investor to put back a loan). Given the large volume of inputs, loan setup is an expensive process for many servicers. Often, the cost of loan setup exceeds the first year's servicing revenue.

The payoff unit is responsible for processing loan payoffs, including recording the mortgage satisfaction and returning the original note to the borrower. Failure to process the mortgage satisfaction in accordance with state laws may result in monetary fines or heightened litigation risk.

If a loan pays in full during the month, some investors require the servicer to remit a full month's interest even though the borrower only paid interest through the payoff date. This interest expense can significantly increase servicing costs in periods of high payoffs. The examiner should assess the bank's efforts to minimize this interest expense.

Under new Regulation Z requirements effective in January 2014, servicers must promptly credit periodic payments from borrowers as of the day of receipt, adhere to new requirements regarding partial payments, and provide accurate payoff balance information under specified circumstances.

Customer Service

Customer service creates and maintains a positive relationship with borrowers. The new Regulation X and Z amendments include various customer service requirements, including those related to customer complaints, error resolution, and information requests; borrower outreach and communication requirements; requirements related to loss mitigation; the transfer of information during servicing transfers; and facilitating communication with successors in interest of a deceased borrower with regard to the property securing such borrower's mortgage loan.

Customer service efforts are especially important before and after servicing portfolio purchases or sales and during periods of high business activity. The customer service unit can facilitate an effective customer retention program. This unit identifies existing loan customers who are likely to refinance their loans and contacts them with offers to refinance. This practice can help preserve servicing volumes in times of increased refinancing activity.

Care must be taken to avoid practices that may be considered to constitute predatory servicing and that may separately violate one or more federal statutes, such as the FTC Act, the Fair Debt Collection Practices Act, FCRA, RESPA, and TILA. Examples of predatory servicing practices include the following:

- Failure to properly credit mortgage payments that are made on time, as a pretext for imposing unjustified late fees, and knowingly reporting borrowers to credit bureaus for the resulting false delinquencies.
- Force-placing high-cost insurance coverage on borrowers despite documentary evidence that satisfactory insurance is in effect. (When escrow accounts are insufficient to make these higher insurance premiums, monthly mortgage payments are increased, leading to further delinquencies and late fees.)
- Charging fees for services not specifically sanctioned in loan documents.
- Charging late fees when the only delinquency is attributable to earlier late fees or delinquency fees.
- Threatening borrowers with unjustified foreclosures (i.e., those caused solely by the servicer's own predatory servicing practices).
- Failure to respond to customer inquiries and complaints about these practices in an adequate or timely manner, including as defined by RESPA.

- Failure to pay insurance or taxes (on loans with escrowed funds) in a timely manner, which could subject borrowers to unnecessary penalties.

Other Servicing-Related Topics

Other servicing-related topics include the provision of required disclosures (e.g., periodic billing statements, notice of interest rate adjustments), the management of third-party servicing arrangements, Ginnie Mae mortgage buyback options, servicing recourse, and servicing QC.

Third-Party Arrangements

Vendors That Are Not Servicers

A servicer may employ outside vendors to perform various tasks. These tasks may include processing tax and insurance payments, providing lock-box services, conducting property inspections, performing legal work on foreclosures, or acting as custodian for loan documents. When delegating authority of business functions to third parties, a bank remains responsible for the consequences of the third parties' actions. Among other considerations, a bank must ensure that third parties comply with applicable laws, regulations (including those pertaining to safety and soundness, privacy, and consumer protection), and bank policy and business practice standards, and do not damage the bank's reputation.

While a bank may use third parties, including vendors, to assist or control costs, these arrangements involve an added level of risk. A bank's arrangements with third parties should comply with internal standards, as well as OCC guidance and applicable law, including new Regulation X requirements that are effective in January 2014. A bank's policies and procedures should address the management and oversight of the life cycle of these arrangements and should cover

- initial selection and due diligence process.
- negotiation of acceptable contract provisions.
- outsourcing of functions.
- oversight and monitoring of vendors, including scorecards and reports measuring performance against key indicators, a certification or approval process, and on-site visits.
- periodic assessment of performance and resolution of deficiencies.
- monitoring of the financial strength of vendors.
- internal audits or other independent reviews of the effectiveness of the bank's outsourcing program and the quality of the vendor risk management program.

Third-Party Servicers

A bank can incur significant loss exposure if it does not properly manage its arrangements with third-party servicers or sub-servicers. The practices of a third party become the bank's responsibility. This risk can be greater if a third party does not have a proven record. Problems arising from a third-party arrangement can result from negligence, incompetent servicing staff, or simply poor servicing practices. Occasionally, losses result from fraudulent activities such as diversion of loan payoffs, escrow funds, or principal and interest payments. Beginning in January 2014, Regulation X requires servicers to have specified policies and procedures that facilitate the oversight of, and compliance by, third-party service providers. More generally, examples of servicer activities and red flags that banks should detect and eliminate to prevent losses include

- excessive delay in the servicer's remittance of mortgage loan payments or prepayments so the servicer can earn additional float income.
- diversion of escrow payments intended for payment of taxes or insurance to the servicer's use.
- retention of funds on full prepayments while representing to the bank that the borrower continues to make monthly payments.
- missing, lost, damaged, or out-of-date records.
- sending nonsufficient funds checks to the bank.
- canceling insurance or bond coverage to save money.
- misrepresenting the level of delinquencies and foreclosures.
- poor management of delinquencies, tax and insurance payments, PMI claims, or ARM adjustments.

Banks should be aware that some state laws view the servicer as an agent of the owner of the mortgage loans and thereby hold the owner liable for the actions of the servicer. While some states regulate servicers, the regulations usually focus on consumer protection rather than safety and soundness. A bank should perform due diligence and ongoing monitoring with any new third-party servicer to minimize the risk of problems and losses.

Initial Due Diligence on Servicers and Sub-Servicers

Before entering into a contractual arrangement with a third-party servicer or sub-servicer, a bank should perform an appropriate review for third parties, including

- obtaining financial and historical background information, such as
  - Dun and Bradstreet reports.
  - audited financial statements and SAS 115, "Communicating Internal Control Related Matters Identified in an Audit," reports.
  - attestations on servicing from external auditors, such as Regulation AB or Uniform Single Attestation Program (USAP) reports.
  - servicer ratings from ratings agencies.
- confirming the servicer's approval and check for any recent adverse audit findings or suspensions by HUD, Fannie Mae, Freddie Mac, Ginnie Mae, and all PMI companies. Obtain ratings from these entities for the servicer's default and investor reporting and remitting functions.
- obtaining investor (including private investor) "seller/servicer" reports, as well as the servicer's internal audit reports and QC reports on servicing functions.

- performing an on-site due diligence visit and determining the adequacy of the servicer's internal audit function.
- checking the adequacy of the servicer's errors and omissions (E&O) insurance and surety bond coverage.
- reviewing established quantifiable criteria, such as the number of loan repurchases; the number of times reports or cash remittances are late; and delinquency, bankruptcy, foreclosure, and real estate owned rates.

If, after performing these reviews, the servicer is acceptable to the bank, it should enter into a written servicing agreement with the third party. The servicing agreement should

- require the third party to comply with all applicable laws, regulations, and other applicable requirements.
- clearly specify the servicing policies and procedures the servicer is to use for all common or anticipated servicing situations.
- permit on-site audits of the servicer at any normal business time by the bank, its agents, or the OCC.
- require the use of separate deposit accounts at approved financial banks for both principal and interest and escrow payments. The deposit account statement should be transmitted directly to the bank.
- request that companies providing the PMI make all claim checks payable to the bank or notify the bank of payments to the servicer.
- allow the bank to have direct access to the MIS service bureau or servicer's MIS department for audit purposes.
- specify the dates and frequencies for remittance of principal and interest and payoff funds to the bank.
- state the servicing fees and the manner of payment to the servicer, including identifying the recipient of ancillary income and float revenue.
- permit termination of the servicing agreement for cause and outline the transfer of the mortgage servicing files, records, insurance policies, computer records, and other related documents to the designee of the bank. The definition of "for cause" should be clearly defined to include fraud, embezzlement, diversion of mortgage payments or payoffs, failure to follow any provision of the servicing agreement, and continued careless servicing after the bank has sent a formal written warning to the servicer.
- permit the transfer of the same servicing records at any time without cause by payment of a stipulated termination fee to the servicer.
- require direct notification to the bank for cancellation or nonrenewal of E&O insurance, and/or surety bond.

Ongoing Monitoring of Servicer Performance and Audit

A bank should implement the following monitoring and audit procedures to minimize the risk of loss from a servicer. If applicable, the bank may also use these procedures, as appropriate, for its oversight responsibility over primary servicers in its role as master servicer:

- Review monthly remittance reports and other computer reports from the servicers to detect discrepancies and errors.
- Review and reconcile bank statements monthly against borrowers' payments and remittances from the servicer and escrows held by the servicer.
- Perform annual desk reviews and on-site reviews of the servicer, and have tracking reports on the status of corrective actions related to these reviews.
- Perform quarterly comparisons of the servicer's delinquency, foreclosure, real estate owned, and prepayment rates to the national averages from the MBA delinquency survey and perform any other trend and peer analysis.
- Verify, on an annual basis, mortgage loans, property owners, and loan balances by direct mail.
- Conduct annual reviews of the servicer's (1) external audit reports and attestations and (2) financial reports.
- Review, on an annual basis, the servicer's internal audit and QC reports on servicing.
- Check the servicer's E&O insurance and surety bond coverage annually.
- Verify, through annual reviews, continued approval of the servicer by PMI companies, HUD, Fannie Mae, Freddie Mac, and Ginnie Mae. Obtain ratings by these entities on the servicer's default management and investor reporting and remitting functions.
- Obtain, on an annual basis, investor "seller/servicer" reports.
- Perform annual review of servicer ratings from rating agencies.
- Review results of servicer contingency plan testing, as well as the bank's testing of its own contingency plans in collaboration with the servicer.
- Review the servicer's compliance self-assessments.

When a bank uncovers problems, it should take immediate action. If the bank detects fraud or diversion of funds, it should move immediately to transfer servicing payments and bank accounts to its name or that of another servicer. For less serious problems, a bank should determine the best solution to correct deficiencies. Banks, however, should not hesitate to transfer servicing for cause if the servicer does not follow any of the provisions of the servicing agreement or does not promptly correct problems after notice.

Ginnie Mae Mortgage Buyback Options

Ginnie Mae programs allow issuers to buy back certain delinquent loans from securitized pools for which the bank provides servicing. To maintain the government agency guarantee or insurance, however, the issuer must continue to follow the agency's servicing guidelines. At the issuer's option, and without Ginnie Mae's prior authorization, the issuer may repurchase certain delinquent pooled loans (e.g., those past due 90 days or greater) for an amount equal to 100 percent of the remaining principal balance of the loans. Continued sales treatment is not permitted under ASC 860 for such loans, irrespective of the intent to exercise the buyback option. See appendix C, "Mortgage Banking Accounting," for additional discussion.

Early pool buyout decisions should be supported by internal analyses evidencing the economic benefit to the bank. Typically such buyout activity is supported by the guaranteed yield on the loan, the estimated remaining time to foreclosure, and the likelihood of reinstatement of the loan to performing status. The analysis of individual loans should consider the collateral, the status of guarantees, and liquidity ramifications to the bank. Banks should have limits on their total investment in early pool buyout loans. Monitoring processes should ensure timely liquidation and disposition of these loans. Management should gauge the impact should these short-term liquidation assets reinstate to performing status and become long-term assets that may not fit the bank's portfolio objectives.

The bank should establish controls to prevent the purchase or removal of a loan from the pool before allowed by investor-established time frames. Premature purchase or removal of a loan harms investors by inappropriately reducing the outstanding balance of the investors' portfolio.

Servicing Recourse

Generally, a bank is subject to recourse when the agreement governing the servicing of mortgages requires the bank to be responsible for losses, even though it has no interest in the mortgage loans. The bank is also subject to recourse when mortgage-servicing assets are transferred to another servicer if the bank guarantees to absorb any credit-related losses on the transferred servicing assets. Under a specific set of circumstances, as described in the recourse provisions of the OCC's risk-based capital rules, however, mortgage servicer cash advances may not be considered recourse.[23] These advances, which usually cover foreclosure costs and other expenses that facilitate the timely collection of the loan, are not recourse if (1) the servicer will be fully reimbursed at the top of the cash flow waterfall and (2) any nonreimbursable advance is an insignificant amount of the outstanding loan balance for a single loan.

Servicing Quality Control

Banks should have a QC unit that independently reviews the work performed by each servicing function. The QC unit should test a representative sample of transactions, report its findings to appropriate levels of management, and require timely responses for significant findings.

Servicing contracts used by many investors contain requirements that an independent external auditor attest that the servicer's operations are of satisfactory quality. Often, investors mandate the annual performance of an opinion-level attestation engagement that conforms to the American Institute of Certified Public Accountants' AT Section 60, "Compliance Attestation." This review is to be documented by a letter from an independent public accountant representing that the loans were serviced in accordance with the USAP for Mortgage Bankers. If the independent external auditor determines that a servicer has successfully met the minimum servicing criteria prescribed by the USAP, those findings may be used in the servicer's audited financial statements and accepted by outside investors. The servicer's internal audit staff sometimes performs some of the USAP procedures on behalf of the external auditor.

---

[23] See the applicable regulatory capital rules for the appropriate capital treatment of servicer cash advances.

In December 2004, the SEC finalized and adopted Regulation AB,[24] which codifies and expands rules and regulations for asset-backed securities that are registered with the SEC and sold to the general public. Most publicly issued, nonagency residential mortgage-backed securities are subject to Regulation AB. Regulation AB rules include, among other things, requirements for periodic reports and standards for assessment of servicing compliance and related accountant attestation.

Another indicator of the quality of servicing operations is the residential servicer ratings assigned by ratings agencies such as Standard & Poor's, Moody's, and Fitch. These are generally available only on large operations. Some investors (including Fannie Mae and Freddie Mac) may conduct their own on-site reviews of servicing activities.

Mortgage Servicing Assets

Mortgage servicing assets (MSA), sometimes referred to as mortgage servicing rights (MSR), are financial assets that are originated, purchased, and sold by various financial institutions. MSAs are complex, intangible assets that arise from owning the rights to service mortgage loans that have been securitized or sold to third-party investors. The market value of MSAs is affected by market supply and demand factors. MSA values are economically represented as the discounted present value of estimated future net cash flows over the life of the underlying mortgage loans. See appendix C, "Mortgage Banking Accounting," for information on MSA recognition and valuation.

A bank can retain the right to service mortgages it has originated (retail and wholesale) and sold, acquire servicing in bulk acquisitions, or acquire servicing from third-party production flow. When a mortgage bank makes a bulk servicing acquisition, it purchases the MSR of a portfolio of mortgage loans, leaving ownership of the underlying mortgages or securities with the investor. When a bank acquires servicing rights through third-party production flow, it is purchasing the servicing on an ongoing basis from another originating institution.

MSAs expose servicers to interest rate, price, and operational risks. The risk of changes in the fair value of MSAs due to changes in interest rates is normally considered interest rate risk. It could be considered price risk, however, if the bank is actively buying and selling its MSAs. MSAs pose operational risk because the servicing and valuation functions are operations intensive and model dependent.

To mitigate these risks, banks that capitalize MSAs must implement an effective MSA risk management structure. Effective risk management of the MSA includes systems for valuation of the MSA asset and managing the risks in this asset.

---

[24] For more information on Regulation AB, see www.sec.gov/rules/final/33-8518.pdf.

Risk Management

A bank's MSA risk management structure should address the following areas:

- Internal controls
- MIS
- MSAs from originations
- MSAs from acquisitions
- Valuation
- Model validation
- Hedging
- Selling MSAs
- Regulatory capital

For guidance on MSA accounting, examiners should refer to appendix C. For additional guidance on risk management of MSAs, examiners should refer to OCC Bulletin 2003-9, "Interagency Advisory on Mortgage Banking."

Internal Controls

A bank's internal control process should provide for adequate segregation of duties among MSA acquisition and sale, valuation, hedging, and accounting. The valuation and hedging risk management functions should be separate from accounting and finance. Each organization is unique and should approach segregation in a manner suitable to its size and complexity. The audit function can assist in developing an appropriate control environment.

Oversight of MSAs should be subject to review by a risk committee composed of persons representing various disciplines, such as accounting, finance, hedging, risk management, legal, compliance, servicing, secondary marketing, and asset-liability management. Audit should periodically evaluate the oversight structure and effectiveness. It is critical that the bank's asset-liability management function be represented because of the significant interest rate risk in this asset. Responsibilities of the risk committee should include

- identifying limits for board and senior management approval.
- monitoring risk for escalation trigger and threshold breaches.
- approving the selection of valuation models and changes to the models.
- assessing the appropriateness of proposed MSA acquisitions or sales.
- approving initial capitalization and monthly valuation results.
- approving valuation assumptions and changes to them.
- ensuring that there is adequate documentation and independent testing of valuations.
- reviewing critical accounting policies and estimates.
- reviewing economic performance of the servicing business.
- reviewing MIS.

It is very important that appropriate information and data be provided to management to effectively administer MSAs. The nature and extent of management reporting varies, depending on the breadth and complexity of a bank's activities. MIS reports that should be provided to executive management include

- historical and projected changes in interest rates and their impact on the valuation of both the MSA and the hedging instruments.
- the current sensitivity of the MSAs and hedging instruments to changes in interest rates and mortgage prepayment speeds.
- an analysis of MSA fair values from multiple sources.
- trends in key valuation assumptions, such as prepayments, servicing costs, ancillary income, delinquencies, defaults, and discount rates.
- a comparison of actual versus projected cash flows (static pool analysis) and economic results.

MSAs From Originations

For many banks, the MSA primarily results from the capitalization of servicing on originated loans that have been securitized or sold into the secondary market with servicing retained. Management should have operating procedures that address MSA initial capitalization rates, including frequency, stratification (e.g., product type, coupon bands, original maturity), and valuation methodology. Policies, procedures, and valuation methodology should be consistent among initial capitalization rates, models used for MSA acquisitions and sales, and ongoing valuation.

MSAs From Acquisitions

Many banks actively acquire MSAs from other institutions through bulk acquisitions or production flow. Formal policies and procedures should guide these acquisition activities. A bank should accurately and consistently document its acquisition of MSAs regardless of source. Documentation provides for proper communication, review, and approval of key assumptions and judgments. Documentation also provides a means for subsequent validation by independent parties, such as internal audit, independent accountants, and regulatory examiners.

Before proceeding with bulk acquisitions, the bank should conduct a due diligence review of the targeted servicing portfolio. The review should document and analyze all of the salient characteristics of the portfolio, including

- contractual servicing fees.
- excess servicing fees.
- mortgage product types.
- loan size.
- weighted average coupon.
- weighted average maturity.
- seasoning.

- payment performance.
- prepayment forecasts.
- geographic concentrations.

In addition, the review should assess the economic value of the servicing rights, including key assumptions, judgments, and estimates. These records should support the initial carrying amount of each acquisition. Management should continuously monitor prepayment speeds and other key assumptions to evaluate their effects on each portfolio.

For production flow activities, management should review the pertinent characteristics of the servicing being acquired. These reviews, which are similar to the due diligence for bulk acquisitions, should adequately support the carrying value of the acquired MSAs.

Valuation

Under GAAP, as described in ASC 860, "Transfers and Servicing," a servicer recognizes MSAs only when the economic benefits exceed "adequate compensation" for performing the servicing. Adequate compensation is defined as the amount of benefits of servicing that would fairly compensate a substitute servicer should one be required, which includes the profit that would be demanded in the marketplace. Economic benefits include the contractually specified servicing fee as well as other sources of cash flow such as float, late fees, and other ancillary income related to the servicing of the mortgage loans.

The bank must estimate the economic benefit that it will receive as compensation for servicing a portfolio of mortgage loans on behalf of an investor and compare that amount to the profit that would be demanded in the marketplace. The servicing agreement between the servicer and the investor specifies the compensation and all cash flows to the servicer. The servicing agreement typically expresses the servicing fee as a number of basis points per month relative to the outstanding principal balance of the serviced portfolio (e.g., 25 basis points per month of the outstanding balance of mortgage loans serviced).

Valuation of MSAs should be supported by adequate documentation. Documentation of MSAs should include the policies and procedures for determining the fair value of servicing and should require

- quarterly reviews of valuations and impairment.
- comparisons with external market data, such as market trades, third-party valuations, industry publications, surveys, and interest-only securities.
- supportable estimates of future cash flows (interest-only securities).
- reconciliations between actual and expected cash flows (static pool analysis).
- detailed support for any changes in the valuation process.
- comparisons between actual yields and market yields.

Static and option-adjusted spread (OAS) cash flow models are the two predominant approaches to the valuation of MSAs if market prices are not readily available. Valuation models depend on various input data, such as prepayment speeds, discount rates, delinquency rates, float earnings, and escrow earnings. All input assumptions to the valuation model must be documented to support the valuation conclusion for MSAs and to provide a means for independently validating those conclusions. See appendix C, "Mortgage Banking Accounting," for additional guidance on the appropriate accounting of MSAs.

Static cash flow analysis is a common practice for valuing MSAs. This analysis involves estimating net servicing income and discounting the projected cash flow stream to its present value using an appropriate discount rate. The discount rate should consider the required rate of return for an asset having similar risk characteristics. The discount rate should also consider the risk premium for the uncertainties associated with servicing operations.

Most mortgage loans are subject to prepayment risk. Many are repaid well before contractual maturity as homeowners move, refinance, or simply pay the loan ahead of schedule. To estimate the servicing income it will receive, a bank must project the level of servicing fees it can expect from the loan pool as individual loans prepay over time.

Prepayment speed is the key component in a valuation model and represents the annual rate at which borrowers are expected to prepay their mortgage loan principal. Common prepayment speed measures used by the industry include Public Securities Association (PSA), conditional prepayment rate (CPR), and single monthly mortality (SMM). Refer to the "Glossary" for definitions of these prepayment measures.

If a bank's estimate of fair values is not based on realistic prepayment speeds and other key assumptions, MSA values will not be supportable. For example, if the bank uses an unsupported slow prepayment speed or low discount rate, the capitalized book value of the MSAs may be overstated. Conversely, a faster prepayment speed or a higher-than-market discount rate can understate the MSAs.

OAS analysis is a form of stochastic (probabilistic) simulation that assumes interest rate movements are essentially random, though subject to certain constraints in their movement or distribution. An OAS model values MSAs based on a full range of interest rate environments that can occur over the life of the asset. As interest rates fluctuate, the cash flow expectations for MSAs change. OAS is further defined in the "Glossary."

The primary advantages of OAS include

- use of a probabilistic model consistent with the current term structure of interest rates and the assumed level of volatility.
- development of explicit pricing and valuation for embedded options, such as the prepayment option.
- use of simulation methodology that is more theoretically sound, approximating the methodologies used to value hedge instruments and mortgage securities.

The primary disadvantages of OAS include

- lack of precise market prices for specific MSAs. The OAS used in the model, like the discount rate used in static analysis, is arbitrary.
- requirement of more resources than static analysis in terms of computing power, software, and model sophistication.
- lack of set standards for OAS computation. OAS model results are highly dependent on input assumptions such as volatility, prepayment speed, default rates, inflation, the appropriate risk-free rate (Treasury or LIBOR), and the setting of model parameters, all of which can result in different OAS and MSA values.
- lack of consistency in OAS model methodology that may result in asset valuation differences.

In choosing between static and OAS analysis, bank risk managers should understand the advantages and disadvantages of each. Technical understanding of the details of implementing the solution is critical. Neither method can be a "black box" into which the user simply plugs assumptions and receives results. Risk managers must understand the internal workings of the model and the implications of the input choices they make.

Model Validation

Models play a critical role in the process of managing and accounting for MSAs. A model's reliability depends on accurate information and the use of reasonable, supportable assumptions. Using models requires substantial judgment and expertise.

Banks should establish validation procedures over the information and assumptions entered into the models, the logic and processing of the information within the models, and the accuracy of reports generated. Management should employ appropriate IT controls to limit access and maintain data integrity. Validation procedures should include independent review of the model logic, comparison against other models, and comparison of model results against actual results and conditions. OCC Bulletin 2011-12, "Sound Practices for Model Risk Management," provides detailed guidance regarding model validation.

Hedging

MSAs are subject to wide changes in fair value as interest rates and prepayment assumptions change. As interest rates decline, borrowers tend to refinance and prepay their mortgage loans. This can drastically reduce the estimate of net servicing income from MSAs and reduce their value. As interest rates rise, MSA values tend to increase, but generally not as much as they decline when rates fall. This negative convexity of MSAs makes them more complex to hedge.

Many banks have established hedge programs to mitigate the effects of interest rate and price risk on MSA values. Banks should understand the nature and magnitude of the risks in their MSA and, if engaged in hedging, the costs and benefits of their particular hedge strategy, and the effectiveness of that strategy. See appendix B, "Hedging," for additional information.

Selling MSAs

Management should periodically assess its strategic decisions to retain or sell servicing. Factors underlying this decision may include the bank's MSA valuation relative to current market prices, management's interest rate risk appetite, strategic servicing portfolio considerations, and capital management issues. Servicing is normally sold in a bulk sale, on a flow basis, or through sales of individual loans with servicing released. Bulk sales are made in the secondary market and involve aged servicing. "Flow" refers to a bank selling loans under a master commitment as loans are produced or pools are formed.

In an "assignment of trade" flow sale arrangement, the seller of the loans and associated servicing assigns a forward sale commitment of MBS to the buyer of the servicing. The seller delivers the loans to the buyer, who is then responsible for creating the MBSs and delivering them to the broker/dealer while retaining the servicing.

Regulatory Capital

Banks should consult and follow the applicable regulatory capital rules for MSAs. As discussed, the regulatory capital rules for MSAs will change effective January 1, 2014, and January 1, 2015, for advanced approaches banks and non-advanced approaches banks, respectively. Banks with a large concentration of MSAs relative to capital will likely be subject to additional regulatory scrutiny because of the volatility of this asset.[25]

Interest-Only Strip (Excess Servicing)

An interest-only (IO) strip is defined in ASC 860 as "a contractual right to receive some or all of the interest due on a bond, mortgage loan, collateralized mortgage obligation, or other interest-bearing financial asset." The IO or excess servicing consists of forward-looking estimates of interest earned on the underlying assets, less

- servicing fee paid to servicer.
- administration and trustee fees.
- coupon paid to investors.
- credit losses.

For example, consider a 30-year, fixed-rate, conventional loan. If the loan rate is 6 percent, the coupon paid to investors is 5.5 percent, the servicing fee is 0.25 percent (25 basis points), and the other fees and credit loss estimate is 0.21 percent (21 basis points), then the excess yield is 0.04 percent (4 basis points). This excess servicing yield would be separately recognized as an IO asset.

---

[25] On October 11,2013, the OCC published its Basel III capital rule 78 Federal Register 62018 (Ocotber 11, 2013), which revises its current rules on bank regulatory capital. The effective date of this rule is phased in over a five-year period, starting on January 1, 2014, for advanced approaches banks and January 1, 2015, for all other banks. Until these effective dates begin, examiners should apply the OCC capital rule as described in this booklet.

Assets created to recognize excess servicing represent earnings and capital to the bank when they are recognized. Therefore, overly optimistic or unreasonable assumptions used to capitalize the IO could result in overstated earnings and capital. A bank should have satisfactory policies, procedures, and control systems in place to ensure that such assets are realistically valued and that the book value is based on prudent assumptions. See appendix C, "Mortgage Banking Accounting," for additional guidance.

Examination Procedures

This booklet contains expanded procedures for examining specialized activities or specific products or services that warrant extra attention beyond the core assessment contained in the "Community Bank Supervision," "Large Bank Supervision," and "Federal Branches and Agencies Supervision" booklets of the *Comptroller's Handbook*. Examiners determine which expanded procedures to use, if any, during examination planning or after drawing preliminary conclusions during the core assessment.

Depending on the focus of any particular review, examiners may need to consult other *Comptroller Handbook* booklets. For instance, examiners undertaking reviews for compliance with consumer protection laws should further consult the relevant *Consumer Compliance* booklet for more information and complete examination procedures, including the booklets addressing the Real Estate Settlement Procedures Act and the Truth in Lending Act, as applicable.[26]

Examiners should evaluate the impact of mortgage banking operations on the bank by assessing the risks posed by current and anticipated activities. Many of the steps in these procedures require gathering information from the bank or reviewing information obtained from examiners in other functional areas. Given that interrelationships exist between the bank departments (e.g., loan production and secondary marketing) and within the bank as a whole (e.g., liquidity and asset quality), and that business processes and operational risks cross business line boundaries, examiners are encouraged to perform integrated cross-discipline examinations. Performing integrated examinations and discussing the findings with other examiners can reduce the burden on the bank, avoid duplication of effort, and contribute to a comprehensive and holistic perspective on the risk profile and quality of risk management. Sharing examination findings also can be an effective cross-check of data and can help examiners assess the integrity of the bank's MIS.

Scope

The scope of mortgage banking supervisory activities depends on the examiner's knowledge of those activities, the amount of total and product exposure, and the cumulative amount of risk posed to the bank. The core examination procedures provide the steps necessary for a comprehensive mortgage banking examination in smaller or less complex operations and serve as the base for mortgage banking examination procedures for larger or more complex operations. The procedures include in-depth analysis and testing to promote examiners' assessments of the quantity, aggregate level, and direction of risk(s).

The scope of the review may be expanded as necessary in cases in which the bank offers new or significantly changed products, a particular concern exists, or there are larger, more complex operations. In these situations, examiners should select the appropriate expanded procedures, internal control questionnaire, or verification procedures to augment the core

---

[26] While the expanded procedures include some consumer compliance requirements, they are not intended to be comprehensive.

procedures. Examiners are also encouraged to refer to other booklets of the *Comptroller's Handbook* as needed.

Operating subsidiaries or service corporations are, in most cases, examined together with their parent bank. The OCC supervises banks by business line, not according to corporate form. Activities conducted in subsidiaries are subject to the same level of scrutiny that is applied to activities conducted directly in a bank.

OCC examiners conducting a mortgage banking examination should (1) test subsidiaries for compliance with established policies, practices, procedures, and internal controls in conjunction with other examination procedures and (2) sample transactions between the operating subsidiary and the parent bank. Thus, a sample of mortgage loans includes loans originated at mortgage operating subsidiaries as well as loans originated at the bank itself.

While reviewing mortgage banking activities, examiners should remain alert for lending practices and product terms that could indicate unfair, deceptive, abusive, or predatory lending.

Objective: To determine the scope of the examination of mortgage banking and identify examination objectives and activities necessary to meet the needs of the supervisory strategy for the bank. Assess the level of risk, evaluate the quality of risk management, and determine the aggregate level and direction of risk of the bank's mortgage banking activities and the potential for a more thorough review in any of the functional areas.

1. Coordinate examination objectives and scheduling with other areas such as consumer compliance, retail lending, and IT. Coordination should include requests for information, meetings, and scope of transaction testing.

2. Review the following documents to identify any previous problems and determine the adequacy and timeliness of management's response to the issues identified, and any findings or issues requiring follow-up:

   - The examination scope memorandum issued by the bank examiner-in-charge (EIC).
   - Previous mortgage banking examination reports and related working papers.
   - Pertinent OCC and other regulatory reports, electronic or otherwise.
   - Internal memorandums and senior management reports on the mortgage banking unit since the last examination.
   - Reports issued by internal and external auditors, investor reviews (e.g., Fannie Mae, Freddie Mac, Ginnie Mae, FHLBs, HUD, VA), and significant private investors.
   - Financial Crimes Enforcement Network reports on SAR filings.
   - Policies and procedures for all functions within the mortgage banking unit.

3. Obtain and review reports management uses to supervise mortgage banking activities. Determine any material changes in the following since the last supervisory activity:

   - Types of products and product mix
   - Terms on products (i.e., introductory interest rates)
   - Growth in overall and individual products
   - Expansion initiatives
   - New products
   - Marketing or acquisition channels (e.g., Internet, direct mail, third-party originators)
   - Underwriting criteria and any automated technologies used in execution
   - Monitoring and risk management processes
   - Secondary marketing (e.g., pricing, pipeline or warehouse inventory, loan delivery, hedging)
   - Servicing volumes
   - Servicing performance metrics for internally originated loans and loans serviced for others
   - New or expanded servicing arrangements
   - Compliance with MERS requirements
   - Market focus
   - Contingency plan test results for IT and business processes
   - SAS16 reports for third-party service providers
   - Rating agency assessments for third-party service providers (where available)

4. Investigate management's perception of the market conditions and whether the bank can remain successful without making changes.

5. Assess the risk profile using the core examination procedures in each functional area to help assess the scope of the examination and potential for a more thorough review.

6. Determine whether the bank has a separate mortgage banking committee. If so, review committee minutes for significant activities. If not, review the committee minutes where mortgage banking results are reported.

7. Obtain copies of complaints reported to the OCC's Customer Assistance Group, review bank consumer complaint logs, and evaluate the information for significant issues and trends.

   Note: Complaints serve as a valuable early warning indicator for compliance, credit, and operational issues, including unfair, deceptive, abusive, and predatory practices.

8. Determine whether there is any litigation, either filed or anticipated, associated with the bank's mortgage banking activities and the expected cost or other implications.

9. Determine whether the bank offers debt suspension or cancellation ("debt waiver") products. If so, consider compliance with 12 CFR 37, "Debt Cancellation Contracts and Debt Suspension Agreements." Refer to the retail lending examination procedures for specific guidance.

10. Determine during early discussion with management

    • how management supervises the mortgage banking operation.
    • whether there have been any significant changes in policies, processes, personnel, control systems, etc.
    • whether any internal or external factors could affect the unit.
    • whether bank officers are operating in conformance with the established guidelines and following appropriate management practices.

11. Based on the performance of the previous steps and discussions with the bank EIC and appropriate supervisors, determine the scope and objectives of the examination.

12. As examination procedures are performed, conduct appropriate transaction testing for compliance with applicable law, established policies and procedures, and the existence of appropriate internal control measures. Identify any area with inadequate supervision or undue risk.

    Examiners should conduct transaction testing when the EIC determines that the OCC should verify a bank's compliance with its own policies and procedures or with regulatory policies, regulations, or laws.

    Testing procedures may be conducted periodically on portfolios or targeted segments of the portfolios when there is elevated risk, an increase in delinquency and loss rates, new lines of business, new acquisition channels, or rapid growth, or when internal audit is inadequate.

    Judgmental or statistical sampling may be used. The sample size and targeted portfolio segment may be modified to fit the circumstances. The sample selected should be sufficient in size to reach a supportable conclusion. For information on sampling methodologies for specific transaction testing, consult the "Sampling Methodologies" booklet of the *Comptroller's Handbook*.

    Examiners conducting testing should remain alert for what could be unfair, deceptive, abusive, or predatory lending practices. If weaknesses or concerns are found, consult the bank's EIC or compliance examiner.

13. Select steps necessary to meet examination objectives from among examination procedures provided under the following sections of this booklet:

- "Management and Supervision"
- "Internal and External Audits"
- "Information Technology"
- "Loan Production"
- "Secondary Marketing"
- "Servicing"
- "Mortgage Servicing Assets"

Note: The following examination procedures are seldom used in their entirety. Select only those procedures appropriate to the complexity and risk profile of the mortgage banking operation.

The first three sections of the examination procedures, "Management and Supervision," "Internal and External Audits," and "Information Technology," apply to all mortgage banking operations. A review of these areas must be completed to effectively conclude on the quality of risk management in any of the four functional areas of loan production, secondary marketing, servicing, and mortgage servicing assets.

Management and Supervision

Objective: Assess the effectiveness of management and board supervision of mortgage banking operations, including practices employed to increase the performance and ultimate profitability.

Core Examination Procedures

1. Determine the level of compliance with or divergence from strategic business plans through risk assessments and impact analysis. Significant deviation from plans may lead to a change in the quantity and quality of products, services, controls, management supervision, and technology. Management should have a clear and demonstrable understanding of the anticipated strategic changes' impact on the financial condition of the operation.

2. Review staffing levels and expertise relative to origination volume, servicing size, or complexity of operations. Insufficient staffing levels, experience, and operational efficiency can lead to high error rates and pose significant risk to the bank.

3. Assess the nature and number of customer complaints relative to the amount of production and servicing. Determine whether the bank has accurately assessed the reasons for such complaints and instituted appropriate steps to provide relief to existing customers and prevent further events from occurring.

4. Review the key risk limits for each of the major functional areas. Absence of meaningful risk limits is usually indicative that the bank does not understand the nature of the risk and is vulnerable to unwittingly accepting excessive risk, such as credit, operational, or interest rate risk and all of the attendant negative results.

5. Assess the depth and timing of MIS reporting. Insufficient and lagging reporting efforts suggest a high level of management and oversight risk. Management is disabled from effectively integrating appropriate risk management processes without a clear knowledge of profitability, servicing values, and production expectations by type and channel.

6. Review the functional organization dynamics and assess the separation of duties among the primary operating functions (origination, underwriting, secondary marketing, valuation, hedging, and finance). Insufficient functional independence may lead to conflicts of interest and expose the bank to various risks, such as credit, operational, and liquidity risk.

7. Determine whether the bank has a high level of mortgage banking income relative to total banking income. An overly dependent or increasing level of dependency could be problematic given the volatility associated with mortgage banking earnings, the potential for rapid changes in interest rates and funding arrangements, and access to capital in the event of adverse market conditions.

8. Evaluate the model development, usage, and adjustment processes. Significant dependence on models, whether internally developed or purchased, and operating systems without external independent reviews could place the bank in a position of false confidence. Incorrect assumptions or algorithms and outdated systems may lead the bank to decisions that could have adverse effects on credit, pricing, and interest rate decisions.

9. Review the volume of mortgage originations, pipeline or warehouse size and turnover rate, and the amount of the servicing portfolio. Significant changes may indicate management's desire to accelerate earnings, or an absence of appropriate management oversight.

Expanded Examination Procedures

Policies and Controls

1. Review policy and procedural guidelines for the mortgage bank operation. Determine whether they are communicated to relevant staff and how compliance is monitored. Ascertain whether guidelines have been established to

   - define permissible mortgage banking activities.
   - identify individual responsibilities.
   - define reasonable risk limits and monitor compliance.
   - require segregation of duties.

2. Review corporate or bank plans, policies, procedures, and systems for asset-liability management, operational risk management, and consumer compliance. Determine the extent to which the policies, procedures, and systems incorporate mortgage banking activities.

3. Review the strategic plan for mortgage banking activities. Determine whether

   - the plan is reasonable and achievable in light of the bank's capital position, physical facilities, data-processing systems, capabilities, size and expertise of staff, market conditions, competition, and current economic forecasts.
   - the goals and objectives of the mortgage banking business are compatible with the overall business plan of the bank or its holding company.

4. Review the budget process and financial performance of the mortgage banking unit. Determine

- whether bank executive management and the board have communicated performance goals to the mortgage banking unit.
- whether management tracks and evaluates the mortgage banking unit's financial performance as a separate line of business.
- whether staff periodically compare current financial results to the unit's financial plan and past performance.
- how staff analyze and document significant deviations from the financial plan.

5. Determine whether management has established a system that reflects all risk characteristics to ensure that sufficient capital is maintained for mortgage banking operations. Determine whether the bank has met the capital requirements of different investors with which it has relationships and assess whether the risk-based capital requirements are calculated correctly.

6. Determine whether the risk management process is effective and based on sound information. Evaluate its comprehensiveness and whether it adequately addresses significant risks in each functional area of the mortgage operation.

7. Determine whether mortgage banking functional areas have adequate independence and segregated reporting lines.

8. Determine whether comprehensive procedures are in place to ensure compliance with laws and regulations.

9. Review the mortgage banking unit's new product development process to ensure that it considers all applicable risks (credit, interest rate, liquidity, price, operational, compliance, strategic, and reputation).[27] Determine whether management

- considers customer needs and wants.
- prepares financial projections and risk analyses.
- considers accounting and regulatory requirements applicable to the product.
- obtains legal opinions.
- considers technology and MIS requirements risk impact.

Note: Before implementing any marketing initiative, including the rollout of a new product or change to an existing product, management should review all marketing materials, consumer disclosures, and product features and terms for compliance with laws and regulations and to identify and address potentially unfair, deceptive, abusive, and predatory lending practices that may adversely affect reputation and compliance risk.

---

[27] See also OCC Bulletin 2004-20, "Risk Management of New, Expanded, or Modified Bank Products and Services."

Personnel

10. Assess the expertise and experience of the mortgage banking unit's management team and key staff. Review management succession plans and determine whether designated successors have the necessary background and experience.

11. Review the organizational chart for mortgage banking activities. Determine

   - whether decision making is centralized or decentralized.
   - which individuals are responsible for major decisions and who makes final decisions.
   - whether sufficient independence exists among the various functional areas.
   - whether actual staffing levels and turnover rates are appropriate based on industry or peer data.

12. Review compensation plans, including incentive components, for mortgage banking managers and staff. Determine whether the plans

   - comply with applicable laws, regulations, and internal standards designed to mitigate risk and reward qualitative factors, not just the quantity of loans originated.
   - comply with applicable laws, including Regulation Z and Regulation X.
   - have been reviewed and approved by the board of directors.
   - consider qualitative factors rather than just production volume.
   - include controls to ensure that originators are not improperly encouraged to direct borrowers to particular products in a discriminatory, predatory, or otherwise unlawful manner.
   - include systems to ensure that overages, if allowed, have sufficient controls and monitoring.
   - are designed to recruit, develop, and retain appropriate talent.
   - discourage employees from taking risks that are incompatible with the bank's risk appetite or prevailing rules or regulations.
   - are consistent with the long-term strategic goals of the bank.
   - include compliance with bank policies, laws, and regulations.
   - consider performance relative to the bank's stated goals.
   - consider competitors' compensation packages for similar responsibilities and performance.
   - consider individual overall performance.

Management Information Systems

13. Evaluate the systems for managing risk within the mortgage banking unit. Determine to what extent the bank uses simulation modeling to assess the impact of interest rate changes or other economic variables on the mortgage operation.

14. Review MIS and determine management's capacity for evaluating and monitoring mortgage banking activities. Evaluate MIS reports for detail, accuracy, and timeliness. Determine whether

    - MIS and operating systems are adequate to monitor current operations and handle future product growth.
    - board receives MIS reports on profitability, monthly production volume, inventory aging, hedged and unhedged positions, mark-to-market analyses, delinquencies, foreclosures, status of reserves, MSAs, operational efficiency, and policy exceptions.
    - current MIS allocates all revenues and costs (including overhead and administrative support) by functional area (production, secondary marketing, servicing, etc.) and production channel (retail, wholesale, correspondent), and how management uses this information to administer mortgage operations.
    - management has adequate knowledge of product profitability, including production, servicing costs, and servicing values, and whether that knowledge is incorporated into the overall risk management process.

15. Assess the extent to which the board and management use the data obtained from MIS in their decision-making process.

16. Assess the adequacy of physical facilities, data-processing systems and platforms, and human resources capabilities. Determine adequacy relative to

    - current business volume.
    - future business plans, including strategic initiatives to meet any shortcomings.

Internal and External Audits

Objective: Determine whether a comprehensive audit program has been implemented and whether the board or audit committee has established effective audit guidelines and processes for mortgage banking activities.

Core Examination Procedures

1. Determine whether an audit review has been performed since the last examination. Assess the scope and frequency of internal audits. Consider statutory requirements and regulatory guidelines, purpose and objectives of audits, control and risk assessments, audit cycles, and reporting relationships and requirements.

2. Determine whether audit staff and related functions have a direct reporting line to the board of directors to dissuade the possibility of managerial pressure and preserve the integrity of the audit process.

3. Determine whether management takes appropriate and timely action on the audit findings and recommendations and whether it reports the action to the board of directors or its audit committee.

4. Evaluate the independence and competence of those who manage and perform the audit functions. Determine the level of experience of bank auditing personnel, specifically in the areas of mortgage banking and capital markets.

5. Determine whether audit personnel actively review appropriate MIS to assist in targeted audit programs. Optimally, audit staff should have access to all systems such that they can create their own MIS reporting independent of the targeted area for review.

6. Determine whether the nature and depth of the relationship between the internal and external audit function is promoting a thorough review of the targeted area and detailing all pertinent areas of concern. Areas of review might include the contract outlining the scope of the work to be performed, fees, and the protocol for changing terms of engagement for increased work assignments.

7. Review the board or audit committee minutes, as well as audit information packages submitted to the board or audit committee to determine whether the audit findings are reviewed, discussed, and acted on by the board of directors. Actions that suggest active participation by the board of directors might include the review and approval of audit strategies, policies, programs, and compensation structures for external auditors.

Expanded Examination Procedures

Policies and Controls

1. Review the bank's internal audit program for mortgage banking activities. Determine whether it includes adequate objectives, procedures, scheduling, and reporting systems.

2. Determine the extent to which the internal audit program covers the following mortgage banking areas, as applicable:

   - Production
   - Pipeline and warehouse operations
   - Hedging activities
   - Servicing
   - MSAs
   - Secondary marketing activities
   - Internal control
   - Financial and regulatory reporting
   - Accounting treatment
   - Inter-company transactions
   - MIS
   - IT and IT environment
   - Compliance with applicable laws, regulations, and guidance, including assessing whether any lending practices are unfair, deceptive, abusive, or predatory

3. Determine whether the audit program specifically targets those mortgage lending activities exhibiting higher risk, including risks from nontraditional mortgage products.

4. Determine whether auditors periodically review and verify

   - accuracy of data input, record keeping, and related MIS.
   - appropriate accounting for and financial reporting of operations.
   - information security processes and requirements (refer to the *FFIEC Information Technology Examination Handbook* "Information Security" booklet).
   - system architecture and performance.
   - loan documentation management.
   - outsourcing arrangements and services (refer to the *FFIEC Information Technology Examination Handbook* "Outsourcing" booklet).
   - continuity of operations, including backup and recovery (refer to the *FFIEC Information Technology Examination Handbook* "Business Continuity Planning" booklet).

Personnel

5. Review the education, experience, and ongoing training of the internal audit staff and draw a conclusion about its expertise in auditing mortgage banking activities.

6. Evaluate the independence of the internal audit staff by considering whether it has necessary authority and access to records and to whom it reports audit findings.

Management Information Systems

7. Determine whether the internal auditors periodically verify the accuracy of MIS reports.

8. Determine whether the internal audit function itself has sufficient MIS to report and monitor significant findings for appropriate management resolution.

Processes

9. Determine whether the board and management have established internal and external audit coverage for the mortgage banking unit and its associated IT environment.

10. Determine whether internal or external audit provides adequate audit coverage of primary income- and expense-related activities most likely to have a significant impact on earnings or capital. Consider any significant recommendations from other examination areas that were not addressed by internal or external audit findings.

Internal Audit

11. Review internal audit working papers. Evaluate the effectiveness of the audit by considering the scope, frequency, and working paper documentation, as well as the conclusions reached.

12. Determine whether the internal audit staff reviews the audit, inspection, or examination reports prepared by the external auditors, HUD, Freddie Mac, Fannie Mae, FHLBs, private investors, and regulators.

13. Determine to what extent the internal audit follows up on criticisms and recommendations in those reports.

14. Review the criticisms and recommendations in the internal audit report. Determine whether, and the extent to which, management changes operating and administrative procedures as a result of report findings. Evaluate how the internal audit unit assesses the appropriateness of management's corrective action.

External Audit

15. Review the results of the most recent engagement letter, external audit report, and management letter for potential issues or concerns to ascertain the consistency and thoroughness of issues identified related to the mortgage banking operation.

16. Determine to what extent the external auditors rely on the internal audit staff and the internal audit report.

17. Determine whether the external auditors review all functional mortgage banking areas.

18. Review the findings in the external audit report. Determine whether the auditors rendered an opinion on the effectiveness of internal controls and assessed the overall condition of the mortgage banking operation.

19. Determine whether management promptly and effectively responds to the external auditor's recommendations, and whether management makes appropriate changes to operating and administrative procedures as a result of the report's finding(s).

Information Technology

Objective: Assess the adequacy of the mortgage banking function's IT structure, operating environment, and control practices.

Note: These procedures are intended to provide an overview of IT in the mortgage banking function. The procedures are not all-inclusive and should be adjusted accordingly. Refer to the *FFIEC Information Technology Examination Handbook* as needed.

Core Examination Procedures

1. Determine whether the bank adopted new Internet-based systems for mortgage loan origination, processing, pricing, or delivery, or enhanced existing usage of such systems. Significantly increasing broker or correspondent relationships through an electronic application exposes the bank and customers to multiple forms of fraud.

2. Assess the level of remote access for independent agents (i.e., mortgage brokers, correspondents, credit repositories, title insurance companies, settlement firms, etc.) and information walls to assure third-party confidentiality.

3. Review the number and nature of outsourcing relationships. Vendors can be problematic for a bank to manage given the technical challenges of connecting to each third party and the potential for increased electronic threats.

4. Determine whether the bank uses a third party to process mortgage applications and the safeguards possessed to ensure the security of the customers' personal information.

5. Assess the level of access controls over customer information from internal as well as external threats.

6. Review the bank's incident response process to system problems. Rapid identification and mediation are imperative to recovery and monitoring for future events.

7. Determine whether the bank has properly segregated IT duties. Failure to appropriately segregate IT duties from the production process can expose the bank to fraud schemes and, ultimately, affect its earnings and capital.

8. Determine the existence, testing, and updating of the business continuity processes. Examine the assumptions, change control processes, data synchronization procedures, crisis management methodologies, and incident response times for level of continuity.

Expanded Examination Procedures

1. Review internal and external IT audit comments and reports issued that address the technology supporting the mortgage banking business.

    Note: IT-related audit comments and reports may be issued by a specialized IT audit group or integrated with general internal or external audit comments and reports.

2. Review internal IT risk assessments of the technology systems that support mortgage banking activities.

3. Obtain and review technology management reports to assess performance issue trends of key mortgage banking systems.

4. Obtain and review a listing of recent mortgage banking IT projects, e.g., new systems, enhancements, and upgrades.

5. Review meeting minutes from the board of directors or designated committee overseeing mortgage banking activities.

    Note: The IT examiner should coordinate this review with the mortgage banking EIC.

6. After review of the above information, and discussion with the mortgage banking EIC, determine the scope of the IT examination.

7. Determine whether key mortgage banking systems are operated internally or by a third-party vendor. If the mortgage banking system is managed by a third party, review the service contract and assess the effectiveness of the bank's vendor management program. Refer to OCC Bulletin 2013-29, "Third-Party Relationships: Risk Management Guidance," and the "Outsourcing Technology Services" booklet of the *FFIEC Information Technology Examination Handbook.*

8. Assess the effectiveness of the IT control environment managed by the bank's IT department, with emphasis on

    *   IT management.
    *   IT audit.
    *   systems development life cycle.
    *   data input, access, processing, and change controls.
    *   data and system validation.
    *   network performance monitoring.
    *   information security.
    *   business continuation and disaster recovery planning and testing.
    *   user access controls.
    *   systems administrator practices.
    *   level and quality of IT technical staff.

9. Assess access control and change management policies and procedures for internally developed and off-the-shelf software used by the mortgage banking function.

10. Discuss any IT-related issues and concerns with the mortgage banking EIC and bank management.

11. Compile IT conclusions and matters requiring attention (MRA) and communicate to the mortgage banking EIC.

Loan Production

Objective: Assess the risks associated with loan production and determine whether loan production activities are executed in conformity with board-approved strategies and processes and comply with legislative and regulatory requirements.

Core Examination Procedures

1. Assess the level of wholesale originated (broker or correspondent) mortgage loans relative to overall production. Significant increases or a disproportionate percentage can present the bank with substantial credit, pricing, recourse, and liquidity risk.

2. Assess the volume of nonconforming, subprime, Alt-A, or nontraditional mortgage loans originated by the bank and by the industry. The bank should have a robust mortgage origination process (i.e., processing and underwriting) and several funding options to avoid potential liquidity issues. Rapid increases in such loans may signal a significant buildup of credit, operational, and compliance risks within the bank and across the system.

3. Review the bank's strategy to originate for the portfolio versus originating for sale, and determine the extent to which mortgage loans originated for sale are transferred to the portfolio. Portfolio increases beyond strategic plans may be representative of systemic or staffing issues in the origination process. Significant variations in standards used to underwrite loans for sale versus loans for the portfolio may be cause for concern.

4. Determine whether the bank has high or an increasing level of policy exceptions. The pressure to acquire assets and achieve revenue targets may be driving the bank to ignore characteristics that have been proven to cause higher levels of default and repurchase requests.

5. Determine whether the bank is loosening underwriting standards without other compensating factors and adequate funding sources. Excessive underwriting flexibility without investor or senior management approval is likely to prove harmful to the bank at different levels.

6. Determine whether the bank has a high level of missing documents on closed loans. High volumes and poorly defined pre-funding review processes can lead to high levels of rejections or repurchase requests.

7. Review the number and nature of QC, audit, and consumer compliance findings. Banks should ensure that consumers have clear and balanced information about the menu of products being offered by the bank. Failure to do so may be in violation of federal and state laws and regulations.

8. Determine whether the bank has sufficient policies, procedures, and staff to comply with requirements related to the origination mortgage loans set forth in federal law (including Regulations X and Z), state law, and investor requirements. The bank should pay particular attention to the assessment of consumers' ability to repay the loan, appraisal requirements, loan originator registration and licensing obligations, loan originator compensation limitations, and disclosure requirements.

Expanded Examination Procedures

Policies and Controls

1. Determine whether the board or its mortgage banking committee, consistent with its duties and responsibilities, has adopted adequate loan production policies. Determine whether policies adequately address

    - the types of loans the bank will originate or purchase.
    - loan sources.
    - underwriting guidelines.
    - pricing methodologies.
    - compliance activities.
    - documentation standards.
    - real estate appraisal and evaluations.

2. Determine whether management recognizes the risks of nontraditional and subprime mortgages and whether appropriate portfolio and risk management practices are in place.[28] Determine whether

    - policies have been developed that specify acceptable product attributes, production, and portfolio limits, as well as risk management expectations. Consider whether the bank
      - manages risk appropriately by means of operating practices, accounting procedures, and policy exception limits and reporting.
      - uses appropriate MIS to identify risk layering and establish appropriate limits on risk layering.
      - establishes growth and volume limits by loan type, especially for products and product combinations requiring heightened attention due to easing terms or rapid growth.

---

[28] The CFPB 2012 rules amending Regulation Z, in particular the ability-to-repay requirements, impose significant limitations on nontraditional mortgage products.

- concentrations of nontraditional or subprime mortgage products exist and, if so, whether they are effectively monitored. Consider concentration limits on
  - loan types.
  - third-party originations.
  - geographic area.
  - property occupancy status.
  - key portfolio characteristics, such as loans with high CLTV and DTI ratios, loans with potential for negative amortization, loans to borrowers with credit scores below established thresholds, and nontraditional mortgage loans with layered risks.

3. Determine whether national bank policies and procedures provide adequate guidance to avoid unfair, deceptive, abusive, or predatory lending practices, including the following:

- Lending predominantly on the liquidation value of collateral rather than the borrower's ability to service the debt.
- Refinancing loans frequently and sequentially.
- Refinancing special subsidized mortgages that contain terms favorable to the borrower into a loan with less favorable terms.

4. Determine whether policies and procedures address, if applicable, the circumstances (and associated controls and monitoring processes) in which the bank may make loans involving features or actions that may raise concerns regarding unfair, deceptive, abusive, or predatory lending practices. Such features or actions include the following:

- Financing single-premium credit life insurance or similar products.[29]
- Allowing negative amortization.
- Requiring balloon payments in short-term transactions.
- Charging prepayment penalties in the later years of a loan or beyond the rate reset period on hybrid ARMs.
- Increasing interest rates upon default.
- Inserting arbitration clauses.[30]
- Making high-cost loans (e.g., loans subject to HOEPA).

If weaknesses or concerns are found relating to unfair, deceptive, abusive, or predatory lending practices, consult the bank's EIC or compliance examiner.

---

[29] When finalized, amendments to Regulation Z, effective January 2014, will prohibit such single-premium financing.

[30] Amendments to Regulation Z effective June 2013 prohibit mandatory arbitration clauses in specified transactions.

Note: For additional information refer to appendix C to 12 CFR 30, "OCC Guidelines Establishing Standards for Residential Mortgage Lending Practices," and 12 CFR 160.101, "Real Estate Lending Standards," and the following OCC advisory letters:

- AL 2000-7, "Abusive Lending Practices"
- AL 2002-3, "Guidance on Unfair or Deceptive Acts or Practices"
- AL 2003-2, "Guidelines for National Banks to Guard Against Predatory and Abusive Lending Practices"
- AL 2003-3, "Avoiding Predatory and Abusive Lending Practices in Brokered and Purchased Loans"

5. Evaluate management oversight of origination, processing, and underwriting functions to ensure supervisor accountability for the quality and timeliness of production functions. Consider

- benchmarking standards for the production function.
- processes to detect and prevent errors before closing and delivery.

Personnel

6. Review the organizational chart and reporting structure for the loan production area. Determine whether

- responsibilities and reporting structure for the origination, processing, underwriting, and closing functions are clearly defined.
- each function is sufficiently independent and not unduly influenced by sales and origination.
- the QC unit is independent of the origination function.

7. Review the qualifications, any required licensing or registration, experience levels, and training programs for originators, processors, underwriters, closers, and QC staff for adequate abilities to execute their respective responsibilities in a safe and sound manner.

Management Information Systems

9. Assess the quality of the MIS used to monitor and administer loan production functional areas, including the adequacy of source document(s) to process application reconcilement procedures.

10. Evaluate the disaster recovery plan to determine whether it covers all major production functions performed in-house. Consider whether backup systems exist in case primary systems fail, and assess the existence of any unnecessary risk exposure.

Processes

Origination

11. Assess the mortgage banking unit's credit culture and lending philosophy, including to what degree it is willing to relax credit standards or offer below-market pricing to increase mortgage production volume.

12. Determine whether the bank's origination activities are primarily retail- or wholesale-oriented. Determine key differences in the programs, including price, product type, and interest rate lock period.

13. Review the sources and types of mortgage products offered. Examiners should

   - evaluate product volume, trends, and concentrations.
   - determine the volume of, and growth in, higher-risk or nontraditional products, such as
     - loans with interest-only features.
     - payment-option ARMs.
     - reduced documentation of the borrower's assets, employment, or income.
     - higher LTV ratios and simultaneous second liens.
     - higher DTI ratios.
     - lower credit risk scores.
     - longer-term amortization.
     - negative amortization.
     - loans secured by non-owner-occupied properties.

   Note: When evaluating lending activities, examiners should remain alert for practices and product terms that could indicate unfair, deceptive, abusive, or predatory issues.

14. Determine whether the bank complies with applicable laws in originating loans, including

   - providing accurate initial consumer compliance disclosures (e.g., good faith estimate and informational booklet, truth-in-lending statement) to the applicant within prescribed time frames.
   - providing full and fair product information to consumers. Consider
     - the availability of full and fair product descriptions when customers are shopping for mortgages.
     - whether promotional materials and product descriptions provide sufficient information to enable consumers to prudently consider the costs, terms, features, and risks of mortgages, including nontraditional and subprime mortgages, in their product selection decisions.
     - how information is disclosed regarding payment shock, negative amortization, prepayment penalties, balloon payments, cost for reduced documentation, and responsibility for taxes and insurance.

  – whether customers are inappropriately directed or steered to consummate any particular transaction.
  – compliance with special rules for certain mortgage transactions (e.g. HOEPA).

Note: Examiners should consult compliance examiners for assistance with these procedures, if needed. Examiners also should consider the asset size of the bank to assess whether the OCC is primarily responsible for assessing compliance with the requirements of federal consumer financial laws.

15. Determine whether the bank sufficiently documents the proposed disposition of each mortgage at the time it is acquired or originated, i.e., whether to hold it in warehouse for sale or retain it in the permanent portfolio.

16. Evaluate controls designed to prevent originators from altering loan pricing parameters set by the secondary marketing unit.

17. Determine the methods used to evaluate and compensate loan originators. Determine whether

  • bank pays loan officers based on transaction terms and conditions, an action prohibited by mortgage loan originator compensation standards set forth in Regulation Z.
  • performance and compensation programs consider qualitative factors such as loan quality, completeness of application information, and timeliness and accuracy of initial consumer disclosures, as well as origination volume.
  • compensation programs incorporate controls to ensure that originators are not improperly encouraged to direct borrowers to particular products in a discriminatory, predatory, or otherwise unlawful manner.
  • management adequately holds originators accountable for quality.

18. Review management's analysis of origination costs. Determine whether all direct and indirect costs are appropriately measured and accounted for. Examiners should

  • determine whether the analysis covers all major product types and sources of production.
  • determine whether management calculates the amount of time the bank must service a loan before it recaptures all origination expenses.
  • evaluate management's comparison of key production functions (e.g., origination costs, underwriting efficiency, and processing time) with budget and industry averages.
  • review management's analysis of origination costs within the organization and whether costs are assessed by product unit.
  • determine whether the bank defers loan fees in excess of cost in accordance with ASC 310 for retained mortgages. See appendix C, "Mortgage Banking Accounting," for additional guidance.

Processing

19. Review management's system for monitoring processor workflow and efficiency. Determine whether

   * industry standards are used as a benchmark.
   * bank has procedures requiring processors to notify pipeline management of withdrawn mortgage applications.
   * there are processes, monitoring, and reporting systems to ensure that loans are closed before the expiration of interest rate locks.

20. Determine the method used to ensure that all required loan documents are obtained and accurately completed before the scheduled loan closing. Determine

   * how often required loan documents were not obtained and accurately completed within the bank's prescribed time frames.
   * whether the volume of exceptions is excessive relative to the total pipeline and volume of closed loans.
   * volume of underwriting suspense items caused by processing errors. Assess whether the volume of these exceptions is high relative to the bank's internal guidelines and industry standards.
   * whether management has evaluated the underlying cause of any errors and has taken appropriate corrective action.

Underwriting

21. Review management's process for measuring underwriter efficiency and quality. Determine whether

   * performance is measured against objective benchmarks and industry standards.
   * management reviews investor feedback to evaluate underwriter performance.

22. Review systems in place to ensure that underwriting practices comply with applicable law, bank policy, and the underwriting criteria specified by the purchaser(s) of the bank's mortgage products. Determine

   * whether the bank has a contractual relationship with each purchaser.
   * whether the bank uses automated underwriting systems, automated valuation models (AVM), and other automated underwriting processes.
   * whether mortgage insurance is obtained in accordance with investor requirements (i.e., original LTV higher than 80 percent) and for loans sold with recourse or those that are retained by the bank (if required by policy).
   * number and dollar volume of loans originated that do not conform to policy. Evaluate the process for approving policy exceptions and determine the reasonableness of the volume of loans approved with policy exceptions.

23. Determine whether loan terms and underwriting standards are consistent with prudent lending and the repayment capacity of borrowers. Determine whether a bank's qualifying standards recognize the potential impact of payment shock on borrowers. Additional consideration should be given to borrowers with high LTV ratios, high DTI ratios, low credit scores, reduced documentation, and any combination thereof.

24. Determine whether the analysis of borrower repayment capacity includes an evaluation of the ability to repay the debt by final maturity. For nontraditional and subprime mortgage products, the analysis of repayment capacity should be determined at the fully indexed rate, assuming a fully amortizing schedule. For products that permit negative amortization, the repayment analysis should be based on the total amount the bank has committed to lend. This would include the initial loan amount plus any balance increase that may accrue from the negative amortization provision.

25. Review the procedure for handling loans that do not conform to policy. Determine whether the bank requires, and obtains, senior management's approval for policy exceptions. Review monitoring systems, reporting, and tracking of performance for loans approved with policy exceptions.

26. Determine whether the bank has developed and deployed processes to mitigate exposures and protect their collateral positions where municipal lending programs are offered that could create a super-senior lien priority. For new mortgage loans, mitigating efforts should include reducing LTV limits to reflect the maximum advance rates offered by the lending program and consideration of the lien's payment requirements in the borrower's financial capacity.

27. Determine whether customers denied credit are provided a proper notice under the ECOA and FCRA.

Appraisal and Evaluation

28. Determine whether there is an effective internal control structure to ensure appropriate collateral valuation policies and procedures that comply with the appraisal provision of Regulation Z (12 CFR 1026.42), OCC appraisal regulations (12 CFR 34, subpart C, for national banks and 12 CFR 164 for FSAs), and OCC Bulletin 2010-42, "Interagency Appraisal and Evaluation Guidelines."

29. Review the appraisal and evaluation function to determine the independence of the function and the competency of the individuals administering the function. Determine whether

- those preparing a valuation or performing a valuation management function do not have a prohibited conflict of interest in the transaction.
- required independence in the appraisal function is fostered through reporting lines and compensation systems in the organizational structure.

- appraisers and evaluators, whether in-house or third-party providers, are appropriately independent from loan production and pressure from other sources that may attempt to influence the outcome of an appraisal or evaluation assignment.
- appraisers and evaluators are selected and engaged on the basis of their competency for valuing property on a case-by-case basis. Geographic and property-type competency, educational background, and experience are important elements to consider in selecting the appropriate provider.
- the bank has a process to ascertain that persons it engages to perform appraisals or provide evaluation services have no direct or indirect interest, financial or otherwise, in the property or transaction.
- the information the bank provides in its engagement of an appraiser or evaluator does not inappropriately influence the appraiser or suggest the property's value.
- persons independent of the loan production function oversee the selection of appraisers and persons providing evaluation services.
- the appraisal review process is appropriately independent of the loan production process.

30. Review the bank's process for establishing and maintaining its list of individuals qualified to perform appraisals, evaluations, and valuation reviews. Determine whether

- the bank has a process for evaluating the quality of work of appraisers and individuals providing evaluation services.
- findings are documented and are used by management in making periodic adjustments to the list.

31. Review the types of appraisals and evaluations that are in use. Determine whether management has established criteria for determining that the valuation methodology is appropriate to the risks associated with a particular transaction.

- If applicable, determine whether the valuation tools meet the GSE or third-party investor valuation standards pertaining to that category of real estate. In the case of a GSE, for a loan using the appraisal exemption section (12 CFR 34.43(a)(10)(ii) for national banks and 12 CFR 164.3(a)(10)(ii) for FSAs), was the loan sold to the GSE?
- If AVMs are used as a part of the evaluation product, a thorough review of the use of AVMs in the evaluation process is necessary. See the "Interagency Appraisal and Evaluation Guidelines" for more information. The following is a starting point for the review and is not meant to be all-inclusive:
  - Determine whether the bank did a thorough validation of models and continues to validate (and document) results periodically.
  - Consider (1) documentation of the validation's analysis, assumptions, and conclusions; (2) back-testing a representative sample of the valuations against market data on actual sales; and (3) whether the validation process covers properties representative of the geographic area and property type for which the tool is used.

- Determine whether the institution has established a process to assess whether the results of an AVM should not be used as a part of an evaluation (e.g., property types, geographic location, and price tiers). For information pertaining to high-priced mortgage loans, see 12 CFR 34, subpart G, for national banks and 12 CFR 164, subpart B, for FSAs.

32. Review the adequacy and effectiveness of the appraisal review process. Determine whether

   - the depth of the appraisal review is based on the size of the loan, complexity, and other risk factors specific to the individual transaction.
   - appraisals ordered by a different financial services institution are thoroughly reviewed to ensure that the appraisal meets acceptable quality standards and complies with the appraisal regulations, agency guidelines, and the bank's internal policies.
   - reviewers are knowledgeable and competent to perform reviews of appraisals and evaluations.
   - the bank's procedures address resolution of disagreements between the appraiser or evaluator and the reviewer with respect to market value or any assumptions provided in the appraisal or evaluation report.
   - there are review policies and controls that ensure that each appraisal and evaluation is reviewed to assure sufficient information and analysis before making the final credit decision.
   - the appraisal review is sufficiently documented.

Closing

33. Determine the adequacy of the bank's process for closing and funding loans, including its compliance with applicable law.

34. Determine how management monitors loan closer performance and ensures that loan closers follow the underwriter's instructions.

35. Determine whether there is a process in place to ensure that settlement statements reflect all actual charges and adjustments in connection with the settlement and require that all charges or adjustments subsequent to settlement are disclosed to the lending institution through the preparation of an amended HUD-1.

36. Determine whether insured closing letters from title insurers are used and whether this letter sets forth the title insurance company's responsibilities for negligence, fraud, and errors in closings performed by approved agents or attorneys.

37. Determine whether the bank has formed bona fide affiliated business arrangements (ABA) with third parties to offer real estate settlement services. Determine the volume and nature of these arrangements. Determine whether the ABA disclosure is provided (12 CFR 1024).

38. If the bank has formed ABAs, determine whether the bank assessed compliance with the standards described in HUD's 1996 policy statement on "Sham Controlled Business Arrangements" and concluded that the structure, operating agreement, and activities of these entities do not violate Section 8 of RESPA. (See OCC Bulletin 2005-27, "Real Estate Settlement Procedures Act: Sham Controlled Business Arrangements," for additional guidance.)

39. Determine whether appropriate initial and ongoing due diligence is performed on third-party settlement agents, including

- reviewing the qualifications of the closers, including training, licenses, types of properties handled, and geographic familiarity.
- assessing the financial strength of the third party, adequacy of professional insurance, business reputation, complaints, litigation, etc.
- checking against investor exclusionary lists, fraud databases, and internal watch lists.
- ensuring that on individual transactions, the settlement agent is qualified given the complexity of the transaction, type of product, and geographic familiarity.

40. If the bank uses third-party settlement agents, determine whether appropriate management processes are in place, including

- ensuring that approved settlement agents are independent of the lending process.
- ensuring that the settlement agent has adequate systems and training programs in place to comply with applicable laws and regulations, to adhere to bank closing instructions governing the closing process, to provide for adequate information security, and to address customer privacy requirements.
- auditing the closing process so that conclusions can be drawn about the agent approval process and adequacy of controls surrounding vendor management.
- ensuring an adequate QC process that tests documentation from sales contract through disbursement of funds, accuracy of the settlement statement, and release and recording of liens.
- tracking and analyzing whether missing or inaccurate documents are received in a timely manner and whether exceptions to policies or procedures are resolved in a timely manner.

41. Determine whether a process is in place to ensure that closing instruction letters are tailored to the transaction, and that they address documenting the source of down payments and all applicable charges to ensure that the HUD settlement statement is completed accurately.

42. Determine whether there is a requirement that the settlement agent notify the bank if (1) the settlement agent has knowledge of previous, concurrent, or subsequent transactions involving the same borrower, seller, or subject property that relate to the transaction being closed by the settlement agent or (2) all irregularities or suspicious activities concerning the settlement of the subject property have been identified, reported, and remediated.

43. Determine whether the bank has a post-closing review process to evaluate closing packages for accuracy and to ensure that all front-end closing documents are obtained. Assess the timeliness and effectiveness of the post-closing review process.

Wholesale Activities

44. Review the list of wholesale sources (brokers or correspondents) of loans approved by the bank. Determine the types and dollar volume of loans purchased from each wholesale source.

45. As part of a newly created wholesale relationship, perform an initial due diligence review and an annual review thereafter. Determine whether the bank reviews the following information before purchasing loans from a wholesale source:

- General competence
- Business practices and operations, including potential conflicts of interest
- Reputation
- Background checks on principals and loan officers
- Financial capacity and condition
- Historical default and foreclosure levels
- Early payment defaults (EPD)
- Nondelivery history
- HUD, Fannie Mae, or Freddie Mac investor status (when applicable)
- Documentation deficiencies
- Fraud
- Record of compliance with applicable licensing, consumer protection, and other laws
- Results of quality-control reviews

46. Determine how the bank's policies and procedures are communicated to third parties with respect to application processing and appraisal ordering and administration. Determine how the bank communicates its policies and standards designed to avoid unfair, deceptive, predatory, and abusive lending practices (e.g., lending predominantly on the value of collateral rather than the borrower's ability to service the debt, misleading disclosures).

47. Determine the process for evaluating and monitoring the quality of mortgages purchased from wholesale sources. Determine whether the bank underwrites mortgages or delegates underwriting responsibilities to the correspondent or a third party. Determine

- how the bank monitors, on an ongoing basis, the quality of mortgages and completeness of file documentation for loans purchased from wholesale sources.
- whether the bank maintains records of post-purchase reviews, including the volume of rejected loans from each source.

- whether the bank rejects noncompliant loans (loans not meeting contractual requirements) and returns them to the seller. If the bank retains noncompliant loans, determine their ultimate disposition.
- whether loans made through third parties reflect the standards and practices used by an institution in its direct lending activities.
- whether adequate systems are in place to verify that third parties are not being paid to generate incomplete or fraudulent mortgage applications or are not otherwise receiving referral or unearned income or fees prohibited by RESPA.
- whether the bank takes appropriate action against a third party with ongoing credit or documentation problems. Such actions should include terminating the relationship when appropriate.

48. Assess the quality of loans acquired from different wholesale sources. Review

- historical default and foreclosure levels.
- history of nondelivery.
- HUD, Fannie Mae, or Freddie Mac investor status (when applicable).
- documentation deficiencies.

49. Assess the bank's risk(s) for funding wholesale mortgages. Determine whether

- collateral is received before payment.
- systems are in place to prevent unnecessary loss exposure.

Pricing Methodologies, Overages, and Concessions

50. Determine whether overages are a component of the bank's earnings and origination activities:

- Review the percentage of mortgages originated since the last examination that resulted in an overage and the average overage collected.
- Determine whether mortgage loan originators receive compensation based on overages (including salaries, commissions, or similar financial incentives).

51. Determine whether adequate systems are in place to monitor and supervise overage and concession activities, and to prevent such compensation from determining mortgage loan originator compensation to the extent prohibited. Determine whether

- the bank has detailed documentation and tracking reports, accurate financial reporting systems, and comprehensive customer complaint tracking systems in place.
- the imposition of overages is consistent with applicable laws and regulations.
- management reviews overage and concession activity for illegal disparate treatment and impact, both for individual customers and protected classes.

Note: If concerns are noted, consult with the EIC or consumer compliance examiners.

Portfolio Management

52. Review monitoring systems for the credit quality of loan production. Determine

    - the number and dollar volume of existing past-due loans, first and early payment default, and loans repurchased since the last examination by each retail and wholesale source.
    - how the bank's credit quality compares with industry averages, as well as against government agency-provided data.
    - whether the bank has any significant concentrations (product type, underwriting criteria, geography, etc.) and whether management is monitoring this exposure.

53. Ascertain the number and dollar volume of loans rejected by investors and the reasons why investors declined to purchase these loans. Determine whether the volume of rejected loans appears excessive in relation to total production volume.

54. Determine whether the bank monitors loan documentation and underwriting exceptions by loan production source.

55. Assess the effectiveness of credit risk management and determine whether management is effectively supervising and analyzing the cause of delinquencies and repurchases. Determine whether

    - key financial statistics (e.g., credit score, LTV, housing, and total debt coverage ratios) and their relationship to credit quality are tracked and analyzed.
    - management is obtaining and analyzing past-due information on mortgages. Determine how management assesses the impact on delinquencies from changes in underwriting practices, origination channels, and new products.
    - management is employing vintage analysis to actively track and monitor delinquencies, foreclosures, and losses.
    - products and sources of production are compared over comparable periods of seasoning.
    - management is monitoring the volume of unplanned nonsalable mortgages (due to underwriting or documentation problems) and analyzing the contributing factors and sources of problems.

56. Determine whether management has sufficient MIS to detect changes in the risk profile of nontraditional mortgages and analyzes potential portfolio performance in a stressed environment. Consider whether

    - the bank's MIS provides early warning reporting and vintage analysis to detect changes in the portfolio's risk profile.
    - reporting systems allow management to isolate key loan products, layered nontraditional loan features, and borrower characteristics to allow early identification of performance deterioration.

- portfolio volume and performance results are tracked against expectations, internal lending standards, and policy limits.
- sensitivity analysis is performed on key portfolio segments to identify and quantify events that can increase risks within a segment or the entire portfolio.

Production Quality Control

57. Determine whether the QC program meets investor guidelines specifying scope, timeliness, content, and independence. Consider whether the QC plan covers all

- channels of production.
- mortgage products.
- underwriting methods.
- employees involved in the origination process.
- vendors or contractors involved in the origination process.

58. Review a sample of reports issued by the QC unit. Determine whether QC reports

- are analyzed according to mortgage broker, loan officer, underwriter or processor, branch office, builders, appraisers, settlement agents, product, geographic area, and other identified concentrations.
- are presented to personnel outside the production unit.
- accurately identify noncompliance with underwriting standards or procedures, whether underwriters properly refer suspected fraudulent loan activity, and whether reappraisal requests are properly initiated.
- provide qualitative analysis and make conclusions regarding trends, common deficiencies, and deficiency concentrations by branch, underwriter, broker, or correspondent.
- adequately document findings and conclusions.
- require corrective action for noted material exceptions.

59. Review the adequacy of the bank's QC program and determine whether it is independent of the production process (determining whether the bank performs the program internally or uses an outside vendor). Determine whether

- the QC unit tests a sample of closed loans from all origination channels to verify that underwriting and closing processes comply with bank policies, government regulations, and the requirements of investors and private mortgage insurers.
- lenders supplement investor-required random sampling with discretionary sampling. If discretionary sampling is used, determine whether it is based on the lender's specific needs, such as sampling of specific offices, brokers and correspondents, staff persons, appraisers, higher-risk loans, nontraditional loans, and loans that may involve fraud.

- QC findings are effectively communicated and whether corrective action or response is required for significant deficiencies.
- management takes timely corrective action to resolve adverse QC findings.

60. Determine whether the bank has any material exposure to mortgage insurance providers. Ensure that management has a process in place to quantify the exposure and assess the credit risk of the insurance providers. Assess and determine

- PMI providers the bank uses as credit enhancements to the bank's portfolio (currently and in the past).
- aggregate exposure report by number and dollar for each provider.
- aging reports on claims submitted and the disposition of those claims.
- list of deferred payment obligations, if any.
- allowance for loan and lease losses (ALLL) assessment and methodology.
- internal and external audit with management responses.

Fraud Detection

61. Determine the number of mortgage fraud referral cases identified since the last examination. Discuss significant cases with management to assess root causes and corrective actions taken.

62. Determine the number of SARs relating to mortgage fraud submitted since the prior examination. Ensure that the bank's SAR submission process is effective.

63. Determine whether the individual or group responsible for fraud risk management adequately

- trains originators, processors, underwriters, and servicing personnel to help identify loans with a higher risk for fraud, fraud schemes, and inconsistencies in borrower and property data that indicate potential fraud.
- investigates fraud referral cases and resolves them promptly and effectively.
- tracks loans repurchased because of fraud or misrepresentation.
- identifies and communicates to the accounting unit fraud losses considered "operational losses" (as distinct from those considered "credit losses").

64. Determine whether effective systems, such as timely MIS, are in place to detect possible fraud. Determine whether

- bank uses pre-funding QC in addition to post-funding QC reviews for loans that are at higher risk for fraud. If so, determine the following:
  - Whether an appraisal and evaluation compliance review process is incorporated into any pre-funding QC program.
  - If a bank determines there is a high risk for inflated appraisals in certain loans, determine whether the bank uses a second valuation method (such as an AVM, broker price opinion, or another appraisal) as a validation tool.

- bank tracks all loan participants in instances of suspected fraud and determines each participant's involvement in the incident.
- bank organizes data so that patterns of fraud can be recognized.
- management uses automated tools to help detect mortgage fraud, such as
  - information databases.
  - AVMs.
  - mortgage fraud databases—industry or internal.
  - fraud scoring models.

65. Determine whether adequate systems are in place to report mortgage fraud to appropriate authorities. Determine whether

- required SARs are promptly submitted to the appropriate authorities and whether investors are appropriately notified of fraudulent activity, as required by investor agreements.
- processes are in place to report fraud to title insurers and the bank's insurer.
- whether there is a process in place to make a referral to the appropriate state appraiser board if suspected fraud involves a state-licensed appraiser.

Secondary Marketing

Objective: Assess the risks associated with secondary marketing and determine whether secondary marketing activities are executed in compliance with applicable laws, rulings, regulations, guidance, investor requirements, and board-approved strategic mandates.

Core Examination Procedures

1. Determine whether the bank has a high or increasing rate of EPDs. Operational processes in loan production may warrant review to determine whether there are high underwriting exception rates, which may be symptomatic of inadequate staffing expertise levels.

2. Assess new and updated purchase and sale agreements for variances (from industry norms) in standard representations and warranties on loans sold. More restrictive standards or increased indemnification requirements against loss could represent poor performance characteristics on behalf of the bank or, potentially, a contraction in the liquidity for the product(s) in question.

3. Review the bank's trend of loan repurchases. As with EPDs, the bank may be faced with loan production-related issues. Increasing rates of repurchases can pose a significant threat to continued liquidity and capital.

4. Review the bank's product development initiatives and their intended outlets. Limited buyers for new products could prove to be a burden on the bank's balance sheet if a high volume of commitments has been made to customers and buyer appetite diminishes.

5. Review the bank's pricing process for exception rates, frequency of pricing adjustments, and pricing exception authority. Clear and measureable standards should be codified in order to avoid price and interest rate risk.

6. Determine whether the warehouse turn rate (average days in the warehouse) is experiencing delays of more than 60 days. Delivery of loans beyond this time frame may prove very costly because of nondelivery into agreed-upon commitments and costs associated with hedging.

7. Review the best execution analysis for realistic assumptions and a balanced delivery strategy. Unreasonable profit expectations may place pressure on the group to take unnecessary risks and further exacerbate a potentially volatile gain on sale margin.

Expanded Examination Procedures

Policies and Controls

1. Determine whether the board and management have adopted mortgage banking policies and controls governing secondary marketing activities that address the following issues:

   - Product development, pricing, pipeline or warehouse management, hedging, securitization structures, loan documentation and delivery, and repurchase management.
   - Limits, exceptions, approval requirements, and strategies to monitor and control risk.
   - Comprehensive accounting policies in accordance with GAAP and call report instructions that address independent valuations, pipeline, warehouse, and hedging activities.

2. For banks that offer nontraditional mortgage loans and loans to subprime borrowers, determine whether management has developed policies that specifically address sales and securitization practices and risk management expectations. Consider

   - operating procedures and guidelines.
   - measurement and monitoring of activities and risk levels.
   - inclusion of key risk exposures in management reports.
   - assurance of appropriate internal controls to verify the integrity of management processes.

3. Evaluate the process for granting exceptions to policies and limits. Determine whether

   - prior approval is required before policies or limits are violated.
   - policy limit exceptions are reported to appropriate senior management, explained and documented, and monitored and tracked.

Personnel

4. Review the organizational chart and reporting structure for the secondary marketing area. Determine whether

   - overall responsibilities for all secondary marketing functions are centralized or otherwise meaningfully structured.
   - responsibilities for product development, pricing, pipeline or warehouse management, hedging, documenting, and delivering mortgage products to investors are clearly defined.

5. Given the size and complexity of the mortgage banking function, review the qualifications, knowledge, technical skills, and experience levels of secondary marketing managers and staff.

Management Information Systems

6. Assess the quality of the MIS used to monitor and administer secondary marketing activities. Determine whether the reports

   - are complete, accurate, and timely.
   - include information on pipeline and warehouse hedged and unhedged positions, mark-to-market analyses, various rate shock scenarios, and policy compliance.

7. Evaluate the disaster recovery plan to determine whether it covers all major secondary functions performed in-house. Consider whether backup systems exist in case primary systems fail, and assess the existence of any unnecessary risk exposure.

Processes

Product Development

8. Review new products developed or implemented since the last examination. Consider whether management offers or plans to offer

   - interest-only loans.
   - payment-option ARMs or other potential negative amortization loans.
   - reduced-documentation or no-documentation loans.
   - simultaneous second liens.
   - expanded-approval, A-minus, Alt-A, or subprime loans.
   - other nontraditional products.

9. Determine whether the review and approval process for new products is sufficiently comprehensive. Consider

   - whether legal counsel and compliance personnel have reviewed new products, advertisements, solicitations, and marketing to determine whether they comply with applicable laws and regulations.
   - whether the audit function has reviewed the proposed internal controls.
   - whether the accounting function has opined on financial recording and reporting implications.
   - whether IT staff has evaluated system capacity and information security implications.
   - whether vendor oversight and monitoring have been addressed.
   - whether business process resiliency requirements have been assessed and business continuity plans have been developed.
   - management's analysis of credit, interest rate, operational, compliance, reputation, and legal risks.
   - whether new products offered are consistent with the bank's internal policies, strategic plan, and risk appetite.

- when mortgage loans are marketed or closed by a third party, whether standards have been developed to provide assurances that third parties also comply with applicable laws and regulations, including those on marketing materials, loan documentation, and closing procedures.
- when external parties (e.g., private mortgage insurers) are required for delivering the loan, management should develop an internal approval process for each party; perform an initial and ongoing analysis of each insurer for viability, capital, profitability, and general financial condition; and develop and practice internal QC standards targeting the bank's compliance with third-party requirements and appropriate MIS for reporting purposes.
- appropriate monitoring tools and MIS to measure the performance of various marketing initiatives.

10. Evaluate how management ensures that new loan products the bank intends to sell meet the guidelines established by investors. Consider

- product liquidity and depth of the market for the new product.
- management's analysis of its ability to price, deliver, and service the product.
- whether unique characteristics of products, such as the potential for payment shock, negative amortization, and interest accrual, are recognized.
- whether new products are evaluated to ensure that terms and features, marketing materials, and loan documentation standards are appropriate for targeted borrowers.

Mortgage Pricing

11. Evaluate mortgage pricing and determine its consistency with the bank's strategic plan:

- Determine how management prices mortgages (security price screens, upstream investor rate sheets, internal model, etc.) and determine whether mortgages are priced below, above, or at market prices.
- Determine the frequency of price changes for retail, wholesale, and broker channels. Evaluate the timing of changes relative to significant market interest rate movements.
- Determine whether profit and loss records for individual transactions are periodically reconciled to general ledger records.
- Review management's analysis of expanded HMDA reporting on higher-priced loans.

12. Assess the reasonableness of the mortgage loan pricing process. Determine whether

- secondary marketing unit is responsible for establishing mortgage prices and whether it ensures that originators are prohibited from overly influencing or dominating pricing decisions.
- management analyzes its pricing decisions in relation to the mortgage banking operation's or the bank's overall profit plan and competitors.
- pricing decisions are evaluated relative to their impact on current and future profitability.

- origination channels are allowed to engage in overage pricing. If applicable, evaluate overage pricing policies and procedures and compliance with applicable laws.
- pricing concessions are made. If applicable, evaluate policies and procedures for the activity and compliance with applicable laws.

Pipeline and Warehouse Management

13. Determine whether daily position reports are prepared that identify pipeline commitments, warehouse inventory, forward sales commitments, mortgage purchase programs,[31] and other hedge positions. Review their accuracy and determine whether they are provided to senior management. Determine whether the reports

- adequately detail risk exposures, limit excesses, and exception approvals.
- provide the dollar amount and percentage of total volume generated for each product type.
- segregate and classify closed loans as either permanent portfolio or held-for-sale.

14. Evaluate how much interest rate, price, and operational risk management is willing to accept for the pipeline and warehouse. Consider

- how management quantifies and monitors risk in the pipeline and warehouse (for example, EaR, economic value or equity at risk, VaR, or percentage of capital at risk).
- whether the bank takes speculative positions with warehouse inventory (e.g., warehouse loans that are held beyond the bank's normal time frames in anticipation of improved market conditions or to increase net interest income). If so, verify that the positions are appropriately valued, monitored, and reported and are within prudent, approved dollar limits.
- whether the bank assumes excessive risks in relation to the volume and complexity of daily operations and management philosophy and expertise.

15. Review the warehouse inventory and aging reports, and assess the quality and marketability of loans in the warehouse. Consider

- number, dollar volume, and percentage of delinquent loans in the warehouse inventory.
- number and dollar volume of loans that have a coupon significantly below current market rates.
- volume of loans that have been in the warehouse more than 60 days.
- reasons why portions of the warehouse inventory are not marketable, if applicable.
- whether the warehouse inventory has other characteristics that might make it difficult to market.

---

[31] These programs function in a similar manner to traditional warehouse lines of credit; in these transactions, however, the mortgage loans securing the lines are legally structured as being purchased by the bank rather than being held as collateral to secure the funding. See appendix C, "Mortgage Banking Accounting."

- volume and frequency of loan transfers to the permanent portfolio.
- whether reconcilements between warehouse subsidiary ledgers and the general ledger account are performed at least monthly.

16. Assess the accounting treatment for the pipeline, warehouse, and associated forward sale commitments and other hedge positions. See appendix C, "Mortgage Banking Accounting," for additional guidance. Consider whether

- management values pipeline commitments (interest rate lock commitments) and the warehouse portfolio pursuant to GAAP and call report instructions at least quarterly.
- transfers of loans from the warehouse to the permanent portfolio are accounted for pursuant to GAAP.

17. Evaluate the timeliness and accuracy of pipeline commitment reporting. Consider

- the process for identifying and reporting pipeline commitments on MIS reports.
- whether commitments are specifically identified by product type and interest rate.
- whether locked-rate commitments and floating-rate commitments are separately identified.
- reconcilements of signed pipeline commitments with pipeline position reports.
- timeliness of information system updates to ensure that changes in pipeline commitments (including repricing of previous rate locks) are appropriately captured.

18. Review warehouse reconciliation reports. Determine whether

- reconciling items are reasonable and explained.
- errors are promptly corrected (e.g., mortgages funded more than once or funded but not closed).

19. Review warehouse turnover and aging reports:

- Determine the reason(s) loans remain in the warehouse after 60 days and assess reasonableness. Assess management plans for disposition.
- Evaluate management's method for monitoring and hedging risk in these loans.
- Ensure that significantly aged loans are appropriately valued, including necessary discounts for illiquidity if applicable.

20. Evaluate the method for handling warehouse loans ineligible for sale due to delinquency or documentation problems, including valuation, accounting, and disposition.

21. Determine whether the bank appropriately risk weights loans obtained in a mortgage purchase program that do not qualify for sale accounting treatment.

22. Determine whether exposures in mortgage purchase or finance programs are appropriately risk weighted under the applicable capital rules.

Hedging Practices

23. Determine whether the board of directors or executive management has approved all hedging programs and activities and the individuals who perform them.

24. Determine types of limits that have been established for traders.

25. Determine how management monitors and forecasts pipeline fallout activity and incorporates this information into hedging strategies. Evaluate

    - management reports that contain fallout ratios for each product type under forecast interest rate scenarios.
    - impact of unanticipated fallout on hedging results.

26. Determine whether the bank effectively hedges pipeline and warehouse loans and applies appropriate accounting treatment. See appendix B, "Hedging," and appendix C, "Mortgage Banking Accounting," for additional guidance. Consider

    - types of hedge instruments, including use of forward sales commitments or options to hedge pipeline or warehouse loans.
    - effectiveness of management's hedging strategies, including profits or losses on the net hedged position.
    - hedge correlation analysis.
    - pair-off activity, including causes and frequency. Assess whether management incurs pair-offs as part of a well-defined best execution strategy or as a result of ineffective hedging and delivery.
    - accounting for hedge instruments (e.g., forward sales and options) to determine compliance with GAAP and call report instructions.
    - reasonableness of hedge instrument valuation, including independence of personnel providing valuations.
    - management's monitoring of basis risk and whether the bank assumes excessive risk for any hedging product.

27. Evaluate the secondary marketing programs used to sell mortgages to investors. Consider

    - volume of sales under each program.
    - master sales commitments with investors. Take steps to
      - determine commitment amounts, maturities, and terms.
      - assess the bank's ability to meet mandatory commitments and determine potential financial exposure.
      - review investor requirements for underwriting, delivery, documentation, and servicing.

28. Determine whether the bank uses financial models to establish risk limits and hedging strategies. Evaluate

- whether assumptions are reasonable.
- whether volatility assumptions are consistent with those implied by the market.
- how frequently assumptions and other model inputs are updated and the basis for those updates.
- whether model assumptions incorporate budgeting and management decisions. If so, determine the extent to which they are incorporated.
- whether all valuation, simulation, and hedging models are validated pursuant to OCC Bulletin 2011-12, "Sound Practices for Model Risk Management."

29. Assess the adequacy of systems in place to manage counterparty credit risk associated with broker/dealer transactions. Determine whether

- management uses an approved dealer list.
- limits are placed, by dealer, on the volume of allowed unsettled trades.
- there is a periodic review of counterparty financial information to allow the bank to assess the dealer's continuing ability to perform on securities transactions.

30. Assess the adequacy of systems governing secondary marketing hedging (e.g., forward sales and options). Consider

- whether individual trade tickets are properly prepared and submitted to an independent operating unit for processing.
- whether third-party trade confirmations are received and reviewed by an independent operating unit.
- whether the bank has established prudent follow-up procedures for unconfirmed trades and confirmation discrepancies.
- reconcilements of outstanding trades to the daily position report.
- whether traders are prohibited from entering trade data into bank systems.
- whether management back-tests the effectiveness of hedging activities and appropriately identifies the underlying sources of gains and losses associated with the hedging program.

31. Assess the adequacy of management's strategies for hedging loans with special risks, i.e., nontraditional mortgage products, ARMs, or loans with interest rate caps and floors.

Securitization Structures

32. Assess the associated risk of security structures used for nonconforming mortgages. (Examiners should refer to the "Asset Securitization" booklet of the *Comptroller's Handbook*.) Consider

- credit enhancements for the securitization structure, including an assessment of the structure's cash flow waterfall.

- the source(s) and cost of third-party guarantees.
- whether the bank regularly reviews the financial condition of third-party guarantors.
- interest rate characteristics of the securitization structure, and methods used to monitor and control this risk.

33. Determine whether the bank participates in guaranteed mortgage securitization programs. Consider

- systems in place to ensure compliance with the Federal Accounting Standards Board (FASB) (ASC 860).
- whether the bank defers origination fees and costs in accordance with GAAP (ASC 310).

34. Determine how management ensures that securitization structures meet applicable legal, accounting, and investor requirements.

Secondary Marketing Profitability

35. Determine whether any profitability requirements have been placed on the secondary marketing department and whether an undue level of reliance is placed on secondary marketing activities to support business-line profitability.

36. Determine whether the bank has systems in place to manage the risks secondary marketing may take to meet profitability goals. Determine whether

- profitability targets are formulated with an understanding of the risks that would be assumed to achieve such targets. Consider whether the unit engages in higher-risk strategies, such as not hedging significant portions of the pipeline or warehouse or using aggressive assumptions on servicing fees to recognize larger gains on sale.
- secondary marketing personnel are compensated on overall mortgage company profitability rather than secondary marketing profitability.

37. Determine whether a best execution analysis is performed when hedge activity is initiated and when loans are sold. Evaluate the appropriateness of this analysis. Determine whether management uses purchased software or internally developed applications to automate the mathematical part of the best execution decision.

38. Determine whether the best execution analysis considers

- guarantee fees, published buy-up and buy-down grids, excess servicing valuations, market prices for securities, and the market price for cash-settled whole-loan transactions.
- other factors, such as the overall effectiveness of executing the trades and the ongoing business relationship with individual investors.

39. Determine whether the bank buys up or buys down guarantee fees under its best execution strategy. Assess the appropriateness of this activity and compare actions with the unit's strategic plan.Evaluate the reasonableness of excess yield valuation supporting the buy-up and buy-down analysis and the process for determining whether retention is the best option.

Loan Documentation and Loan Delivery

40. Review the bank's post-closing document tracking system to assess the significance of missing documents and resulting risk exposure. Consider

   - volume, trends, and types of documents that have been missing more than 120 days and management's efforts to obtain missing documents.
   - volume and types of missing documents relative to similar-period production volume.
   - financial impact that missing documents have had on the bank (i.e., penalties, repurchase requests, and recourse implications). Assess the potential exposure arising from investor documentation requirements and the bank's documentation management process.

41. Determine whether an independent process has been implemented to verify the accuracy of the post-closing documentation tracking systems.

42. Evaluate the Ginnie Mae pool certification process. Consider

   - whether effective procedures are in place to ensure compliance with Ginnie Mae pool certification requirements and guidelines established by other investors.
   - volume of uncertified Ginnie Mae pools, including the breakdown of uncertified pools by month of issuance.
   - whether Ginnie Mae has required the bank to post a letter of credit because of excessive uncertified pools.

43. Review pool certification requirements for other investors. Consider

   - bank's obligation for final pool certification for other investors.
   - any requirements to post letters of credit, provide indemnification, hold back sales proceeds, or make other pledges of collateral.

44. Ensure that a quality assurance or internal audit review is conducted to verify that mortgage pools are certified in a timely manner.

45. Determine the effectiveness of systems in place for loan delivery. Consider

   - systems for ensuring compliance with investor requirements.
   - systems for monitoring commitment deadlines.
   - penalties assessed for late delivery.

Recourse Transactions, Repurchases, and Indemnifications

46. If the bank transfers loans with recourse,

   - determine the number and dollar volume of loans transferred or sold to other entities for which the bank has retained recourse.
   - review investor agreements to determine whether there are any credit-enhancing representations and warranties.
   - determine the type of program into which mortgage loans are sold with recourse.
   - determine whether the bank has adequate MIS to track all recourse obligations.
   - verify that the bank appropriately follows risk-based capital rules for any credit-enhancing representations and warranties, including sales to FHLB programs.
   - determine whether management has instituted effective processes to ensure that recourse transactions (including indemnifications for any future losses) are accurately reported on the bank's call report.
   - when GAAP does not permit the transaction to be given "sales treatment," determine whether management accurately reports the transaction as a financing on the call report.
   - when GAAP does permit the transaction to be given "sales treatment," determine whether management accurately reports the transaction as a sale on the call report.

47. Assess the level and trends of delinquencies and losses on mortgages sold with contractual recourse and trends in repurchase demands due to EPD, underwriting, or another deficiency.

48. Assess the adequacy of the recourse or repurchase reserve(s):

   - Determine whether the reserve or reserves were established in accordance with ASC 860 (recourse) or ASC 460 (repurchase and indemnification guaranties) to reflect the fair value of the recourse or guarantee obligation.
   - Evaluate the reasonableness of the bank's method of establishing and maintaining the recourse or repurchase reserve(s).
   - Determine whether losses on loans sold with recourse or repurchased or indemnified under sales representations and warranties are recognized in a timely manner and recorded against the recourse or repurchase reserve(s).
   - If recourse is limited, determine whether systems are in place to prevent payments to purchasers above the bank's contractual obligation.

49. Determine whether management has established adequate reporting to monitor risk from repurchases or indemnifications. Determine whether management reports include information on

   - volume of repurchases or indemnifications, including status of pending cases.
   - overall loss amounts.
   - status of repurchased loans, including delinquencies, aging analysis, source of loan, LTV, and any recourse to others.

- cause of repurchase (fraud, documentation, credit, regulatory compliance, or other).
- corrective action taken to prevent future repurchases.
- external analysis of repurchase reserves.
- aging of requests for repurchase(s) from investors.
- status of negotiations with mortgage insurance companies on insurance requests.

50. Review repurchase and indemnification demands during the past year:

- Determine whether repurchased loans are identified in a centralized database and how these loans are valued and accounted for pursuant to GAAP and call report instructions.
- Determine whether repurchased loans are included in the warehouse or whether they have been transferred to the bank's loan portfolio.
- Review management systems to track investor repurchase and indemnification demands (by investor), including related correspondence and management negotiations with the investor regarding the demand.
- If approval authority for accepting repurchase or indemnifications demands from investors has been established, determine whether monitoring systems exist to ensure that individuals do not exceed approval authority.
- Review costs of repurchasing, curing, and re-selling loans since the last exam.
- If the bank indemnifies loans in lieu of repurchase, ensure that monitoring systems are in place to track these loans and that the indemnification exposure is appropriately reported on the call report and follows appropriate risk-based capitalrequirements.

51. Determine whether systems exist to identify loans for which the bank may have a right to reimbursement from third parties, such as correspondents, brokers, or mortgage insurance companies.

Servicing

Objective: Assess risks associated with mortgage servicing and determine whether servicing activities are executed in compliance with applicable laws, rulings, regulations, guidance, investor requirements, and board-approved strategic mandates.

Core Examination Procedures

1. Determine whether the bank has sufficient policies, procedures, and staff to comply with all servicing standards prescribed by federal (Regulation X and Z), state, and investor requirements. The bank should pay particular attention to practices surrounding disclosures, servicing transfers, escrow management, error resolution procedures, borrower information requests, force-placed insurance, default management, and continuity of contact practices.

2. Review the delinquency, default, or foreclosure rates for loans in the bank's portfolio and for LSFOs with comparable portfolios and industry data. As a part of this exercise, evaluate the bank's servicing portfolio concentrations (agency, nonconforming, or nontraditional product type, subprime mortgages, high CLTV, low credit score, high DTI, property types, geography, etc.). Ongoing reviews defined by clearly established risk assessment procedures should measure the need for additional staff, systems, and, potentially, a sub-servicer.

3. Review default management procedures for proper implementation of collection strategies on early-, mid-, and late-stage delinquency accounts. The bank should be employing consistent policies, procedures, and practices in its collection techniques to ensure compliance with applicable law (Regulation X and Z).

4. Determine whether the bank is experiencing a high or rapidly increasing cost to service. Current and projected profitability may need to be adjusted based on management's analysis of profitability on a product-by-product basis and how that analysis drives strategic business decisions (e.g., buying or selling servicing).

Expanded Examination Procedures

Policies and Controls

1. Determine whether the board of directors or its mortgage banking committee, consistent with its duties and responsibilities, has adopted mortgage banking policies that adequately cover all facets of the servicing operation, including servicing nontraditional loan products or loans to subprime borrowers. Policies and controls should be in place to ensure compliance with applicable law, including the prevention of predatory servicing practices such as the following:

    *   Failure to properly credit mortgage payments that are made on time, as a pretext for imposing unjustified late fees, and knowingly reporting borrowers to credit bureaus for the resulting false delinquencies.
    *   Force-placing high-cost insurance coverage on borrowers despite documentary evidence that satisfactory insurance is in effect. (When escrow accounts are insufficient to make these higher insurance premiums, monthly mortgage payments are increased, leading to further delinquencies and late fees.)
    *   Charging fees for services not specifically sanctioned in loan documents or in excess of what is normal and customary.
    *   Threatening borrowers with unjustified foreclosures (i.e., those caused solely by the servicer's own predatory servicing practices).
    *   Failure to respond to customer inquiries and complaints about these practices adequately or in a timely manner.
    *   Failure to pay insurance or taxes (on loans with escrowed funds) in a timely manner, which could subject borrowers to unnecessary penalties.

2. Review policies and procedures in place to ensure the accuracy and integrity of information furnished to consumer reporting agencies

3. Review the organizational chart for the servicing unit. Evaluate the qualifications and experience of senior management and key staff for major functional areas. Determine whether staff members have the special skills required to service nontraditional loan products or other special categories of loans or borrowers (e.g., service members), if applicable.

Personnel

4. Review the organizational chart and reporting structure for the servicing department. Determine whether

    *   overall responsibilities for all servicing marketing functions are centralized or otherwise meaningfully structured.
    *   responsibilities for investor accounting and reporting, document custodianship, escrow account administration, collections and default management, loan setup and payoff, OREO administration, and customer service are clearly defined.

Management Information Systems

5. Review the most recent management reports in which the operating results for the servicing unit are described. Determine whether the amount of detail provided is sufficient to supervise each servicing function.

Processes

Portfolio Supervision and Assessment

6. Determine the characteristics of the servicing portfolio, paying specific attention to the following:

   - Investors (Ginnie Mae, Fannie Mae, Freddie Mac, FHLBs, private investors)
   - Types of products (30-year fixed, 15-year fixed, ARMs, balloons, jumbos, hybrids)
   - Types of borrowers (prime versus nonprime)
   - Level of nontraditional mortgages, such as interest-only or payment-option ARMs
   - Level of mortgage loans with risk-layering features, such as reduced-documentation and simultaneous second-lien loans
   - Whether transactions with investors are with or without recourse
   - Geographic dispersion and concentration of borrowers
   - Lien priority of loans where municipal lending programs are available
   - Range of interest rates on the loans
   - Projected life of the loans
   - Average loan size
   - Average age of the loans
   - Delinquency level
   - Foreclosure level
   - Bankruptcy level
   - Loss experience
   - Amount of OREO

7. Evaluate the asset quality of the servicing portfolio:

   - Compare the level of delinquencies, foreclosures, bankruptcies, losses, and OREO with historical levels and with comparative industry data, including both regional and national averages, if available.
   - Evaluate the extent and impact of geographic concentrations.
   - Evaluate the extent and impact of concentrations in nontraditional mortgage products or loans to subprime borrowers.

8. Review the most recent analysis of servicing revenues and costs for each product type. Determine whether costs are estimated on an average or incremental basis. Determine

   - whether revenue analysis considers income from contractual servicing fees, ancillary fees and charges, earnings from payment float, and the benefits derived from compensating balances from custodial funds.
   - whether cost analysis includes all direct and indirect servicing expenses.
   - servicing unit's current and projected profitability, whether management has analyzed profitability on a product-by-product basis, and if so how that analysis is factored into strategic business decisions (e.g., buying or selling servicing).
   - whether cost analysis includes realistic assumptions for servicing nontraditional and subprime loan products.

9. Ensure that a master servicing agreement is on file for each investor.

10. Determine whether investors require an independent external audit attesting that loans were serviced in accordance with the USAP for mortgage bankers. Obtain and review reports prepared and determine whether appropriate corrective action was taken, if applicable.

11. Determine whether the bank has a QC program covering the major functional areas of the servicing unit. If so, assess its scope and effectiveness.

12. Evaluate the disaster recovery plan to determine that it covers all major servicing functions performed in-house. Consider

    - whether backup systems exist in case primary systems fail.
    - existence of any unnecessary risk exposure.

13. Review the list of outside sub-servicers and vendors employed by the bank to perform servicing functions:

    - Verify that management assesses the financial condition of each sub-servicer and vendor.
    - Evaluate the bank's contingency plan to ensure that it addresses servicing responsibilities if sub-servicers or vendors fail to perform.
    - Assess the quality of work performed by vendors and sub-servicers and any associated risk(s).
    - Confirm that vendors and sub-servicers are complying with applicable law and the bank's policies and procedures.

Investor Accounting and Reporting

14. Review the list of investors for which the bank services loans:

   - Determine whether a servicing contract is in place with each investor.
   - Review a sample of the servicing contracts to determine investor servicing requirements, funds remittance schedules, contractual servicing fees, guarantee fees, and servicer representations and warranties.

15. Review the procedures for receiving payments from borrowers, depositing the funds into segregated custodial accounts, and remitting funds to investors:

   - Assess the bank's system for ensuring that borrowers' payments are applied accurately, including those for nontraditional loan products, and that investors receive payments on schedule.
   - Assess the adequacy of custodial account processes, including daily balancing, monthly reconcilements, assigned authority for disbursements, and segregation of administrative duties.
   - Verify that custodial balances are deposited into the types of accounts and financial institutions specified in investor guidelines.

16. Determine that periodic interest rate changes are properly implemented on mortgages having rates or payments subject to change (such as adjustable-rate, hybrid, or payment-option loans), and determine whether the bank maintains adequate documentation of adjustments and notifies the borrower in a timely manner, in accordance with Regulation Z requirements.

17. Track the flow of funds from the investor accounting cutoff date, the remittance of funds to investors and security holders, and the recognition of servicing revenue. Determine whether

   - loan delinquencies have prompted the use of corporate funds to meet remittance requirements to investors and security holders.
   - bank appropriately recognizes servicing revenue.

18. Review a sample of investor account reconciliations and assess management's process for reconciling investor accounts. Determine whether

   - schedule is maintained that lists all investors for which servicing is being performed.
   - each investor account is reconciled at least monthly.
   - a supervisor reviews and approves the reconciliations.
   - bank resolves outstanding items in a timely manner.
   - bank reviews the aging of unreconciled items regularly and charges off uncollectible balances.

19. Determine whether investor accounting and reporting internal control processes are adequate. Determine whether

- monthly investor reports are accurate and timely.
- adequate processes are in place to ensure that investors receive payments on schedule.
- management has established adequate processes to prevent delinquent loans from being prematurely removed from mortgage pools.
- a monthly report is sent to each applicable investor detailing principal and interest collections from homeowners, bankruptcy, delinquency rates, foreclosure actions, property inspections, loan losses, OREO status, etc.

20. Review reconciliations of investor accounts that are out of balance or have significant stale reconciling amounts:

- Ascertain whether there are stale, unreconciled items that should be charged off.
- Determine whether management reviews the aging of unreconciled items regularly and charges off nonbankable, uncollectible balances.

21. Review management's analysis and monitoring of Ginnie Mae early pool buyouts. Determine whether

- early pool buyout decisions are supported by internal analysis demonstrating the economic benefit to the bank.
- such buyout activity is supported by the guaranteed yield on the loan, the estimated remaining time to foreclosure, and the likelihood of reinstatement of the loan to a performing status.
- analysis of individual loans considers the collateral, the status of guarantees, and liquidity ramifications for the bank.
- financial impact of this strategy is appropriate for the bank.
- monitoring processes ensure timely liquidation and disposition of these loans at minimal loss to the bank.
- management monitors the potential of these short-term liquidation assets to reinstate and become long-term assets that may not fit bank portfolio objectives.

22. Determine the number and dollar volume of delinquent Ginnie Mae loans the bank purchased from the servicing portfolio. Determine whether

- these Ginnie Mae buybacks are appropriately reported on the call report.
- there are limits on the total investment in early pool buyouts.

Document Custodianship

23. Evaluate the procedures for safeguarding loan documents. Determine whether

    - loan documents are stored in a secured and protected area.
    - bank's safekeeping facilities are appropriate.
    - bank maintains a log of documents held in safekeeping.
    - log identifies which documents have been removed and by whom.
    - copies of critical documents are stored separately from original documents.
    - processes for loan file imaging are adequate.

Escrow Account Administration

24. Review the effectiveness of the system for ensuring the timely payments of taxes, insurance, and other obligations of borrowers.

25. Determine whether escrow account administration complies with 12 USC 2609 (RESPA), "Limitation on Advance Deposits in Escrow Accounts":

    - Evaluate the process for establishing the required escrow account balance at loan inception.
    - Determine whether bank sends each borrower an annual statement itemizing the elements required by 12 USC 2609(c).
    - Determine whether bank accurately analyzes each escrow account annually. Evaluate the appropriateness of the bank's calculation method and assumptions.

26. Determine whether the bank sends the borrower a statement showing the amount of any overage or shortage in the account and an explanation of how the bank will correct it in a timely manner:

    - Review the method for correcting shortages and surpluses in escrow accounts.
    - Ensure that overages and shortages in escrow accounts are administered in accordance with 12 USC 2609 (RESPA) requirements.

27. Review the method for substantiating that insurance is in place for each property. Determine whether the bank uses a blanket insurance policy or forced-placement hazard insurance (a bank-purchased policy covering a specific property or a portfolio of properties) for borrowers with expired insurance. Consider whether

    - sufficient notice to borrowers is given if evidence of insurance is not provided.
    - force-placed insurance is required and, if applicable, the impact on payment shock for nontraditional mortgage products.
    - controls exist for a process to ensure accurate identification of insurance shortfall and the timely cancellation of a force-placed insurance policy once the borrower provides evidence that adequate insurance coverage is obtained.

28. Review the method for substantiating that required flood insurance is in place for each property. Determine the adequacy of management's process to force-place flood insurance on loans lacking required flood insurance and loans with an insufficient amount of flood insurance, pursuant to 12 CFR 22.7 and 12 CFR 172.7, as appropriate.

29. Review the procedures for ensuring that tax and insurance payments are made on delinquent loans. Evaluate their effectiveness.

30. Evaluate the adequacy of systems in place for preventing the use of escrow custodial balances to meet other bank obligations.

31. Determine the volume of serviced loans that do not have an escrow requirement. Evaluate how the bank documents that tax and insurance payments are current for these loans.

32. Review management reports to determine the number and dollar volume of loans for which the bank does not have a hazard insurance policy in place. Determine how management protects the bank against losses on those loans.

33. Review management reports detailing loans lacking required flood insurance and loans with an insufficient amount of flood insurance. Determine how management protects the bank against losses on these loans. Coordinate findings with OCC consumer compliance examiners.

34. Determine the number and dollar volume of loans with a delinquent tax bill. Determine how management monitors delinquent taxes on nonescrowed accounts. Determine how management protects the bank and investor's lien position on those properties.

Collections and Default Management

35. Review key reports for collection and default management. Consider whether reports include key performance indicators for the collection department and for individual collectors against established standards. Consider

   - daily and monthly metrics for inbound and outbound collection calls.
   - reporting systems to track and monitor loss mitigation activities, bankruptcies, and foreclosures.

36. Review collection strategies for early-, mid-, and late-stage delinquent accounts. Consider whether

   - call programs are appropriately prioritized by risk (e.g., high-risk and large-balance accounts).
   - staffing plans adequately address peak calling periods—this could vary depending on the geographic location and concentration of the servicing portfolio.
   - collection calls are initiated in a timely manner for first and early payment defaults.
   - systems identify accounts with no contact within a specified time frame.

37. Review procedures for collecting delinquent loans, including nontraditional loans and subprime loan products. Determine whether

    • collection efforts follow applicable law and investor guidelines.
    • bank documents all attempts to collect past-due payments, including the date(s) of borrower contact, the nature of the communication, and the borrower's response or commitment.
    • bank conducts appropriate property inspections for delinquent loans.
    • bank uses nonabusive collection practices.
    • management uses adequate methods to ensure that the bank complies with applicable state and federal laws and regulations.

38. Determine whether early contact is made with (1) borrowers who have nontraditional loan products subject to payment shock and (2) borrowers who have other kinds of loans whose low initial start rates have not yet reset. Determine whether additional contact is made after increased payment requirements go into effect.

39. Determine whether behavior-scoring modeling is used in the collection process. Consider whether

    • behavior-scoring models are subject to model validation or review by internal audit.
    • behavior scores provide appropriate portfolio segmentation by risk (e.g., low-, medium-, and high-risk accounts).
    • sufficient attention is paid to collecting high-risk accounts.
    • customers' payment patterns are considered in the behavior-score model.
    • refreshed credit scores are periodically obtained for the portfolio and are appropriately included in the behavior-score model.

40. Evaluate the collection unit's call monitoring program, whether performed internally or outsourced, to monitor the quality and effectiveness of collection calls. Consider whether monitoring processes include identifying

    • consistency of collection techniques used across portfolio risk segments.
    • effective and efficient use of time in administering collection calls.
    • compliance with collection policies and procedures and regulatory and investor requirements.
    • collectors with performance issues.
    • specific training needs.

41. Evaluate the collection unit's risk management process, including

    • monthly review of delinquencies, including roll rate analysis.
    • refreshing credit scores.
    • review of extension reports.
    • review of first and early payment defaults.

- third-party vendor agreements that include performance standards.
- internal quality assurance process.

42. Review outstanding investor advances and advances to cover borrowers' escrow account obligations for taxes and insurance, and determine whether there are advances with uncollectible balances that should be charged off.

43. Determine whether servicers review governing documents for securitization trusts to determine the full extent of their authority to restructure loans that are delinquent or in default or are in imminent risk of default. Consider whether the authority under the governing securitization documents is used to take appropriate steps when an increased risk of default is identified, including

- proactively identifying borrowers at heightened risk of delinquency or default, such as those with impending interest rate resets.
- contacting borrowers to assess their ability to repay.
- assessing whether there is a reasonable basis to conclude that default is "reasonably foreseeable."
- exploring, where appropriate, a loss mitigation strategy that avoids foreclosure or other actions that result in a loss of homeownership.

44. Determine whether effective policies, procedures, and workflows have been established to administer loss mitigation, bankruptcy, and foreclosure activities in accordance with regulatory and investor guidelines. Consider the bank's use of the following loss mitigation techniques:

- Reinstatement or repayment plans
- Partial mortgage insurance advance claim payments
- Forbearance agreements
- Mortgage modifications
- Loan assumptions
- Pre-foreclosure or short sales
- Deed in lieu of foreclosures

45. Determine the number of foreclosure actions that have not been completed within the time periods allowed by investors and GSEs. Determine the reasons for delay and whether the bank has notified the investors.

46. Review the list of delinquent loans for which foreclosure action is delayed because of forbearance or as a function of a GSE foreclosure moratorium. Select and review a sample of forbearance files. As appropriate, determine whether

- bank has sound reasons for delaying foreclosure action.
- forbearance actions comply with investor guidelines and determine whether the bank obtains investor approval, if necessary.

- bank appropriately documents the reasons for forbearance.

47. Consider the average foreclosure costs for each product type. Assess the adequacy of foreclosure reserves relative to the volume of loans currently in foreclosure and those severely delinquent, as well as average historical foreclosure costs:

- Affirm that the bank makes charge-offs, recoveries, and provision expenses directly to the foreclosure reserve.
- Determine whether the bank processes its reimbursement claims to investors in a timely manner, if applicable.

48. Review loan delinquency reports. Select and review a sample of files for borrowers delinquent 121 days or more. Assess the bank's foreclosure process:

- Determine whether the bank initiates foreclosure proceedings in a timely manner and properly notifies borrowers and investors of the initiation of foreclosure actions.
- Determine whether foreclosure practices comply with investor guidelines.
- Determine whether the methods used by management to ensure that foreclosure procedures comply with applicable state and federal laws and regulations are effective.
- Determine the number of foreclosure actions that have not been completed within the time periods allowed by investors and GSEs, and determine the reasons for delay and whether the bank has notified the investor.
- Determine whether the bank has established a foreclosure reserve.
- Determine whether uncollectible investor advances are charged off in a timely manner.

49. Assess the bank's process for handling delinquent loans in forbearance status. Determine whether

- bank has sound reasons for delaying foreclosure action.
- forbearance actions comply with investor guidelines, and whether the bank obtains investor approval, if necessary.
- bank documents the reasons for forbearance.

Loan Setup and Payoff

50. Determine how management ensures that loans, including nontraditional loan products, are set up accurately and in a timely manner (normally within 15 days of loan closing, or moderately longer for purchased servicing).

51. Determine the volume of loans not set up on the bank's servicing system before the first payment due date. Determine

- reason(s) loans were not set up in a timely manner.
- whether adequate systems are in place to notify the mortgagor where to send note payments.
- impact on the servicing unit's operating performance.

52. Determine whether the bank has incurred fines for failing to file mortgage release and satisfactions in accordance with applicable state laws and whether the amount of fines paid is reasonable.

Administration of Other Real Estate Owned

53. When title has been or will be obtained to an OREO property, determine whether the bank follows applicable law, regulations, and financial reporting rules.

54. Select and review a sample of investor-owned OREO properties. Determine whether OREO property administration and marketing practices comply with investor guidelines.

Customer Service

55. Determine the level of customer complaints pertaining to mortgage banking that the bank has received since the previous examination. Determine whether

- any customer complaints may indicate predatory servicing practices.
- customer service segregates complaints on nontraditional loan products.

56. Determine whether the customer service unit appropriately informs the bank's senior management of significant and recurring complaints. Determine whether

- customer complaints are appropriately resolved.
- processes and reporting history of dropped calls indicate whether system or staffing is sufficient to handle call volume during peak periods.
- specific training needs are identified and implemented.

Mortgage Servicing Assets

Objective: Assess the risks associated with MSAs and determine whether MSA activities are executed in compliance with applicable laws, rulings, regulations, guidance, investor requirements, and board-approved strategic mandates.

Core Examination Procedures

1. Review the bank's level of MSAs relative to capital and determine the ability to conform to mandated regulatory capital requirements.[32] Failure by management to identify alternative contingencies could pose significant risks to the bank's capital position and access to viable liquidity options.

2. Review the MSA valuations and determine whether they differ significantly from comparable portfolios and industry mark to market. The use of unsupported prepayment speeds, discount rates, and other key assumptions in MSA valuation models can prove problematic in creating realistic profitability targets.

3. Determine whether the bank has employed frequent changes in the MSA valuation process. Such inconsistency is likely a result of inadequate staffing experience levels, management inconsistency, and lack of meaningful benchmarks, and can lead to earnings volatility.

4. Review the prepayment speeds, discount rates, or other key assumptions used in MSA valuation models. Unsupported or overly optimistic levels may be indicative of a bank whose earnings are disproportionately driven by MSAs.

Expanded Examination Procedures

Policies and Controls[33]

1. Review mortgage banking policies and procedures to ensure that directors and managers have adequately addressed the following:

   - Comprehensive standards for MSAs and IO strip assets (hereafter collectively referred to as MSA), including standards for initial capitalization, valuation, acquisition and sale, hedging, and ongoing administration.
   - Risk limits and controls.
   - MSA valuation and impairment analyses that use reasonable and supportable assumptions.
   - Comparison of modeled MSA results with the actual cash flow experience.

---

[32] Follow applicable regulatory capital rules for MSAs noting that as of January 1, 2014, and January 1, 2015, these rules are changing for advanced approaches banks and non-advanced-approaches banks, respectively.

[33] For additional guidance, refer to appendix B, "Hedging"; appendix C, "Mortgage Banking Accounting"; and OCC Bulletin 2003-9, "Interagency Advisory on Mortgage Banking."

- Review and approval of results and assumptions by management.
- Appropriate amortization practices, as applicable.
- Approval process for significant sales and purchases of MSAs.
- Independent review of MSA accounting, controls, and risk management.

2. Determine whether management has appropriate systems, MIS, limits, reporting, and internal controls in place to oversee hedging activities, including monitoring the effectiveness of hedging strategies and reviewing concentrations of hedge instruments and counterparties.

Personnel

3. Assess management's knowledge and technical skills related to managing MSA and hedging activities.

Management Information Systems

4. Assess the quality of the MIS used to monitor the bank's MSAs, hedges, and risk exposure.

5. Identify all models used for MSA capitalization, valuation, hedging, and bulk acquisitions. Determine whether any inconsistencies among these values are identified, supported, and reconciled.

6. Determine whether the board receives information on hedged and unhedged positions. Evaluate the adequacy of board reports on MSA and hedge valuation, interest rate shock scenarios, and policy compliance.

7. Evaluate the disaster recovery plan to determine that it covers all major servicing functions performed in-house. Consider whether backup systems exist in case primary systems fail, and assess the existence of any unnecessary risk exposure.

Processes

Mortgage Servicing Asset Valuation

8. Determine the adequacy of the MSA valuation process. Any of the following concerns should result in additional scrutiny:

- Use of unsupported prepayment speeds, discount rates, and other key assumptions in MSA valuation models.
- Questionable, inappropriate, or unsubstantiated items in the valuation models.
- Disregard of comparable market data, coupled with over-reliance on peer group surveys as a means of supporting assumptions and the fair value of MSAs.
- Frequent changing of assumptions for no compelling reason.

- Undocumented policies and procedures relating to the MSA valuation process and oversight of that process.
- Inconsistencies in MSA valuation assumptions used in valuation, bidding, pricing, and hedging activities, as well as in the bank's other mortgage-related activities, when relevant.
- Poor segregation of duties, from an organizational perspective, between the valuation, hedging, and accounting functions.
- Failure to properly stratify MSAs for impairment-testing purposes.
- If accounting for MSAs under the amortization method, inadequate amortization of the remaining cost basis of MSAs, particularly during periods of high prepayments.
- If accounting for MSAs under the amortization method, continued use of a valuation allowance for the impairment of a stratum of MSAs, when repayment of the underlying loans at a rate faster than originally projected indicates the existence of an impairment for which a direct writedown should be recorded.
- If accounting for MSAs under the fair value method, failure to recognize changes in fair value through earnings.
- Failure to assess actual cash flow performance.
- Failure to validate or update models for new information or necessary version changes.

9. Review MSAs recorded as a result of retail production or third-party production flow activities. Determine whether

- bank has clear operating procedures for capitalizing the value of newly originated servicing assets in conformance with GAAP. Ensure that initial capitalization rates address the key characteristics of the servicing assets.
- bank's documentation supports how management arrived at the particular fair value and the fair value technique employed.
- market prices or assumptions used to determine the fair value of MSAs and loans are reasonable and based on the characteristics of the individual pools at the time the bank booked the MSAs.
- discounted cash flow valuation techniques include data on the characteristics of the underlying mortgages, projected servicing revenues and costs, prepayment estimates, and the discount rate.
- assumptions for ancillary income, float, earnings on escrows, servicing costs, foreclosure expenses, and other revenue and expense items are realistic, including for nontraditional loan products.

10. Evaluate any bulk acquisitions of MSAs since the previous examination. Determine whether

- valuation assumptions include data on the characteristics of the underlying mortgages, projected servicing revenues and costs, prepayment estimates, discount rate, etc.
- assumptions were reasonable at the time the bank booked the servicing assets.

- bank's documentation for valuation assumptions includes an explanation of how the bank arrived at the valuation assumptions employed.

11. For MSAs accounted for under the amortization method, determine whether the bank amortizes the capitalized values of MSAs in proportion to, and over the period of, estimated net servicing income or loss.

12. For MSAs accounted for under the fair value method, determine whether the bank recognizes changes in fair value through earnings on at least a quarterly basis pursuant to a satisfactory valuation methodology.

13. Review the list of all MSAs sold since the last examination. Evaluate the documentation supporting the sale. Review the sales contracts (bulk or flow) to determine whether the bank has any continuing obligations to the purchaser, beyond normal representations and warranties.

14. Determine whether the bank has separately capitalized IO strip assets representing excess servicing value. If so, determine whether assumptions and processes for capitalizing and valuing the IO strips are reasonable considering the characteristics of the underlying loans. Ensure that the IO strip assets are reported appropriately on the call report.

Hedging Mortgage Servicing Rights

Note: Examiners should refer to appendix B, "Hedging," and appendix C, "Mortgage Banking Accounting," for additional guidance.

15. Determine whether the MSA and IO strip assets are hedged. Assess effectiveness and resulting level of risk from hedged or unhedged positions.

16. Determine whether hedging activities are well developed, consistent with policy, documented, and communicated to responsible personnel.

17. Evaluate the adequacy of hedging strategies, MIS, monitoring, reporting, and hedging instruments. Consider

- methods to determine hedge effectiveness.
- documentation of hedging activities.
- valuation sensitivities and measurement methods.
- correlation analysis.
- model validation and testing.

18. Determine whether management has adequately considered the risk IO strips present to earnings and capital in different interest rate environments. Assess whether management is hedging these risks in consideration of their unique characteristics, as noted in the MSA hedging section above.

19. Review overall hedging activities, as well as profit and loss reports for these activities:

   - Determine the overall financial success of hedging activities.
   - Compare actual results with management projections.
   - Assess overall net returns and income volatility.

20. Determine whether the bank is attempting to achieve ASC 815 hedge accounting treatment and whether appropriate documentation is maintained.

Conclusions

Conclusion: The aggregate level of each associated risk is (low, moderate, or high). The direction of each associated risk is (increasing, stable, or decreasing).

Objective: To determine, document, and communicate overall findings and conclusions regarding the examination of mortgage banking.

1. Determine preliminary examination findings and conclusions and discuss with the EIC, including

   - quantity of associated risks (as noted in the "Introduction" section).
   - quality of risk management.
   - aggregate level and direction of associated risks.
   - overall risk in mortgage banking.
   - violations and other concerns.

2. Complete the risk assessment matrix for each applicable functional area:

   - Loan production
   - Secondary marketing
   - Servicing
   - MSAs

Summary of Risks Associated With Mortgage Banking				
Risk category	Quantity of risk (Low, moderate, high)	Quality of risk management (Weak, satisfactory, strong)	Aggregate level of risk (Low, moderate, high)	Direction of risk (Increasing, stable, decreasing)
Credit				
Interest rate				
Liquidity				
Operational				
Compliance				
Price				
Strategic				
Reputation				

Examiners should refer to guidance provided under the OCC's large bank and community bank risk assessment programs. See appendix F for risk assessment factors to consider when completing the matrix. Also consider conclusions from any cross-discipline reviews, including consumer compliance, IT, etc. Examiners should consider these conclusions when assessing the aggregate risk for the bank and the CAMELS[34] ratings.

3. If substantive safety and soundness concerns remain unresolved that may have a material adverse effect on the bank, further expand the scope of the examination by completing verification procedures.

4. Discuss examination findings with bank management, including violations, recommendations, and conclusions about risks and risk management practices. If necessary, obtain commitments for corrective action.

5. Compose conclusion comments, highlighting any issues that should be included in the report of examination. If necessary, compose a matters requiring attention (MRA) comment. Consider

   - adequacy of policies and procedures.
   - quality of management and board supervision.
   - aggregate risks posed by the mortgage banking operation.
   - compliance with laws and regulations.
   - profitability levels and future plans.
   - adequacy of MIS and control systems, including internal and external audit and internal QC reviews.
   - any violations and significant deficiencies noted.

6. Update the OCC's information system and any applicable report of examination schedules or tables.

7. Write a memorandum specifically setting out what the OCC should do in the future to effectively supervise mortgage banking operations in the bank, including time periods, staffing, and workdays required.

8. Update, organize, and reference work papers in accordance with OCC policy.

9. Ensure that any papers or electronic media that contain sensitive bank or customer information are appropriately disposed of or secured.

---

[34] The CAMELS rating system assesses capital adequacy, asset quality, management, earnings, liquidity, and sensitivity to market risk.

Internal Control Questionnaire

An internal control questionnaire (ICQ) helps an examiner assess a bank's internal controls for an area. ICQs typically address standard controls that provide day-to-day protection of bank assets and financial records. The examiner decides the extent to which it is necessary to complete or update ICQs during examination planning or after reviewing the findings and conclusions of the core assessment.

Management and Supervision

1. Have management and the board of directors established general operating policies and procedures as well as defined responsibilities for the mortgage banking operation?

2. Have management and the board defined permissible business activities?

3. Have management and the board articulated a risk appetite, established risk thresholds, and set trigger points for escalating oversight and response?

4. Have management and the board communicated performance goals to the mortgage banking unit?

5. Have management and the board implemented a risk management program for the mortgage banking unit?

6. Is mortgage banking integrated into the bank's overall enterprise-wide risk management program and risk limits?

7. Does each mortgage banking function have adequate independence and segregated reporting lines?

8. Is comprehensive MIS in place?

9. Do key officers throughout the mortgage company possess the skills and experience necessary to supervise mortgage banking activities?

10. Has management established an appropriate oversight program for third parties performing outsourced activities?

11. Does management track and evaluate the mortgage banking unit's financial performance as a separate line of business?

12. Does management award bonuses to mortgage banking employees based on qualitative factors rather than just production volume?

13. Are comprehensive procedures in place that ensure compliance with laws and regulations?

14. Are there sufficient internal controls to ensure that assets are safeguarded?

15. Are there sufficient procedures to ensure accounting is accurate?

16. Has management established a system to ensure that the mortgage company maintains adequate capital?

17. Has management established procedures to monitor that the bank has met the capital requirements of the different agencies (GSEs) with which it has relationships?

Internal and External Audits

18. Has the board established internal and external audit coverage for the mortgage banking operation?

19. Has management addressed all outstanding audit findings?

Information Technology

20. Does management use IT for originations or delivery into secondary markets or to maintain borrower information? Are alternate IT sites maintained and tested? Have any internal processes been outsourced? If so, refer to the *FFIEC Information Technology Examination Handbook* booklets:

    - "Outsourcing Technology Services": due diligence, contracts, subcontractors, vendor management (e.g., service level agreements).
    - "Information Security": privacy, access controls, regulatory compliance
    - "Business Continuity Planning": planning, infrastructure, testing

    The booklets and examination procedures are available at: http://ithandbook.ffiec.gov/

    Each booklet also contains an appendix of all laws, regulations, and agency guidance for that topic.

    Depending on the scope and complexity of the bank's use of IT for this business line, IT examiners may be required to adequately assess the IT environment and any associated operational risks.

Loan Production

21. Has the board or its mortgage banking committee, consistent with its duties and responsibilities, adopted written policies and limits that govern

    - types of loans the bank will originate in-house (retail) or purchase from outside sources (wholesale)?

- sources the bank will use to acquire loans?
- underwriting standards and procedures for approving exceptions to written policies?
- legal and compliance obligations that arise from loan production activities?

22. Is the operation and supervision of each facet of the production process sufficiently separated, e.g., underwriting and originations?

23. Are records maintained that detail the number and dollar volume of loans acquired through retail and wholesale sources?

24. Does the bank track the number and type of documentation exceptions and unmarketable loans by origination source?

25. Is a system in place for tracking loan delinquencies, foreclosures, and losses?

26. Does management perform appropriate vintage analysis to monitor the quality of loans produced?

27. Does the QC unit report outside of the production unit?

28. Does the bank prepare QC reports monthly?

29. Does the QC function meet investor requirements for content, scope, and timeliness?

30. Has a unit or individual(s) been assigned responsibility for fraud detection?

31. Are losses on portfolio and warehouse loans recognized in a timely manner and taken against the ALLL?

32. Are losses on loans sold with recourse recognized in a timely manner and recorded against the recourse reserve?

Secondary Marketing

33. Has the board of directors or its mortgage banking committee, consistent with its duties and responsibilities, adopted written mortgage banking policies governing secondary marketing activities that comply with applicable law and that define

- secondary marketing programs used to sell mortgages?
- permissible credit enhancements?
- responsibilities of the secondary marketing department for sale and delivery of loans?
- procedures for tracking and obtaining missing loan documents?
- procedures for mortgage pricing?

34. Are profit and loss records for individual transactions periodically reconciled to general ledger records?

35. Are procedures in place to ensure that recourse transactions are accurately reported on the bank's call report?

36. Are procedures in place to ensure that mortgage pools are certified in a timely manner?

37. Are tracking systems for post-closing documentation in place?

38. Are post-closing documents obtained in a timely manner and in accordance with investor requirements?

Secondary Marketing: Hedging, Pipeline, and Warehouse Activities

39. Has the board of directors or its mortgage banking committee, consistent with its duties and responsibilities, adopted written mortgage banking policies governing pipeline, warehouse, and hedging activities that define

    - position and earnings-at-risk limits?
    - permissible hedging activities?
    - individuals authorized to engage in hedging activities?
    - acceptable hedge instruments?

40. Are risk limits reasonable and supported by documented analysis?

41. Does a formal process exist for granting exceptions to policies and limits?

42. Are detailed MIS reports produced on pipeline, warehouse, and hedging activities?

43. Do adequate fallout reports exist?

44. Are loans awaiting sale segregated from loans held in the permanent mortgage portfolio?

45. Are warehouse reconciliation reports produced?

46. Are inventory turnover and aging reports generated?

47. Are procedures in place to ensure that warehouse loans are accurately reflected on the bank's call report?

48. Are pipeline commitments and warehouse loans accounted for at the lower of cost or market (LOCOM)?

49. Do the hedge products the bank uses minimize the bank's exposure to interest rate risk?

50. Are hedging strategies supported by correlation analysis when basis risk exists?

51. Is simulation modeling used to quantify risk? If so, are assumptions documented?

52. Are profit/loss reports generated for all mortgage banking hedging activities?

53. Does management back-test the effectiveness of hedging activities?

Servicing

54. Has the board of directors or its mortgage banking committee, consistent with its duties and responsibilities, adopted written mortgage banking policies governing mortgage servicing activities that comply with applicable law?

55. Is a schedule maintained that lists all investors for whom servicing is being performed?

56. Is a written master servicing agreement on file for each investor?

57. Are disbursements from custodial accounts adequately controlled?

58. Are custodial accounts reconciled in a timely manner?

59. Are the duties associated with the administration of custodial accounts properly segregated?

60. Are controls in place to ensure that custodial account funds are deposited only in qualified financial institutions?

61. Are procedures and controls in place to ensure that investors receive payments on schedule?

62. Has management established controls to prevent delinquent loans from being prematurely removed from mortgage pools?

63. Are interest adjustments to ARM loans properly performed?

64. Is a monthly report sent to each applicable investor detailing principal and interest collections from homeowners, delinquency rates, foreclosure actions, property inspections, loan losses, and OREO status?

65. Are loan documents stored in a secured and protected area?

66. Is an inventory log maintained listing documents held in safekeeping?

67. Are copies of critical loan documents maintained in a location separate from the originals?

68. Are procedures in place to ensure that the amount of escrow funds collected from each homeowner does not exceed the limit established by 12 USC 2609 (RESPA)?

69. Is every escrow account analyzed annually and an annual recap of escrow account activity sent to each consumer?

70. If an escrow account overage or shortage is found, is the homeowner notified in writing of the method that will be used to adjust the account?

71. Are controls in place that prevent the bank from using homeowners' escrow account balances to meet other obligations?

72. Are procedures in place to ensure that collection activities conform to investor and legal requirements?

73. If a forbearance arrangement is made with a delinquent mortgagor, is the reason for the forbearance action documented?

74. Is a system in place to ensure that, if required, the investor approves the forbearance arrangement?

75. Has the bank established a foreclosure reserve?

76. Are uncollectible investor advances charged off in a timely manner?

77. When title has been or will be obtained to an OREO property, does the bank follow applicable laws, regulations, and financial reporting rules?

78. Do controls exist to ensure that loans are set up on the servicing system?

79. When a borrower pays off a loan, does the bank file the mortgage release and satisfaction and return the original promissory note to the borrower in a timely manner?

80. Does a customer service unit exist to handle customer questions and ensure that customer complaints are properly resolved?

Outside Vendors

81. If applicable, is the quality of work performed by each outside vendor and sub-servicer monitored on an ongoing basis? Is a comprehensive due diligence review performed at least annually on providers of business critical services or processes?

82. Does management analyze the financial condition of vendors and sub-servicers at least annually?

Mortgage Servicing Assets

83. Has the bank formulated written policies and procedures governing MSAs?

84. Is the board required to approve significant sales and purchases of MSAs?

85. Does management conduct a due diligence review before purchasing a bulk servicing portfolio?

86. Are due diligence reviews documented and reviewed by the board of directors before a transaction is approved?

87. Does the bank have an adequate record-keeping system in place to support and account for MSAs?

88. Are records maintained that document original valuation assumptions for each bulk acquisition of servicing rights?

89. Are records maintained by product type and month of origination for MSAs acquired through retail production (origination) and production flow (purchase) activities?

90. Does the bank have a system in place to track actual prepayment experience on individual pools of mortgages?

91. Do the bank's valuation techniques provide a reasonable estimate of fair value, and do they incorporate market participant assumptions?

92. Does the bank use an appropriate market discount rate for valuing MSAs?

93. Is an impairment analysis performed at least quarterly?

94. Is the impairment analysis performed on a "strata-by-strata" basis?

95. Are the prepayment assumptions used in discounted cash flow calculations realistic and substantiated by an independent third party?

96. Are the assumptions for ancillary income, float, earnings on escrows, servicing costs, foreclosure expenses, and other revenue and expense items realistic?

97. Do assumptions correspond to the bank's actual experience?

98. Are MSAs amortized over their estimated useful life? Is the useful life reasonable, given actual prepayments?

99. Are accounting practices documented and applied on a consistent basis?

100. Has the board approved adequate policies and procedures and established appropriate risk limits?

101. Does the bank have an adequate record-keeping system in place to support and account for its retained interests?

102. Are files maintained that document the assumptions used to record retained interest for each sale of mortgages?

103. Does the bank have a system in place to track actual prepayment experience on individual pools of mortgages?

104. Does an appropriate legal opinion exist to support that mortgage securitizations meet ASC 860's isolation of transferred assets criteria?

105. Are "gain on sale" accounting entries reasonable and are residual interests initially recorded at their relative fair value?

106. Are retained interests (excluding servicing assets) marked to market quarterly?

107. Does the bank rely on models to provide an estimate of the fair value of its retained interests?

108. Do independent and competent personnel conduct valuation modeling?

109. Does the valuation model appropriately reflect the terms and conditions in loan sales documentation?

110. Can management provide reasonable and verifiable support for the following assumptions used in the valuation model?

- Cash yield
- Prepayment curves
- Appropriate loss severities
- Discount rate

111. Does the valuation of residual interests properly reflect the following impacts on cash flows?

- Fees (e.g., trustee, servicer, insurer)
- Release or additions to reserves
- Overcollateralization requirements
- Payments from delinquent loans that are not in default
- Recoveries
- Insurance coverage of losses (e.g., FHA guarantees)
- Credit losses

112. Does management compare model estimates of monthly cash flow with actual cash flow received by the bank and explain significant variances?

Conclusion

113. Does the foregoing information provide an adequate basis for evaluating the activities of the mortgage banking unit? Explain negative answers briefly, and indicate conclusions as to their effect on specific examination procedures.

114. Based on the answers to the foregoing questions, internal control for mortgage banking is considered (strong, satisfactory, or weak).

Verification Procedures

Verification procedures are used to verify the existence of assets and liabilities, or test the reliability of financial records. Examiners generally do not perform verification procedures as part of a typical examination. Rather, verification procedures are performed when substantive safety and soundness concerns are identified that are not mitigated by the bank's risk management systems and internal controls.

Loan Production

1. Execute random sample of originations to assess accuracy of loan data and the appropriateness of a product type delivered to the consumer.

2. Test a sample of loans to ensure that underwriting policies and guidelines are appropriately followed. Determine whether the exception rate is within investors' acceptable standards and consistent with industry practices.

3. Ensure that appropriate controls exist over the real estate appraisal process.

4. Review final approval and funding processes to estimate any conflicts of interest.

5. Review the compensation structures of employees considered to be loan originators to ensure compliance with industry and regulatory requirements.

Secondary Marketing

6. Evaluate pricing, locking methodology, and exception authority to ensure consistency with strategic and regulatory expectations. Review the average lock periods in conjunction with processing times for the company and industry.

7. Random sample loans closed with those originated to measure the degree of rate fluctuation. Significant variation may be symptomatic of "bait and switch" schemes.

8. Random sample loans funded through committed warehouse lines.

9. Review the contractual documents, including the loan purchase and sale agreements and offering circulars, to validate that the bank is legally entitled to deliver loans.

Servicing

10. Evaluate whether MIS reports for servicing operation provide adequate information to monitor servicing activities.

11. Assess the accuracy of cost-of-service information to ensure it includes all costs associated with direct and indirect overhead, capital, and collections. Compare cost of service with industry averages to judge the efficiency of the operation.

12. Assess the effectiveness of loan collection practices and their compliance with applicable federal and state requirements.

13. Evaluate the efficiency of the asset disposal unit and compliance with industry and regulatory standards.

14. Test loss mitigation practices to ensure that they are conducted in a safe and sound manner.

15. Ensure that the cash management function has established appropriate segregated custodial accounts. Determine whether adequate controls exist over custodial accounts, including daily balancing, monthly reconcilements, assigned authority for disbursement, and appropriate segregation.

16. Review servicing advancing practices to ensure that the activity is conducted in a safe and sound manner. Verify that servicing advances are consistent with industry practices and conducted in accordance with the servicing agreement and securitization documentation.

17. Verify that investor accounting and reporting are timely and accurate. Ensure that servicing reports used for reporting conform to the requirements of securitization documents.

Mortgage Servicing Assets

18. Evaluate the reasonableness of model validation procedures performed by bank management. Test model to ensure output is calculated correctly and provides meaningful results.

19. Determine whether the model appropriately reflects the terms and conditions in securitization documentation.

20. Evaluate the independence and competence of staff responsible for valuation.

21. Review the methodology and supporting documentation to assess the reasonableness of cash yield, prepayment, default, loss, and discount rate assumptions, and verify their calculations.

22. Compare the prepayment, default, and loss assumptions used in valuing the retained interests with actual performance of the underlying collateral. If the underlying collateral does not have sufficient performance history, compare assumptions with substantially similar assets. In addition, evaluate whether weaknesses or liberal collection practices identified in servicing reviews are fully considered in these assumptions.

23. Calculate the cash yield of the portfolio based on actual cash received from customers. Compare the cash yield calculated with the cash yield assumption used in valuing the retained interests.

24. Compare model estimates of monthly cash flow to actual cash flow received by the bank. Significant variances require explanation.

25. Compare the discount rate used in valuing the retained interests with the discount rate that other market participants use to value retained interests with substantially similar underlying assets.

26. Verify discounted cash flow methodology. Ensure that expected cash flows are discounted based on when they are received (cash-out method) as opposed to when they are earned by the trust (cash-in method).

Appendixes

Appendix A: Sample Request Letter

Examiners should tailor the following request letter as needed, based on the bank's activities.

Please provide the following information for mortgage banking operations as of the close of business on [date], unless otherwise indicated. Information in an electronic format is preferred. If submitting hard copies, please prominently mark any information or documentation that is to be returned to the bank.

Our intent is to request information that can be easily obtained. If you find that the information is not readily available or requires significant effort on your part to prepare, please contact us before compiling the data.

For many items we request a copy of the current or most recent report available. Please note that during the examination we may request the report from other dates or time periods. For items noted as "make available," we request access to the information but do not require copies that we can retain. Please also note that this list is not all-inclusive, and that we may request additional items during the course of our examination.

Management and Board Supervision

1. Policy and operating procedure manuals for Production, Secondary Marketing, Servicing, and Mortgage Servicing Assets, and related accounting policies and procedures for these areas.

2. Strategic, business, and profit plans for mortgage banking activities.

3. Copy of the organizational chart indicating key managers, office locations, and roles, and telephone numbers for all key managers and examination contacts.

4. List of board and management committees that includes function, members, frequency of meetings, and whether minutes are kept; copies of minutes covering meetings from the last year; information packets associated with these meetings; and any additional director or management special reports (e.g., executive summary for any special analyses performed).

5. Copy of management reports from the most recent fiscal year and year-to-date that outline operational results, performance, profitability, comparisons to expected results and key financial results for the mortgage banking unit.

6. Description of compensation associate with mortgage banking activities (fixed-pay, variable-pay, fixed/variable-pay combination, etc.) programs, and any overage or similar arrangements for originators, processors, underwriters, and other loan production personnel.

7. List of ABAs involved in the mortgage loan process, the nature of the arrangements, and the ABA's name, location, ownership structure, nature of business, and year-to-date operating results to include activity volume and profitability.

8. List of material pending or threatened litigation.

9. Copies of recent reports used to monitor and track the volume of customer complaints since the prior fiscal year.

10. Business continuity and resumption plans for major functions.

11. Copies of fraud risk management practices, key reports, and training programs, and recent fraud reports.

12. List of all service providers or third-party vendors. List should include

    - contact information.
    - overview of the service provided.
    - executed contract detailing the nature of the service provided and the fee structure.
    - bank oversight processes, including quality control reviews.
    - MIS detailing key performance metrics.
    - record of any affiliate relationships with the bank.

Production, Processing, and Underwriting

13. Key management reports (daily, weekly, biweekly, monthly, etc.) used to monitor production volume, efficiency, profitability, quality, underwriting exceptions, etc.

14. Descriptions of products and underwriting criteria.

15. Copies of marketing materials for nontraditional and subprime mortgages.

16. If available, workflows for key mortgage loan production functions, including origination, processing, underwriting, and closing processes.

17. Description of the appraisal and valuation process, including the ordering and review process; the most recent reports used to monitor the independence and quality of appraisals and property valuations for the origination process; and a description of the exception monitoring and reporting process and a list of any exceptions to appraisal policies during the last year.

18. Copy of origination volume reports for the prior year and year-to-date by QM versus non-QM and product type, including government versus conventional, conforming versus nonconforming, fixed versus ARM, portfolio versus sold, servicing retained versus released, etc. Include production volume information for mortgage products with unique characteristics, such as

- payment-option ARMs.
- other mortgages with start rates significantly below the fully indexed rate.
- interest-only mortgages.
- reduced-documentation loans (e.g., "stated," "no income," "no income, no asset," "no document," etc.).
- primary obligors with a credit score(s) < 620.
- loans with combined LTV (first-lien and junior-lien mortgages) > 90 percent without PMI.

19. List of brokers, correspondents, and affiliates used, including the most recent scorecards used to monitor their performance, and volume information by correspondent/broker for the most recent fiscal year and year-to-date.

20. Copies of contracts and agreements between the bank and brokers/correspondents.

21. List of brokers and correspondents terminated during the past year and reasons for action.

22. Copy of management reports used for tracking and monitoring performance of first mortgage loan production with unique characteristics (as noted above).

23. List of early payment defaults during the prior fiscal year and year-to-date.

Secondary Marketing, Pipeline, and Warehouse Management

24. Supporting documentation for all new products offered during the last year.

25. Key management reports (daily, weekly, biweekly, monthly, etc.) for monitoring, managing, and hedging the pipeline and warehouse.

26. Description of the process or model used for loan pricing and applicable model documentation.

27. Most recent rate sheet and copy of Bloomberg or other screens showing market rates as of same date.

28. Most recent pipeline position report.

29. Most recent fallout analysis reports.

30. Most recent warehouse aging report.

31. List of mortgages transferred to portfolio during the last year or carried in the warehouse for longer time frames (e.g., over 90 days); reasons for transfers from the warehouse to the portfolio or for longer-term warehouse holdings (e.g., salability or documentation issues); description of the accounting treatment for these loans.

32. Most recent pipeline mark and warehouse valuation reports, and a description of the valuation process.

33. Current investor contracts.

34. Report showing volume delivered to each investor during the prior fiscal year and year-to-date.

35. Fannie Mae, Freddie Mac, Ginnie Mae, and other investor commitment status reports showing product type and coupon.

36. Ginnie Mae pool certification status, if applicable.

37. Post-closing exception report.

38. Trailing document summary and aging report.

39. List and description of all transactions involving recourse to the mortgage company for more than customary representations and warranties, including all loans sold with early default clauses or similar warranties that extend beyond 120 days.

40. List of all loans repurchased from investors because of sales representations and warranties, as well as loans the bank has indemnified in the event of future losses, during the prior fiscal year and year-to-date.

41. Most recent recourse reserve and ASC 460 ("Guarantees") analysis.

Servicing

42. Most recent analysis of servicing costs and revenues by product type.

43. List of investors serviced, including product types and current outstanding volume.

44. Copy of most recent delinquency and default management reports used to monitor performance by origination source, product, geographic area, risk rating, credit score, etc.

45. Copy of recent vintage analysis used to track and compare delinquency, foreclosure, and loss rates over various seasoning periods.

46. Description of the process and reports used to manage uncollectible servicing advances.

47. Description of deferrals, re-agings, extensions, modifications, loss mitigation, and loss recognition practices, and the most recent monthly report used to monitor these practices.

48. List of loan substitutions and loans purchased from investor pools.

49. List of all loans subject to the Servicemembers Civil Relief Act.

50. Recap of all properties in the process of foreclosure and OREO.

51. Copy of the most recently prepared foreclosure reserve analysis.

52. Most recent copy of investor account reconciliations, with a description of the process for reconciling investor accounts and status reports on reconciliation issues for cash management and investor accounting.

53. Description of the document-tracking system for safeguarding mortgage loan documents and the off-site backup process.

54. Copies of reports used to monitor delinquent property taxes and insurance for mortgage products, and information on tax penalties incurred and hazard insurance claims denied for the prior fiscal year and year-to-date.

55. Copies of reports used to manage mortgage satisfactions, including any exception tracking reports.

56. List of arrangements where the mortgage company is the sub-servicer for another institution and description of the terms and conditions.

57. List of external sub-servicers and vendors used to perform servicing functions, including terms, conditions, and responsibilities, and copies of the most recent monthly reports used to monitor the performance of sub-servicers and vendors.

Mortgage Servicing Assets

58. Copies of key management reports used to monitor and manage MSAs.

59. List of all purchases and sales of MSAs during the prior fiscal year and year-to-date, the dates and terms of the transactions, and due diligence assessments and analytical reviews used for bulk acquisitions of servicing during the prior fiscal year and year-to-date.

60. Copy of the most recent third-party valuation of MSAs, industry surveys, and any other benchmarking reports used for MSA valuation and management.

61. Most recent static pool cash collection analysis that shows the actual cash flows realized from MSAs relative to model projections.

62. Copy of the most recent quarterly MSA valuation analysis.

63. Cash flow model used for fair value measurement of MSA, including prepayment model factors; copies of all model validation reports issued during the last two years; and all MSA valuation model documentation.

64. Copy of the risk management program governing MSAs, e.g., stress test, assumption review, or approval mechanisms.

65. Current MSA capitalization factors or multiples by product type.

66. Summary of hedging strategies and financial instruments used to hedge MSAs.

Internal/External Audits, Third-Party Reviews, and Other Reports

67. Internal/external audits, investor reviews (Fannie Mae, Freddie Mac, Ginnie Mae, FHLBs, HUD, VA, private investors, etc.), consultant reports, rating agency reports, and other internal/external analyses, together with management's response, and copies of the last review performed, regardless of date.

Quality Control

68. Key reports (daily, weekly, biweekly, monthly, etc.) generated by the QC function for monitoring loan quality and adherence to investor underwriting requirements.

69. Copy of the most recent QC committee packet.

70. Copies of internal/external QC summaries and exception reports covering the last year.

Information Technology

71. Organizational chart or overview and list of key contacts for all technology support functions.

72. Schematic of the technology infrastructure environment for mortgage processes, including but not limited to

- loan production.
- secondary marketing.
- servicing.
- MSAs.

Highlight systems or applications supported by third-party service providers.

73. Copies of management tracking reports relating to capacity, performance, and availability of mission-critical systems and applications.

74. Copy of the information security plan and an overview of the information security control structure, including system and data access control.

75. Copy of business continuation and disaster recovery plans for mission-critical systems, applications, and locations, and results of the most recent business continuation plan and disaster recovery tests.

76. A list of current application or data management projects that will affect mission-critical processes.

Appendix B: Hedging

Hedging Objective

Through mortgage banking activities, banks assume market risk by issuing interest rate lock commitments and aggregating closed mortgage loans held for sale. Left unhedged, losses associated with these risks can be significant. In banks with significant mortgage banking operations, secondary marketing responsibilities include executing and managing the day-to-day risks associated with their mortgage pipeline and warehouse positions.

The objective of hedging is to mitigate market risk and protect the value of such mortgages and commitments from the initial commitment date until the loan is funded and sold. The primary objective of hedging mortgage banking activities is to offset changes in the fair value of the mortgage pipeline and warehouse positions in the most cost-effective and efficient manner. Without hedging, changes in fair value of the pipeline and warehouse may lead to volatility in earnings or erosion of gain-on-sale margins. An effective risk management program can help level the peaks and troughs of normal market movements to produce a consistent and predictable revenue flow.

Hedging Process

Mortgage companies that engage in mortgage banking should have formal policies and procedures for hedging pipeline and warehouse risks that are consistent with the overall risk management process of the association. This process should include the following:

- Procedures for identifying and segmenting risks in the pipeline and warehouse.
- Measures to identify the types of risks inherent in the operations.
- Board-approved risk exposure limits indicating acceptable risk limits.
- Systems to measure and monitor risk exposure.
- Procedures to track and evaluate price movements.
- Limits for officers authorized to open and manage hedging positions.
- Management reporting systems that disclose the mortgage pipeline and warehouse risk position on a daily basis.
- Management expertise to design, execute, and maintain an appropriate secondary marketing hedge program.
- Appropriate monitoring and internal control systems to ensure that internal policies are followed.

Risk Metrics

Banks engaged in mortgage banking should develop risk metrics for measuring, monitoring, and estimating the effects of different events on mortgage banking activities. One of the most common risk metrics is based on a parallel rate shock scenario. This scenario analysis estimates the change in value of the pipeline and warehouse holdings and hedge instruments for a specific basis point change in interest rates, such as plus or minus 1, 25, 50, 100 basis points, etc. Although this analysis is useful and captures much of the duration risk, banks with significant and complex mortgage banking activities should establish a broad array of more sophisticated risk metrics. These metrics could include duration/convexity, nonparallel yield curve shifts, prepayment shocks, volatility, and mortgage basis spreads.

Some banks use metrics that assess multiple risk factors concurrently, such as parallel and nonparallel yield curve, volatility, basis, and option-adjusted spread. VaR can be used to estimate the maximum loss that could be incurred on the pipeline or warehouse over a certain time period, such as one day, 10 days, one quarter, etc., at a given confidence level such as 95 percent, 98 percent, or 99 percent. This means that the maximum estimated VaR loss would only be expected to be exceeded 1 percent to 5 percent of the time for a given holding period, depending on the confidence level established by management. EaR measures the maximum shortfall in earnings relative to a specified target that could be experienced because of the impact of market risk on a specified set of exposures for a specified reporting period and confidence level.

Best Execution

Banks are able to achieve better selling execution by aggregating funded loans rather than individual loans. Best execution means getting the best price for a loan sale or a loan securitization delivery. Best execution is achieved in conjunction with hedging loan pricing risks. Hedge selection is driven by the bank's plan for achieving best execution. For example, loan sale executions are based on current mortgage security prices, buy-down and buy-up grids or factors, agency cash program prices and yields, guarantee fees, and the prospects of retaining or releasing servicing rights.

Secondary marketing managers should continually analyze sale execution variables to maximize the delivery options for optimum results. Large or active mortgage bankers use sophisticated models to clarify tactics associated with placing forward hedge coverage by quantifying the value of alternative executions, thus enabling more profitable decisions.

Loan securitization is another form of loan delivery used by large mortgage bankers who retain mortgage servicing. Loans are bundled into a security that is sold to secondary market investors. Conforming loan securitizations require the approval of Fannie Mae or Freddie Mac. The MSRs created are either sold separately (servicing released premium) or retained in portfolio (servicing retained).

Hedge Optimization

Hedge optimization blends best execution (primarily secondary market driven) with bank preferences. These preferences may include approved hedging instruments; level of risk appetite; hedge coverage, including cross-product hedging between loan programs; and desired use of option coverage, including option premium cost, or minimum transaction size. Hedge optimization pulls together all existing hedge positions; current best execution for each loan; potential forward sale and option instruments for every coupon, expiration, and strike price; and bid-ask spreads for all potential trades and preferences for hedging. The optimal set of daily hedge positions should be based on management's criteria and specific risk limits. To minimize hedge cost, the hedger should have a good understanding of the relative cost or value of different instruments before making any trading decisions.

Loan Pool Optimization

Loan pool optimization combines best execution and hedge optimization with preferences for investor delivery. The objective is to create loan pools for delivery into existing trades, create loan pools for delivery into new trades, or to aid in deciding whether to pair off existing trades. Factors management should consider in creating optimal loan pools include delivery appetites, investor-specific restrictions and requirements, and management preferences relative to the retention of servicing rights.

Risk Identification and Segmentation

In the "Secondary Marketing" section of this booklet, primary pipeline and warehouse risks are discussed, including interest rate or price risk, fallout risk, reverse price risk, basis risk, product risk, credit risk, and prepayment risk. In addition to those risks, other hedging-related risks, such as measurement risk, timing risk, and liquidity risk, must be identified, monitored, and controlled. Measurement risk is the risk that the hedger will execute too much or too little coverage. Timing risk is the risk of putting on or taking off the hedge at the wrong time. Liquidity risk is the inability to close a position promptly without incurring significant loss. The use of thinly traded hedging instruments or hedge positions with large concentrations relative to market breadth or float heighten liquidity risk.

Before entering into any hedging strategy, management and the board of directors should have thorough knowledge of the risks and rewards of the hedging programs under consideration. Important areas of focus include the following:

- Adequate management technical expertise
- Benefits hedging will bring to the association
- Advantages and disadvantages of various hedging strategies and hedging instruments
- Hedging techniques the bank plans to use
- Risks associated with hedging strategies and methods
- Sensitivity of hedge instruments to changes in market price
- Costs of hedging
- Potential difficulties in hedge administration

Hedge Coverage

Hedge coverage refers to the portion of the rate-sensitive mortgage pipeline and warehouse that a hedging instrument covers. It is usually expressed as a percentage of the pipeline and warehouse positions. In practice, most secondary marketing managers hedge 100 percent of the rate-sensitive warehouse position. Once these loans are closed and funded, they are exposed to interest rate risk but are no longer at risk for fallout. Coverage is then focused on the mortgage pipeline position and can be expressed as a percentage of the mortgage pipeline.

The primary risks associated with hedging a mortgage pipeline are interest rate risk and fallout risk. When a potential borrower receives a rate lock, the bank has in effect provided a put option to the borrower to sell the loan to the lender at a specified price. The bank is incurring a risk without directly receiving compensation. If rates rise, the borrower is likely to execute the loan transaction. If rates fall, the borrower is less likely to execute. This risk is referred to as fallout risk. Hedging strategies should consider both interest rate and fallout risks.

Secondary marketing managers typically determine the amount of hedge coverage based on historical performance. These managers should periodically perform historical fallout analysis under varying market environments to gauge the level of fallout and identify the reasons changes in the level occurred.

As interest rates fall, the bank suffers losses on unfunded loans in the rate-locked pipeline that do not close because existing mandatory forward sale commitments cannot be filled. In this situation, the hedger needs to pair off or compensate the investor for the failed delivery. This situation illustrates an over-hedged pipeline position and reinforces the importance of understanding the fallout potential of the bank's locked mortgage pipeline.

Conversely, as interest rates rise, fallout declines and pull-through increases because the borrower's rate lock is "in the money," resulting in a higher likelihood of loan closure. In this situation, mortgage bankers suffer losses if too little hedge coverage exists, forcing the sale of uncovered loans into the market at a loss.

An effective hedge program maintains a balanced hedge position to neutralize both primary risks inherent in the mortgage pipeline and warehouse. A common hedge program is as follows:

- Initiating coverage for a given percentage of the rate-locked mortgage pipeline to cover pull-through of loans in the pipeline between rate lock and funding, based on historical fallout analysis.
- Covering 100 percent of the rate-sensitive warehouse loans.
- Adjusting hedge coverage on a daily basis to account for changes in the pipeline or warehouse and to maintain proper hedge coverage ratios.

The secondary marketing manager accomplishes hedging using a variety of hedge instruments. The most commonly used include

- optional best efforts forward sale commitments.
- mandatory forward sale commitments.
- options on forward sales of MBSs.
- U.S. Treasury or Eurodollar financial futures.

Hedging Activity and Effectiveness

The secondary marketing or mortgage pipeline and warehouse policy should specify the bank's risk limit. The level of risk appetite determines the extent to which the bank hedges pipeline and warehouse risk exposure. The level of risk appetite can be specified relative to a specific hedge coverage ratio or dollar loss in economic value.

Hedge ratios are a necessary part of the risk management process, because it is not practical or even possible to offset every rate lock and closed loan in the pipeline and warehouse with an identical hedge instrument. This approach provides the basis for determining more precise cross-product and cross-coupon hedge ratios (delta hedging). This risk measure is effective only to the extent that all mortgage banking positions inclusive of hedge positions are on a duration (delta) equivalent basis. Examiners should scrutinize the bank's hedge instrument activity very closely in conjunction with the risk profile of its mortgage banking activity. Inappropriate use of hedging instruments or combinations of instruments may not result in material risk reduction and may even exacerbate risk. The exposure report may, however, erroneously show these positions as providing full hedge protection. Management reports that indicate only the current notional amount of hedge protection relative to the pipeline and warehouse exposure may not be representative of the underlying net exposure.

The best framework for viewing secondary-marketing-related risks and the impact of hedges in reducing risks is to account for the relative value of all positions (i.e., loan pipeline, warehouse loans, and hedge instruments). A market value or "market value at risk" approach provides the basis for measuring risk embedded in the bank's pipeline and warehouse positions, ensuring that comparisons on an instrument-to-instrument basis are valid.

Scenario analysis measures the price/value sensitivity of the pipeline and warehouse portfolios, including all hedge positions, to changes in interest rates or changes in price of a benchmark MBS. The most common scenarios are yield curve shock scenarios based on instantaneous and parallel shifts in the Treasury or LIBOR yield curve. This type of analysis shows the risk profile of the entire mortgage banking position, which helps assess the effectiveness of the hedge position relative to the bank's risk appetite.

The scenarios are usually determined by selecting a variety of yield curve shifts. Yield curve shifts or interest rate shocks may be more focused on short-term market moves, such as smaller shifts or benchmark security price changes that are more probable, or longer-term market moves, such as larger shifts or benchmark security price changes. Many banks look at both long- and short-term scenarios. The time span from loan commitment until sale is an important factor in assessing and managing interest rate and price risks.

In addition to the valuation and sensitivity of the mortgage loan pipeline and warehouse positions, management should consider the economic value of the related mortgage servicing. This framework also provides a rigorous basis for valuing MSR. The value of the mortgage servicing is often a key factor in the profitability of a mortgage banking operation. Mortgage bankers do not want to risk the value of the mortgage servicing when evaluating the level of tolerance to risk of the entire mortgage banking operation. The overall performance or effectiveness of hedging can usually be gauged by analyzing the profitability of the secondary marketing department over time. Significant income or gain on sale margin volatility may indicate pipeline management issues that stem from hedging activities.

Pipeline and Warehouse Hedging Techniques

Delta (Dynamic) Hedging

Delta hedging is relatively simple to employ because it is concerned with hedging only small changes in interest rates. Delta hedging focuses on a risk measure referred to as DV01, or the dollar value of a 1-basis-point change in interest rates. DV01 is calculated based on the effective duration of a 1-basis-point parallel shift in the yield curve. Thus, this measure does not capture the convexity effect of mortgage-based products that is generated by larger yield curve shifts. The objective of delta hedgers is to reduce or eliminate losses relative to small changes in rates. Typical delta hedging employs a "delta neutral" approach that attempts to immunize mortgage pipeline and warehouse positions in the aggregate against small changes in interest rates.

Delta hedging has limitations. It does not provide adequate hedge coverage for larger changes in rates, and risk exposure to convexity, basis, and volatility are left unhedged. For mortgage assets with embedded prepayment options, a delta hedger needs to rebalance hedges frequently as rates move because convexity causes the mortgage pipeline and warehouse deltas to change with rate shifts. This frequent rebalancing is referred to as dynamic hedging. Fast-moving markets can be problematic for a delta hedge because they require the bank's models to quickly re-estimate the bank's mortgage banking risk positions. Options are generally not used in delta hedges.

Delta/Gamma (Global) Hedging

A global hedging strategy anticipates changes in the pipeline and warehouse relationships caused by market changes. Global hedging also constitutes a more comprehensive approach to delta hedging, because it captures the impact of convexity and volatility risks in the pipeline and warehouse portfolios. Under this strategy, options are used to minimize the impact of convexity and volatility risks in addition to the pipeline and warehouse delta.

Using options typically provides more relief from the frequent rebalancing required under the delta hedging strategy and improves the mortgage banking risk profile under larger rate moves. Disadvantages of using options are the higher cost and reduced liquidity relative to alternative hedge instruments, such as exchange-traded futures and swaps. Option hedging, by contrast, requires more sophisticated modeling to measure and monitor a variety of market risks.

Hedging Instruments

Banks use various instruments to hedge market risk in the secondary market. The board or delegated board committee should identify approved hedging instruments, and the mortgage banking operation should have the expertise to manage such instruments. In addition to explicit board approval, the bank's policies should describe the authorized instruments in detail and the particular purposes for applying each instrument.

The most commonly used hedges are best efforts forward sales agreements, mandatory forward sales agreements, and options on MBSs.

Optional or best efforts forward sales agreement: A hedge that removes fallout risk from the mortgage pipeline. The bank may find that it cannot produce loans in sufficient quantity to securitize or service them. In this situation, the secondary marketing manager may elect an optional forward sale to sell particular loan production. Many small mortgage banking operations use this hedging strategy for its relatively simple interest rate risk mitigation. It also offers the advantages of minimal price or product risk, low cost, and little required monitoring.

Mandatory or firm forward sales agreement: The most common type of forward sales agreement. If the bank chooses not to use forward whole-loan sales, it can substitute the sale of something similar that is not owned for future delivery. This can be accomplished with forward sales of similar mortgages, MBS, or other debt instruments, such as U.S. Treasury securities.

Forward sales of mortgage loans in the pipeline permit lenders to eliminate price and product risks by establishing simultaneously the terms of origination and sale. If closing and delivering mortgage loans were a certainty, a forward sales agreement would represent a perfect hedge; that is, it would provide complete interest rate protection and introduce no additional risks. There is always the possibility of fallout during the origination process, however, especially if interest rates decrease substantially.

In the event a seller is unable to close and deliver mortgages at required yields, the seller may be liable for the pair-off costs that involve buying back the position. This entails repurchasing mandatory delivery commitments. Alternatively, the bank may choose to go back into the wholesale market and buy enough loans to meet the obligation, obtain securities by buying a comparable security, pairing off, or rolling forward the position. Pairing off the hedge position or purchasing loans usually results in a loss. The following paragraphs describe how this type of coverage works.

Example: The bank has $100 million of loans in the pipeline at 6.5 percent and two points (price of 98 percent). The bank's hedger sells a 6 percent MBS for a price of 98.25 percent. If all of the loans close as expected, the bank will realize a gain equal to 0.25 percent plus the value of the servicing in excess of the minimum required servicing spread (for example, 0.25 percent). If all of the loans do not close as expected (i.e., fallout occurs), and other loans with substantially equivalent yields are not immediately available for substitution, one of two simplified scenarios will occur.

Scenario 1: Interest rates have risen since the original hedge trade, causing loan fallout to decline or loan pull-throughs to increase. Before settlement day, the hedger determines that the bank will have a higher percentage of loans closing in the pipeline than originally estimated. Because rates have risen since the initial trade, the pipeline loans attributable to the increase in the pull-through rate (i.e., unhedged pipeline loans) will be sold at the current market price (e.g., 96.00 percent). Therefore, the bank will incur a loss on those loans that were not initially hedged, equal to the difference in the current market price and the price at the original trade.

Scenario 2: Interest rates have declined since the original hedge trade. Before settlement day, the hedger determines that the bank will be unable to pool enough funded loans to meet the forward sale requirements. Because rates have declined since the initial trade, the hedger must purchase a comparable security in an amount equal to the shortfall at current market at a higher price (e.g., 100.00 percent). Therefore, the bank will incur a pair-off loss of 1.75 percent equal to the 98.25 percent sold less 100.00 percent bought. If the unclosed loans actually close at the initial lock-in terms, a gain may be realized to partially offset the pair-off losses.

Options on MBSs and futures: These options give the holder the contractual right, but not the obligation, to buy (call option) or sell (put option) an underlying MBS or financial futures at a specified price on the option expiration date.

One method of reducing pair-off costs arising from the failure to deliver mortgage loans under a mandatory forward sales agreement is to purchase mortgage loan options. For example, an originator may purchase an option to sell a Freddie Mac participation certificate (PC) with a certain coupon at a specified price by a certain date. Here, the originator is long a put option, which is the most common option used to hedge a mortgage pipeline. Basis risk is neutralized assuming that the MBS is identical to the mortgage loans in the pipeline and warehouse.

Banks may use either over-the-counter (OTC) mortgage options or exchange-traded options for hedging purposes. OTC mortgage options are traded in the dealer market. These options are less liquid and have higher premiums than exchange-traded options on U.S. Treasury futures.

Treasury and Eurodollar financial futures contracts closely track the price performance of the underlying "cheapest to deliver" U.S. Treasury security-based or LIBOR-based deposit rates (with terms up to 30 years). Futures positions are marked to market daily. A mortgage option, however, has significantly less risk than an option on Treasury futures because it does not introduce basis risk and can be customized with respect to strike price and maturity.

A synthetic put is another alternative that offers the same benefit. It consists of the simultaneous sale of a mandatory forward and purchase of a call in "like instruments" (agency, coupon, settlement month). Option cost or premium is a function of the specified strike price, current underlying security price, time to expiration, implied volatility, and risk-free interest rate corresponding to the time to expiration of the option. Options can be an effective hedge vehicle, especially during periods of high interest rate volatility.

Put options may be used in a hybrid strategy with forward contracts to hedge pipeline risk when borrower fallout is uncertain. The choice of strike price on these options is dictated by the degree of protection the originator desires. For instance, an at-the-money option will provide greater protection than an out-of-the-money option. An at-the-money option, however, would be obtained at a higher option premium. The trade-off between the degree of protection and the price paid for the option, which is determined by its strike price, is similar to purchasing automobile insurance with a high deductible.

The value of U.S. Treasury securities and Treasury or Eurodollar futures: Contracts whose value is directly linked to the value of a deposit rate based on a comparable-maturity noncallable Treasury security or on LIBOR. Using these contracts to hedge the value of a mortgage security captures duration risk but exposes the hedger to convexity and basis risk. To address the nonlinear profile of mortgages, options may be used in combination with the financial futures.

Interest rate swaps: OTC contracts in which one party receives or pays a fixed rate of interest and another party pays or receives a floating rate of interest, usually three-month LIBOR, over a specified period. Similar to Eurodollar futures, interest rate swaps can provide an effective hedge against duration risk, but they introduce basis risk and convexity risk. As such, options may be used in combination to offset the convexity risk.

Interest rate swaptions: Options to enter into a specified interest rate swap transaction at a predetermined future date. These instruments are similar to options on MBSs, but the underlying financial instrument is an interest rate swap. These instruments address the convexity risk normally attributed to using swaps to hedge mortgages but still introduce basis risk.

Hedge Position Management

Pipeline and warehouse positions are normally classified into categories by program type and risk level. Hybrid ARM products, along with traditional fixed-rate loan products, are exposed to interest rate risk. While ARMs, because of their lower exposure to interest rate and price risk, are not usually hedged, hybrid ARMs are usually hedged because of the interest rate risk in the loans' initial fixed-rate term. The following are common categories for pipeline and warehouse positions:

- Agency conforming, 30-year fixed rate
- Agency conforming, 15-year fixed rate
- Nonconforming, 30-year fixed rate
- Nonconforming, 15-year fixed rate
- Government (e.g., VA, FHA)
- Subprime
- Hybrid ARMs
- ARMs

In addition to the listed categories, banks segregate by salability parameters including loan size, product code, purpose code, investor code, and property type. The basic components of establishing the desired hedge position are security type, delivery month, and coupon, along with a decision related to mandatory versus optional sales.

Pipeline and Warehouse Risk Exposure Reports

To operate the mortgage banking operation in a safe and sound manner, management must have current information detailing the mortgages in the pipeline and warehouse and project how those positions can change in the short term. Position reports that show the pipeline (gross and net of fallout), warehouse, and hedge portfolios are key to effective management and monitoring. Risk exposure reports that include an appropriate range of stressed interest rate shock scenarios are essential in providing adequate oversight.

Management market risk exposure reports should include, but not be limited to, an executive summary report, position reports detailing coverage and exposure, mark-to-market reports, activity registers, and profitability reports. The executive summary report should include pipeline and warehouse aggregate positions along with aggregate hedge or hedge coverage showing net exposure. This report should also include market value changes compared with a benchmark MBS price change and interest rate (Treasury or LIBOR) yield curve shifts. The executive summary should show current positions and risk levels to promote effective oversight of pipeline and warehouse management.

Pipeline and Warehouse Hedging Policy

Board-approved, written policies should govern the use of pipeline and warehouse hedges. Policies should define

- ranges of hedge coverage.
- loss limit thresholds.
- risk limit violation approval with oversight escalation procedures.
- acceptable hedging instruments.
- internal controls to properly approve hedging instruments.

For many banks, mortgage banking is a means of augmenting spread income and generating fee income in addition to traditional bank operations. The primary purposes of secondary marketing are to maximize profits on servicing released sales or to sell mortgages with servicing retained on the best terms available while minimizing or managing market risk. Because mortgage prices can fluctuate significantly over a short period, the secondary marketing manager must maintain strict risk discipline and stay within predetermined risk thresholds. A strong hedging policy with specific loss parameters is essential to define operational boundaries. The secondary marketing manager should execute trades to mitigate risk rather than speculate on the direction of interest rates.

Hedging: Mortgage Servicing Rights

Background

From a regulatory standpoint, supervisory attention is heightened when capitalized MSR represents a large concentration of a bank's capital. Concentration thresholds, however, are often useful in focusing supervisory attention on the evaluation, management, and reporting of the MSR risk exposure.

In accordance with GAAP, ASC 860, "Transfers and Servicing," banks are required to initially measure and recognize servicing assets and servicing liabilities at fair value. A bank must subsequently measure each class of servicing assets and servicing liabilities using one of two methods: (1) the amortization method or (2) the fair value measurement method. Banks electing to use the amortization method are generally not likely to actively hedge the fair value of the MSR portfolio. This section addresses the hedging of MSR, presuming the election of fair value accounting.

Once considered a rare practice within the thrift industry, the hedging of MSR portfolios is now common practice among the large institutions with significant MSR holdings. MSR hedges are financial instruments executed to protect against declines in economic value and earnings. The value of a servicing hedge should rise when interest rates fall, offsetting the decline or impairment in the value of the MSR portfolio that occurs due to an increase in prepayments and the inability of the production of new loans to keep pace with the runoff of the MSR. Conversely, the value of the hedges generally declines in rising rate environments, which is normally offset by a corresponding increase in MSR value as prepayments slow.

A number of mortgage servicers recognize the "natural" or "macro" hedge provided in a declining rate environment by new servicing created from increased originations. Some institutions model and project economic values of the origination operation by estimating gains from servicing valuations based on historical loan production and gain on sale. While it is understood that loan production volume will offset runoff of the servicing portfolio, it is not certain that a natural hedge will cover the entire change in MSR value.

There are several issues to consider with this type of hedge. First, consider how long it takes before an immediate MSR writedown or impairment to earnings can be offset by realized income from new loan originations. The second consideration is the difficulty of predicting the origination volume for the production hedge. Examiners need to understand both issues before rendering an assessment of a natural hedge as part of the overall MSR hedge program.

Fair values of MSR generally rise as rates increase and fall as rates decline, but the change in value is not linear. Rather, the risk profile of MSR is asymmetrical and generally exhibits negative convexity. This means the MSR value increases less rapidly as rates rise than it declines when rates fall. An effective hedge for this profile is the purchase of financial instruments that exhibit positive convexity, that is, instruments that increase in value as rates decline faster than they decrease in value as rates rise. Purchasing positive convexity in financial markets has an associated cost, however, because the instruments often contain long embedded options.

Hedging the MSR portfolio is a dynamic process with a primary objective of preserving the value of the MSR against adverse changes in market conditions by minimizing total risk exposure. The servicing asset has historically been one of the most volatile assets on an institution's balance sheet. It is subject to a high degree of market risk due to fair value changes and the resulting impact on earnings as rates change. Although MSR typically exhibits a negatively convex risk profile, the degree to which this is true can vary with changes in interest rate environments. Consequently, MSR hedgers must have a thorough understanding of the risks involved and regularly assess the risk profile of the asset as rates change.

Types of Hedgeable Risks

Before constructing a hedge strategy, a bank should identify the MSR risk profile, which is determined by the valuation of the asset and its sensitivity to changes in market conditions. The accuracy of the risk profile will impact the effectiveness of the hedge and its performance.

The primary risk to an MSR portfolio is the risk of prepayment that results from changes in interest rates. These changes are the main driver of prepayments due to the borrowers' options to refinance their loans. MSR portfolios typically decline in value when interest rates decline because prepayments increase, thereby shortening the cash flow life of the MSR. The MSR asset is exposed to other risk factors, including the following:

- **Interest rate risk:** The potential change in the value of the MSR and hedge portfolios due to a parallel shift in the yield curve. Interest rate risk includes
  - duration (delta) risk: the portfolio's sensitivity to a change of plus or minus 1 basis point in the level of rates.
  - convexity (gamma) risk: the degree of change in duration that occurs with larger interest rate movements.
- **Yield curve risk:** The potential change in the value of the MSR and hedge portfolios due to nonparallel shifts in interest rates. Yield curve risk includes
  - basis risk: the potential change in the value of the MSR and hedge portfolios due to changes in spread between mortgages and nonmortgage hedge instruments, such as swaps and Treasury securities.
  - volatility risk: the potential change in the value of the MSR and hedge portfolios due to changes in implied volatility (vega) used in pricing interest rate options.

Some risks are unhedgeable. Modeling risk cannot be hedged. Changes made to valuation, prepayment, and other models or assumptions alter the MSR risk profile and can lead to unhedgeable events.

Another unhedgeable event is related to "servicing retention" programs. Some large mortgage servicers employ a servicing retention program in an effort to maintain their servicing portfolio size. While a successful program will regenerate the MSR portfolio, the increase of prepayment activity will result in altering the risk profile of the existing MSR portfolio. It is often difficult to determine the precise impact of retention programs on subsequent prepayment activity. Nonetheless, the hedging strategy needs to account for this activity when constructing the desired hedge coverage.

Delta (Dynamic) Hedging

Delta hedging for MSR is conceptually similar to the strategy described in the mortgage pipeline and warehouse hedging section. In summary, delta hedging is only concerned with hedging small changes in the level of interest rates. Therefore, as rates move, delta hedgers will need to rebalance their hedges frequently, because convexity causes the MSR portfolio deltas to change. Some banks have used U.S. Treasury securities as a delta hedge against their MSR portfolios as a means of reducing risk exposure to falling rates. While this strategy can provide an economic offset to MSR risk, it requires constant rebalancing in order to ensure adequate delta coverage.

This strategy does not address other sources of MSR risk, such as basis risk, convexity risk, yield curve changes, and changes in volatility. In many cases, it is not a complete solution for hedging the MSR. Additionally, volatile markets can be problematic for delta hedgers, because they require robust systems and models to promptly re-estimate the MSR and related hedge positions.

Delta/Gamma Hedging

Because there are no individual financial instruments that exactly offset the risk profile of the MSR asset, hedgers use a combination of instruments to hedge the duration (delta) and convexity (gamma). An example of this type of hedging strategy is the use of a combination of receiver swaps and to-be-announced (TBA) securities. This strategy accounts for the asset's exposure to mortgage/swap basis risk. The receiver swap plus TBA hedge strategy can be further combined with long options to offset some of the negative convexity of the MSR and mortgages.

Using options typically provides more relief from the frequent rebalancing required under the delta hedging strategy and improves the MSR risk profile under larger rate moves. Disadvantages of using options are the relative cost (premiums paid) and the lack of interest income (known as "positive carry") that is normally afforded by other instruments, such as TBAs, Treasuries, and receiver swaps. Option hedging also requires more sophisticated modeling to measure and monitor market risks.

Hedging Instruments

The goal of hedging the economic value of the MSR portfolio is to stabilize value and decrease the negative convexity of the servicing asset. MSR hedgers frequently use an array of hedge instruments (on- and off-balance-sheet) to manage market risk. Below is a description of commonly used hedge instruments, rationales for their use, and their advantages and disadvantages.

Principal-only mortgage strips (PO): POs backed by collateral similar to a servicing portfolio can provide an effective hedge for potential spikes in prepayments. PO hedges not only serve as duration and convexity hedges but also cushion against income variability. PO hedges can have limited liquidity depending on market conditions. It is also sometimes difficult to find a PO strip security with the desired coupon and weighted average maturity.

Receiver interest rate swaps: Receiver interest rate swaps are OTC contracts in which the mortgage servicer/hedger receives the fixed-rate payments and pays the floating rate side of the interest rate swap over a specified period. The servicer benefits when interest rates fall, as the market value of the receiver swap appreciates. The swap market is deep with good liquidity. Swaps have low costs and no convexity, but they create exposure to basis risk.

Interest rate swaptions: Swaptions are options to enter into a specified interest rate swap transaction at a predetermined future date. These instruments are similar to options on MBSs, with the underlying financial instrument being an interest rate swap. Swaptions address the convexity issues associated with receiver swaps but still exhibit exposure to basis risk.

Interest rate floors: Interest rate floors tied to the LIBOR, 10-year Treasury, or constant maturity swaps provide a hedge against duration and convexity. Interest rate floors provide both market value protection and income protection if they go into the money. While this type of hedge exhibits strong positive convexity characteristics, it does not offer a closely matched offset to cash flow variability, and it exposes the portfolio to basis risk between prepayment and interest rate changes. The interest rate floor benefits a servicer as rates decline below a specified level and has an offsetting effect to the runoff of MSR. Interest rate floors have positive convexity but suffer from basis risk and can be costly to purchase.

MBSs and TBAs: These instruments serve as duration hedges. They have little basis risk and normally have positive interest income carry. The disadvantage of using an MBS or TBA hedge is their negative convexity. MBSs require funding considerations, whereas TBAs are off-balance-sheet.

U.S. Treasury securities: These securities are used to hedge duration of the MSR. High liquidity and positive convexity are benefits of using Treasury securities. Disadvantages include increased basis risk and funding considerations.

Call options on U.S. Treasury securities: These call options can provide a hedge for both duration (by taking a long position) and the negative convexity (through the call option) embedded in the MSR risk profile. They are liquid but lack mortgage basis coverage. The main advantages of Treasuries and Treasury call options are that they are liquid, have potentially lower costs compared with other instruments, and can be rebalanced easily. Drawbacks include basis risk and funding as well as leverage considerations when using large, on-balance-sheet hedging positions.

Constant maturity mortgage (CMM) swaps: CMM swaps are hedging instruments that offset delta risk of the MSR. Because the CMM rate represents the yield on a par-priced mortgage, use of these instruments does not introduce basis risk. The CMM swap is traded in the form of a forward rate agreement (FRA). In an FRA, one party agrees to pay or receive a fixed rate instead of receiving or paying the CMM rate at a future date. The movement of the CMM relative to the fixed rate determines gains and losses. CMM products are useful for hedging the exposure to changes in the current coupon mortgage rate. There is limited dealer involvement in this market, resulting in lower liquidity.

Prepayment caps: To reduce monthly exposure to prepayment errors and improve hedging efficiency, mortgage servicers may consider using prepayment cap derivatives. A prepayment cap is based on a hypothetical amortization of a notional balance at a specified prepayment speed, which is expressed as a multiple of the constant prepayment rate. The higher the multiple, the higher prepayments are expected to be. These derivatives offer protection against prepayments being faster than forecast and reduce exposure to adverse fluctuations in servicing values and income. These instruments are relatively new and, as a result, lack market depth and liquidity. While these instruments minimize prepayment risk, they can also introduce counterparty credit risk.

MSR Risk Exposure Reporting

MSR risk exposure reporting is essential for a bank with significant MSRs to manage and monitor its profile. Examiners should review a bank's exposure reports to determine the reports' accuracy and sufficiency for monitoring risk. Examples of risk exposure reports include the following:

- Executive summary reports
- Position reports that detail MSR risk exposure and hedge coverage and show net exposure to various risk measures
- Mark-to-market reports
- Reports on compliance with risk limits
- Hedge performance and effectiveness analysis
- Profitability reports

The executive summary discloses vital information relating to the current level of all applicable market risks and potential exposures. This report should promote effective oversight of the MSR portfolio. An effective executive summary report would include information showing the MSR risk profile net of the hedge coverage. This report should include all risk measures required pursuant to the MSR hedge policy. The following are examples of risk measures:

- **Duration and convexity risks:** Parallel shifts of the Treasury/swap or LIBOR/swap yield curve
- **Yield curve risk:** Nonparallel shifts of the Treasury/swap or LIBOR/swap yield curve
- **Basis risk:** Widening and tightening of mortgage spreads
- **Volatility risk:** Value changes due to increasing or decreasing implied volatility

Larger and more sophisticated banks incorporate more sophisticated and comprehensive risk analytics, such as VaR and EaR approaches, in measuring market risk exposure. In those risk summary reports, the MSR risk exposure is combined with other risk activities or business lines to show the total aggregated exposure to market risk.

MSR Hedging Policy

Poorly conceived or poorly managed hedges can result in substantial risk of loss. Therefore, it is vital that banks that hedge their MSR portfolio risks are governed by prudent, board-approved policies that define

- hedging objectives and risk management strategies.
- risk measures and exposure limits.
- processes for handling limit violations with oversight escalation procedures.
- management reporting requirements.
- management and committee responsibilities.
- approved hedging instruments.
- the internal controls needed to properly control use of approved hedge instruments.

Appendix C: Mortgage Banking Accounting

Introduction

This appendix summarizes the accounting requirements for mortgage banking activities. These requirements evolve over time, and bankers and examiners should follow current accounting standards.

Note: Examiners should contact the Office of the Chief Accountant to obtain information on recent developments not reflected in this appendix.

This appendix is organized by business activity rather than by accounting pronouncement. While it summarizes the pertinent accounting literature for mortgage banking activities, it is not a substitute for the actual accounting standards. This appendix should be used in conjunction with other sections of this booklet to gain a full understanding of the business activity and reporting.

The table below summarizes the applicable accounting guidance for various mortgage banking activities:

Mortgage banking activity	Applicable accounting guidance
Commitments to originate mortgage loans	ASC 815, ASC 815-10-S99-1, ASC 820
Loan origination fees and costs	ASC 948, ASC 310-20, ASC 825
Loans held for sale	ASC 948, ASC 820, ASC 825
Transfers and sales	ASC 860
Guaranteed mortgage securitizations	ASC 860
Sales with recourse	ASC 860
Ginnie Mae buybacks	ASC 860, ASC 310-30
Guarantees	ASC 815, ASC 460, ASC 825
Other real estate owned (OREO)	ASC 360, ASC 860
Interest-only strips	ASC 860
Mortgage servicing assets (MSA) and liabilities (MSL)	ASC 860, ASC 820, ASC 825.
Hedging/derivatives	ASC 815 , ASC 860, ASC 820
Fair value	ASC 820

Commitments to Originate or Purchase Mortgage Loans

Commitments to originate: When a bank issues a commitment to originate a loan, the bank must determine whether the prospective loan is a mortgage loan (e.g., residential) or a nonmortgage loan. If it is a mortgage loan, the bank must further determine whether the loan will be held for investment or held for sale. ASC 815, "Derivatives and Hedging," stipulates that loan commitments to originate mortgage loans that a bank intends to hold for sale are "derivative loan commitments." Accordingly, banks should account for these loan commitments at fair value and recognize changes in fair value in current period earnings.

Mortgage loans originated in the course of mortgage banking activities that are to be sold are to be classified as "held for sale." See OCC Bulletin 2005-18, "Interagency Advisory on Accounting and Reporting for Commitments to Originate and Sell Mortgage Loans," for further information on mortgage commitments.

On November 5, 2007, the SEC issued Staff Accounting Bulletin 109 (SAB 109), which is now codified at ASC 815-10-S99-1. SAB 109 states the staff's view that the expected net future cash flows related to the associated servicing of a loan should be included in the fair value measurement of derivative loan commitments, which are recorded at fair value through earnings. Derivative loan commitments generally include both written loan commitments, such as interest-rate lock commitments and forward sale commitments, which may or may not include servicing.

The benefits of SAB 109 from a mortgage banking perspective is that the fundamental elements used to fair value measure the derivative loan commitment are more closely aligned to the fair value measurement of the forward loan sale commitment used to hedge the derivative loan commitment.

In September 2006, the FASB published Statement of Financial Accounting Standards 157, "Fair Value Measurements" (FAS 157), which is now included in ASC 820, "Fair Value Measurements." ASC 820 defines and establishes a framework for measuring fair value. Banks should follow the guidance in ASC 820 in estimating the fair value of loan commitments. Under ASC 820, "fair value" is defined as the price that would be received to sell an asset, or paid to transfer a liability in an orderly transaction between market participants. In the absence of an active market, loan commitments should be valued using valuation techniques that are appropriate for the circumstances and consider what a market participant would demand to assume the commitments. The method banks use to estimate the fair value of their mortgage banking pipeline should be reasonable, well supported, and adequately documented.

Commitments to purchase: Regardless of whether the underlying mortgage loans will be held for investment or for sale, commitments to purchase mortgage loans from third parties, under either mandatory delivery contracts or best efforts contracts, are derivatives if, on evaluation, the contracts meet the definition of a derivative under ASC 815, "Derivatives and Hedging." Banks should report loan purchase commitments that meet the definition of a derivative at fair value on the balance sheet.

Loan Origination Fees and Costs

Unless a bank has elected to account for a loan at fair value under the fair value option allowed under ASC 825, "Financial Instruments," it should account for deferred fees and costs associated with originated loans in accordance with ASC 310-20, "Receivables, Nonrefundable Fees, and Costs," and ASC 948, "Financial Services—Mortgage Banking." If a mortgage loan is held for sale, loan origination fees and the direct loan origination costs are deferred until the related loan is sold and recognized as a component in the calculation of the gain or loss on sale. If the loan is held for investment, generally such fees and costs are deferred and recognized as an adjustment of the loan's effective yield over the life of the loan.

ASC 310-20 generally does not allow a bank to anticipate loan prepayments in recognizing deferred loan origination fees and costs. That is, the payment terms required by the loan contract shall be used to determine the loan term. An exception to this general principle exists for large numbers of homogeneous loans for which prepayments are probable, and the timing and amount of prepayments can be reasonably estimated. If these conditions are met, the bank may consider estimates of future principal prepayments in recognizing deferred loan origination fees and costs. While mortgage loans held for investment may meet these conditions, the bank should carefully analyze and document the similarities of the loans in its portfolio, and the probability and timing of anticipated prepayments, to determine whether it is appropriate to consider prepayments in recognizing deferred loan origination fees and costs.

If a bank anticipates prepayments in recognizing deferred loan origination fees and costs, and a difference arises between the anticipated prepayments and actual prepayments received, the bank should recalculate the effective yield to reflect actual payments to date and anticipated future payments. The net investment in the loans, which includes the unamortized balance of deferred loan origination fees and costs, should be adjusted to the amount that would have existed had the new effective yield been applied since the acquisition of the loans (the "catch-up" method). The investment in the loans should be adjusted to the new balance with a corresponding charge or credit to interest income.

Loans Held for Sale

Loans held for sale (warehouse): Banks must account for loans held for sale under one of the following methods: fair value under the fair value option (ASC 825), lower of cost or fair value LOCOM under ASC 948-310, or as the hedged item in a hedge qualifying for fair value hedge accounting under ASC 815.

Each reporting period, banks must calculate the fair value of their warehouse loans. The accounting for value changes varies depending on whether the bank elects LOCOM accounting, ASC 815 hedge accounting, or the fair value option (ASC 825). For loans accounted for at LOCOM, the carrying amount should be adjusted through a valuation allowance (if fair value is less than carrying amount) with changes in the valuation allowance reported in net income. More specifically, under LOCOM, decreases in values below cost (unrealized losses) are recognized in net income, but increases in value above cost (unrealized gains) are not recognized in net income. Thus, for loans measured under LOCOM, the reported carrying amount may vary with the market, but it cannot be greater than the loans' cost basis. In contrast, if the bank hedges its warehouse loans, and qualifies for fair value hedge accounting pursuant to ASC 815, the bank will adjust the carrying amount of the hedged loans, through net income, to reflect the change in fair value that is attributable to the hedged risk (e.g., interest rate risk or overall market price risk). Finally, under the fair value option (ASC 825), all changes in the fair value of the loan will adjust the carrying amount and be reflected in net income, because the fair value option is an election to use fair value measurement rather than LOCOM.

As noted earlier, ASC 820 defines fair value as the price that would be received to sell an asset or would be paid to transfer a liability in an orderly transaction between market participants. Generally, the inputs to the fair value of warehouse loans would include quoted market prices for each type of mortgage loan in the secondary market. Secondary market information for prime loans is readily available to banks for the purpose of estimating the market value of their loans held for sale. For nonconforming, Alt-A, A-, home equity, subprime, and "scratch-and-dent" loans, however, secondary market information may be more difficult to obtain. Nevertheless, banks must support their estimate of the fair value consistent with the guidance in ASC 820.

Hedging with forward loan sales commitments: Often, banks that originate loans to sell in the secondary market hedge the interest rate or market price risk inherent in those loans. Banks usually hedge their mortgage loans held for sale (as well as those in the pipeline) through forward loan sales commitments. Forward loan sales commitments may be mandatory delivery or "best efforts" contracts.

In a mandatory delivery forward sales commitment, the bank commits to deliver a certain amount of mortgage loans at a specified price and date. If the bank fails to deliver on the commitment, it must pay a "pair-off" fee to the investor to compensate the investor for the shortfall (an amount based on the difference between the specified price in the commitment and the current market price of the mortgage loans that were not delivered into the contract).

In one type of best efforts contract, the bank commits to deliver specified mortgage loans at a specified price, conditioned on whether the bank actually originates the mortgage loans. If a bank does not originate the mortgage loan or loans, it does not have to compensate the investor. Accordingly, investors pay less for best efforts contracts than mandatory delivery contracts because of the uncertainty associated with the best efforts contracts.

Community banks are the primary users of best efforts contracts because there is less risk, and the administration of secondary marketing is simpler. Larger, more sophisticated banks typically execute mandatory delivery contracts because they can obtain a higher price for their mortgage loans than under best efforts contracts. Larger banks may also have the necessary secondary marketing expertise to properly administer mandatory delivery contracts.

Terms of best efforts contracts and other forms of forward sales commitments vary; therefore, a bank must carefully evaluate such contracts to determine whether the contracts meet the definition of a derivative under ASC 815. Under ASC 815, if the forward sales commitment is considered a derivative, the bank must account for the commitment at fair value. The fair value of mandatory delivery contracts can be determined by direct reference to prices quoted in the secondary market for comparable contracts. The fair value of best efforts contracts is not as readily available; nonetheless, consistent with the guidance in

ASC 820, valuation techniques that are appropriate in the circumstances, and for which sufficient data are available, shall be used to measure fair value.

Transfers and Sales

ASC 860, "Transfers and Servicing," establishes accounting and reporting standards for transfers and servicing of financial assets (e.g., mortgage loans). It also establishes the accounting for securitizations, transfers of receivables with recourse, securities lending transactions, repurchase agreements, and loan participations. ASC 860 employs a financial components approach allowing financial assets to be separated into many parts or components.

Criteria for a Transfer of a Financial Asset to Qualify for Sales Accounting

Under ASC 860, for a transfer of a mortgage loan, a portion of a mortgage loan that meets the definition of a participating interest, or a group of mortgage loans, to qualify for sale accounting, the transferor must surrender control over the transferred loans. If the transferor has surrendered control of the transferred mortgage loans, the transfer qualifies for sale accounting. As a result, the loans should be derecognized from the transferor's balance sheet and any resulting gain or loss on the transfer should be recognized on the financial statements through other non-interest income.

Control over the financial assets is surrendered if and only if all of the following three conditions are met:

- **Isolation of transferred financial assets.** The transferred financial assets have been isolated from the transferor including beyond the reach of creditors in the event of a bankruptcy or a receivership (the FDIC). This isolation analysis should include consolidated affiliates and agents of the transferor as well as all aspects of the transaction.
- **Transferee's rights to pledge or exchange.** The transferee has the right to pledge or exchange the assets it has received, *and* no condition *both* constrains the transferee from taking advantage of its right to pledge or exchange *and* provides more than a trivial benefit to the transferor.
- **Effective control.** The transferor does not maintain effective control over the transferred financial assets. To assess whether the transferor maintains effective control over the transferred financial assets, involvement of its consolidated affiliates or its agents shall be considered in the continuing involvement of the transferor.

If all three conditions are met, the transferor records a sale. If all three conditions are not met, the transaction is accounted for as a secured borrowing.

Recognition and Measurement of a Mortgage Loan Pool Sales Transaction

Provided that the mortgage loan(s) transfer has met the criteria to qualify for sales accounting, the loans should be derecognized from the financial statements and any resulting gain or loss recognized in earnings. Any assets obtained as part of the proceeds from the sale, and any liabilities incurred, are to be initially measured at fair value. The proceeds (also called net proceeds) from the sale consist of cash received and any other assets, including beneficial interests (e.g., securities issued by the trust) and separately recognized servicing assets, less any liabilities incurred, including separately recognized servicing liabilities (albeit recognition of servicing liabilities is infrequent). Any liability incurred, even if it relates to the transferred assets (e.g., guarantees and recourse obligations), is a reduction from the proceeds. Each transaction should be evaluated independently to determine whether the bank should record MSAs or MSLs. Any stand-alone derivative financial instrument (e.g., put or call options held or written, forward commitments, or swaps) entered into concurrently with the transfer of the mortgage loan(s) is either an asset obtained or a liability incurred and, thus, part of the proceeds received in the transfer.

The net carrying amount of the mortgage loans that are sold forms the basis that determines the amount of the gain or loss on the sale or securitization.

Example: Mortgage Banking Bank (MBB) sells a group of individual loans with a fair value of $1,200 and a carrying amount of $1,000 to a securitization entity. Assume the transfer qualifies for sales accounting. In exchange, MBB receives $205 in beneficial interests in the form of securities backed by the transferred loans, a $10 interest-only strip, and a $20 call option. MBB intends to subsequently account for the interest-only strip at fair value through earnings. The call option entitles MBB to obtain from the transferee mortgage loans that are readily obtainable in the marketplace. MBB will continue to service the loans (i.e., servicing retained) under a contract that provides for a compensation level that is more than adequate. The servicing asset has a fair value of $90 and a recourse obligation (liability) of $90. MBB assumes a limited recourse obligation to repurchase delinquent loans. MBB will receive cash of $950 and pay $5 in issuance costs.

Table 1: Calculation of Gain on Sale in Example

CATEGORY	FAIR VALUES				NET PROCEEDS
Cash proceeds	$950		Cash Received		$950
Beneficial interest	205		Plus: Beneficial interest		205
Interest-only strip	10		Plus: Interest-only strip		10
Call option	20		Plus: Call Option		20
Servicing asset	90		Plus: Servicing asset		90
Recourse obligation	(70)		Less: Recourse obligation		(70)
Issuance costs	(5)		Less: Issuance costs		(5)
			NET PROCEEDS		$1,200
CALCULATION OF GAIN ON SALE					
Cash	$950				
Beneficial interest	205				
Interest-only strip	10				
Call option	20				
Servicing asset	90				
Recourse obligation	(70)				
TOTAL	1,205				
Less carrying value of loans sold	(1,000)				
Less: Issuance costs	(5)				
GAIN ON SALE	200				

Loans				1,000	–
TOTAL ASSETS				1,000	1,270
Recourse Obligation				$ –	70
Shareholder's equity				1,000	1,200
TOTAL LIABILITIES AND SHAREHOLDER'S EQUITY				$1,000	$1,270

Qualified Special Purpose Entities

Special purpose entities (SPE) are used often in securitization transactions. Before being amended in 2009, ASC 860 allowed an SPE that met specific criteria to be considered a qualified special purpose entity (QSPE). The key benefit derived from status as a QSPE was that a transferor, or its affiliates, would not have to consolidate a QSPE in its financial statements. The FASB eliminated the QSPE concept in 2009. Entities previously considered QSPEs are now subject to the variable interest entity model in ASC 810, "Consolidations." The requirements in ASC 810 should be applied to determine when a variable interest entity should be considered.

Guaranteed Mortgage Securitizations

Guaranteed mortgage securitizations, as defined in ASC 860, before being amended in 2009, provided an exception that allowed a bank to recognize securitized mortgage loans as securities that subsequently were to be measured under ASC 320, "Investments—Debt and Equity Securities." ASC 860 defined a guaranteed mortgage securitization as "a securitization of mortgage loans that is within the scope of Topic 948 and includes a substantive guarantee by a third party."

Under previous accounting guidance, a guaranteed mortgage securitization did not meet ASC 860 sales criteria because the transferor retained all of the beneficial interests (i.e., the securitized assets) and received no other consideration as a result of the transfer. The FASB eliminated this exception in 2009. Guaranteed mortgage securitizations must now be evaluated consistent with all other transfers within the scope of ASC 860.

Sales With Recourse

"Recourse" is an arrangement between the transferor (seller) and the transferee (buyer) for the transferor to make payments to the transferee under certain circumstances related to the sale of the mortgage loans. Such circumstances can include

- failure of borrowers to pay when due (credit risk).
- the effects of prepayments.
- adjustments resulting from defects (including fraud) in the eligibility of the loans or breach of standard representations and warranties.

Standard representations and warranties are defined in ASC 860 as "representations and warranties that assert the financial asset being transferred is what it is purported to be at the transfer date." Examples of representations and warranties include the following:

- Characteristics, nature, and quality of the underlying financial asset, including any of the following:
  - Characteristics of the underlying borrower.
  - Type and nature of the collateral securing the underlying financial asset.

- Quality, accuracy, and delivery of documentation relating to the transfer and the underlying financial asset.
- Accuracy of the transferor's representations in relation to the underlying financial asset.

Standard representations and warranties are generally applicable for the life of the loan, thus creating ongoing exposure that the transferor must evaluate for the initial and subsequent measurement of the recourse liability.

A transfer of residential mortgage loans with recourse should be accounted for as a sale, with the proceeds of the sale reduced by the fair value of the recourse liability, if the criteria in ASC 860 are met for sales treatment. A recourse liability should be separately recognized on the financial statements and initially measured at fair value.

The guidance in ASC 820, "Fair Value Measurements," should be followed in estimating the fair value of the recourse liability. Consequently, since a recourse obligation is a liability, the fair value would be the price that would be paid to transfer the liability in an orderly transaction between market participants at the measurement date.

To measure the fair value of the recourse liability, the reporting entity should use observable market prices, if available. If not, the entity shall seek to maximize the use of observable inputs and minimize the use of unobservable inputs consistent with the fair value measurement objective of estimating an exit price between market participants at the measurement date in the principal market, or, in the absence of the principal market, then the most advantageous market.

If the entity uses a valuation technique, it should consider relevant market information and the assumptions market participants would use to price the liability. A possible starting point could be for the entity to use historical loss experience, adjusted to reflect expectations of future losses based on current market conditions, and the applicable recourse provisions applied from a market participant's perspective in addition to other supportable documented adjustments.

To identify and interpret the recourse provisions, an analysis of the sales agreement needs to be performed. The recourse provisions are negotiated and written into the sales agreement by lawyers and bankers, thus their involvement is essential to properly understand the financial reporting consequences.

The recourse liability should be subsequently measured according to accounting pronouncements for measuring similar liabilities. Although ASC 860 is not specific, the bank should assess whether the recourse liability is a derivative (ASC 815), a guarantee (ASC 460), or a contingent liability (ASC 450). The bank may also decide to elect the fair value option (ASC 825) on its recourse liability. If ASC 450-20, "Contingencies—Loss Contingencies," is applied, an incurred loss should be recognized when it is probable and reasonably estimable by adjusting the recourse liability through the income statement. The bank should reassess the recourse arrangements each reporting period to determine whether there needs to be an increase or decrease of the recourse liability in accordance with

ASC 450-20. This assessment should be supported by a well-documented financial analysis. Payments or settlements related to representations and warranties for mortgages sold should be charged against the recourse liability.

To determine the appropriate risk-based capital treatment for these transactions, examiners should refer to applicable regulatory capital rules and call report instructions.

Assets with recourse transferred in transactions that do not qualify for sales treatment under GAAP should continue to be reported as assets on the call report balance sheet. The proceeds received are presented as a secured borrowing under ASC 860 and are subject to the applicable regulatory capital rules.

Ginnie Mae Buybacks

Ginnie Mae mortgage-backed securities are backed by residential mortgage loans that are insured or guaranteed by the FHA, the VA, or the Farmers Home Administration. Ginnie Mae programs allow banks to buy back individual delinquent mortgage loans that meet certain criteria from the securitized loan pool for which the bank provides servicing. At the servicer's option, and without Ginnie Mae's prior authorization, the servicer may repurchase such a delinquent loan for an amount equal to 100 percent of the remaining principal balance of the loan. Under ASC 860, this buyback option is considered a conditional option until the delinquency criteria are met, at which time the option becomes unconditional.

When the loans backing a Ginnie Mae security are initially securitized, ASC 860 does not preclude the transferor of the loans from treating the transaction as a sale for accounting purposes, because the conditional nature of the buyback option means that the transferor (seller) does not maintain effective control over the loans. If the transfer meets all the criteria for sales accounting, the loans are removed from the seller's balance sheet. When individual loans later meet Ginnie Mae's specified delinquency criteria and are eligible for repurchase, the seller (provided the seller is also the servicer) is deemed to have regained effective control over these loans, and, under ASC 860, the loans can no longer be reported as sold. The delinquent Ginnie Mae loans must be brought back onto the seller-servicer's books as assets and initially recorded at fair value, regardless of whether the seller intends to exercise the buyback option. An offsetting liability also would be recorded. Whether or not these rebooked delinquent loans are repurchased, the seller-servicer should report them as loans on the call report balance sheet and related schedules. These loans should be reported as held for sale or held for investment, based on facts and circumstances, in accordance with GAAP. These loans should not be reported as "other assets." As required per the call report instructions, the offsetting liability should be reported as "other borrowed money."

A seller-servicer must report all delinquent rebooked Ginnie Mae loans that have been repurchased or are eligible for repurchase as past due in Schedule RC-N in accordance with their contractual repayment terms. In addition, if a bank services Ginnie Mae loans, but was not the transferor of the loans that have been securitized, and purchases individual delinquent loans out of the Ginnie Mae securitization, the bank must report the purchased loans as past due in Schedule RC-N, in accordance with their contractual repayment terms, even though the bank was not required to record the delinquent Ginnie Mae loans as assets before purchasing the loans. Banks should refer to ASC 860 and 310-30 for further guidance on the appropriate accounting for rebooked delinquent loans.

Guarantees

For programs that include a form of financial guarantee (for example, in some FHLB mortgage programs), the guarantee contract must be evaluated to determine the appropriate accounting treatment. Financial guarantee contracts could be subject to ASC 815 depending on the terms of the contract. If the financial guarantee contract meets the definition of a derivative and is subject to ASC 815, it is accounted for at fair value with changes in fair value reported in earnings. See ASC 815 for the criteria that determine when a contract is subject to ASC 815.

Financial guarantee contracts that are not subject to ASC 815 are accounted for under ASC 460. This guidance clarifies that a guarantor is required to recognize, at the inception of a guarantee, a liability for the fair value of the obligation undertaken in issuing the guarantee. Among the types of guarantee contracts to which the provisions of ASC 460 apply are

- financial standby letters of credit, which are irrevocable undertakings, typically by a financial institution, to guarantee payment of a specified financial obligation.
- performance standby letters of credit, which are irrevocable undertakings by a guarantor to make payments in the event a specified third party fails to perform under a nonfinancial contractual obligation.
- representations and warranties that survive the date of closing on loans sold to third parties. Examples would include representations and warranties by the seller to repurchase first payment defaults within a certain time period (e.g., first 90 days) and standard representations and warranties. These representation clauses are typically standard in sale agreements to the GSEs and third-party investors.

Commercial letters of credit and other loan commitments, as well as subordinated interests in securitizations, are not considered guarantees under ASC 460 and, therefore, are not subject to the interpretation. Banks should refer to ASC 460 for further information on the types of guarantee contracts to which the interpretation's initial recognition and measurement provisions do and do not apply.

For financial and performance standby letters of credit and other types of guarantees subject to the interpretation, when a bank issues the guarantee, it must recognize on its balance sheet a liability for that guarantee. The initial measurement of the liability is the fair value of the guarantee at its inception. When a bank issues a guarantee in a stand-alone arm's-length transaction with a party outside the consolidated bank, which would typically be the case for a standby letter of credit, the liability recognized at the inception of the guarantee should be the fair value of the guarantee, which will generally be equal to the premium or fee received or receivable by the guarantor as a practical expedient. If the bank issues a guarantee for no consideration on a stand-alone basis, however, the liability recognized at inception should be an estimate of the guarantee's fair value. In the unusual circumstance where, at the inception of a guarantee, it is probable that a loss has been incurred and its amount can be reasonably estimated, the liability to be initially recognized for that guarantee should be the greater of the fair value of the guarantee (which will generally be equal to the premium or fee received or receivable by the guarantor) or the estimated loss from the loss contingency that must be accrued under ASC 450.

ASC 460 does not prescribe a specific account for the guarantor's offsetting entry when it recognizes the liability at the inception of a guarantee, because that offsetting entry depends on the circumstances. If a bank issued a standby letter of credit or other guarantee in a stand-alone transaction for a premium or fee, the offsetting entry would reflect the consideration the bank received, such as cash, a receivable, or a reduction of a deposit liability. In contrast, if the bank received no consideration for issuing the guarantee, the offsetting entry would be expensed.

For guarantees not accounted for at fair value under the fair value option, however, the accounting for fees received for issuing standby letters of credit has been, and should continue to be, governed by ASC 310. Under ASC 310-20, such fees are termed commitment fees.

Other Real Estate Owned

On receipt of real estate through foreclosure or outside of foreclosure (e.g., deed-in-lieu or upon obtaining physical possession), OREO should be recorded at the fair value of the asset less estimated costs to sell, establishing a new cost basis. Once classified as OREO, the subsequent measurement is at LOCOM. Changes in fair value must be determined on a property-by-property basis. A valuation account should be used for subsequent changes in fair value, but in no event may the valuation account be reduced below zero. Changes in the OREO valuation account are reflected in the call report as gains or losses on sale of OREO.

Any revenue from OREO should be reported on the call report as "other noninterest income," and the expenses as "other noninterest expense." Because the asset is held for sale, depreciation expense would not normally be recognized in accordance with ASC 360, "Property, Plant, and Equipment."

The primary accounting guidance for sales of foreclosed real estate is also covered in ASC 360. This standard, which applies to all transactions in which the seller provides financing to the buyer of the real estate, establishes several methods, depending on the circumstances, to account for dispositions of real estate. If a profit is involved in the sale of real estate, each method sets forth the manner in which the profit is to be recognized. Regardless of which method is used, however, any losses on the disposition of real estate should be recognized immediately.

Interest-Only Strips

An interest-only strip is defined in ASC 860 as "a contractual right to receive some or all of the interest due on a bond, mortgage loan, collateralized mortgage obligation, or other interest-bearing financial asset." Interest-only strips that are not recorded at fair value through earnings pursuant to ASC 860-20 should be evaluated to determine whether they are derivatives in their entirety or hybrid instruments that include embedded derivatives that require bifurcation. The bank would generally account for the interest-only strip at fair value (see the example in the "Transfers and Sales" section).

If not considered a derivative, an interest-only strip is accounted for and subsequently measured like an investment in trading or available-for-sale (AFS) securities under ASC 320. In other words, it is measured at fair value. If it is classified as trading, the unrealized gains and losses are recorded through earnings. If it is classified as AFS, the unrealized gains and losses are reported in other comprehensive income (a component of equity). Finally, like other AFS securities, interest-only strips should be evaluated for other-than-temporary impairment.

Mortgage Servicing Assets

MSAs, also referred to as MSRs, are intangible assets that banks may purchase, assume, or retain in a sale of mortgage loans. In accordance with ASC 860-50, servicing is inherent in all financial assets; as noted below, it only becomes a distinct asset or liability in specific situations.

An entity shall recognize and initially measure at fair value a servicing asset or servicing liability each time it undertakes an obligation to service a financial asset by entering into a servicing contract in either of the following situations:

- A transfer of the servicer's financial assets that meets the requirements for sale accounting. (See the example in the "Transfers and Sales" section.)
- An acquisition or assumption of a servicing obligation that does not relate to financial assets of the servicer or its consolidated affiliates.

An entity shall subsequently measure each class of servicing assets and servicing liabilities using one of the following methods:

Amortization method: Amortize servicing assets or servicing liabilities in proportion to and over the period of estimated net servicing income (when servicing revenues exceed servicing costs) or net servicing loss (when servicing costs exceed servicing revenues), and assess servicing assets or servicing liabilities for impairment or increased obligation based on fair value at each reporting date.

Fair value measurement method: Measure servicing assets or servicing liabilities at fair value at each reporting date, and report changes in fair value of servicing assets and servicing liabilities in earnings in the period in which the changes occur.

The election described in this paragraph shall be made separately for each class of servicing assets and servicing liabilities. An entity shall apply the same subsequent measurement method to each servicing asset and servicing liability in a class. Classes of servicing assets and servicing liabilities shall be identified based on (1) the availability of market inputs used in determining their fair values, (2) an entity's method of managing its risks, or (3) both. Once an entity elects the fair value option method for a class of servicing assets and servicing liabilities, that election shall not be reversed.

ASC 860 provides that a servicing asset results when the economic benefits of performing the servicing are expected to exceed "adequate compensation." The economic benefits of performing servicing normally include

- contractually specified servicing fees.
- earnings on escrow deposits.
- float resulting from timing differences between borrower payments and investor remittances.
- late fees.
- ancillary income.

As defined in the ASC 860 glossary, adequate compensation is the amount of benefits of servicing that would fairly compensate a substitute servicer should one be required, which includes the profit that would be demanded in the marketplace. Adequate compensation does not vary according to the specific servicing costs of the servicer; therefore, a servicer's own costs should not be considered in determining whether a servicing asset or liability is recorded.

Furthermore, adequate compensation does not necessarily equal "normal" servicing fees. That is, normal servicing fees may be more or less than adequate compensation. A servicing asset results when the benefits of servicing (i.e., the expected future cash flows from performing the servicing) are expected to be more than adequate compensation. If adequate compensation exceeds the benefits of servicing, the result is a mortgage servicing liability.

To determine whether servicing fees constitute adequate compensation, servicers should evaluate all available evidence, placing greater weight on information that is objectively verifiable (e.g., servicing fees noted in comparable transactions, average servicing fees, and costs based on recent surveys) than on information that is subjective and based on probabilities and future events. A bank may use the rate required by a backup servicer as a reference point in determining adequate compensation, so long as the backup servicer would provide the same services that the current servicer provides. Because the rate required by a backup servicer may be more or less than adequate compensation, however, it should not be used as the sole benchmark or proxy for determining adequate compensation and whether a servicing asset or liability should be recognized.

Regardless of how a bank acquires an MSA, a bank that elects the amortization method to account for its MSAs must amortize the MSAs in proportion to and over the period of estimated net servicing income. A straight-line approach may not be appropriate if it does not approximate the rate at which a bank realizes net servicing income from the MSAs.

In addition, banks electing the amortization method must assess the MSAs/MSLs for impairment each reporting period. For purposes of assessing impairment, banks must stratify their MSAs/MSLs based on one or more of the predominant risk characteristics. Such characteristics may include, but are not limited to, loan type, interest rate, unpaid balance, origination date, term, and geographic location. Banks should identify a sufficient number of risk characteristics to adequately stratify each MSA/MSL and provide for a reasonable and valid impairment assessment. Each stratum is assessed separately for impairment by comparison with the fair value for that stratum.

Once an entity has determined the predominant risk characteristics to be used in identifying the stratums of servicing assets, those strata should be applied consistently from period to period unless significant changes in economic facts and circumstances clearly indicate that the predominant risk characteristics and resulting stratums should be changed.

Banks recognize "temporary" impairment through a valuation allowance when the net carrying amount of the MSA exceeds its fair value. If the fair value of the MSA increases after recognition of temporary impairment, banks may increase the carrying amount of the MSA (through a reduction of the valuation allowance) but not above its amortized cost basis. If impairment is determined to be other than temporary, a direct writedown of the carrying amount of the MSA should be taken. Thus, an accurate valuation of an MSA is critical to properly accounting for the asset.

Banks should have formal policies stating their impairment assessment practices and their practices in determining an appropriate fair value for both the amortization and fair value measurement method of accounting elected. Procedural discipline and consistency are essential to any method of measuring valuation or impairment. Therefore, a bank's practices should reflect these concepts to ensure the reliability of its MSA impairment assessments. OCC Bulletin 2003-9, "Interagency Advisory on Mortgage Banking," provides guidance on the risks associated with MSA valuation and hedging activities.

Valuation

Banks should follow the guidance in ASC 820 to estimate the fair values of MSAs. In using valuation techniques, banks should include the assumptions about interest rates, default rates, prepayment rates, and volatility that other market participants employ in estimating fair value. Estimates of expected future cash flows should be based on reasonable and supportable assumptions and projections. All available evidence should be considered in developing estimates of expected future cash flows. The weight given to the evidence should be commensurate with the extent to which the evidence can be verified objectively. Valuation techniques used to measure fair value shall maximize the use of observable inputs and minimize the use of unobservable inputs.

Specifically, institutions must estimate the present value of expected cash flows from the MSAs using an appropriate discount rate. The discount rate used should equal the required rate of return for an asset with similar risk. It should consider an investor's required return for assets with similar cash flow risks, such as mortgage-backed interest-only strips for similar underlying mortgages. The discount rate should also consider the risk premium for the uncertainties specifically associated with servicing operations (e.g., possible changes in future adequate compensation, ancillary income, and earnings on escrow accounts).

Most mortgage loans are repaid before contractual maturity as homeowners move, refinance, or pay the loan ahead of schedule. To estimate the income to be received from servicing the loans, a bank must consider loan prepayments in determining the level of servicing fees it can expect from the loan pool. Prepayment speed, a key component in a valuation model, represents the annual rate at which borrowers are forecast to prepay their mortgage loan principal. Common prepayment speed measures used by the industry include the PSA standard prepayments rate, CPR, and SMM.

When estimating the fair value of an MSA, banks should use market-based prepayment speeds. Prepayment speeds should be realistic and substantiated by independent sources. Banks with substantial servicing assets should track their own prepayment experience for different pools and types of mortgages to validate the prepayment assumptions used in their valuation models. If a bank's servicing portfolio experiences prepayment rates that differ from the national industry experience for similar pools because of regional or other market factors, the bank may have to adjust its prepayment speed assumptions to reflect the regional market factors. Banks should apply a consistent method of determining the prepayment speeds used in their valuation models and should ensure that their prepayment speeds are both well supported and adequately documented.

If a bank's estimate of fair values is not based on appropriate discount rates and prepayment speeds, MSA values will not be appropriate. For example, if all other assumptions remain constant, a slower prepayment speed or lower discount rate will result in a higher MSA valuation. Conversely, a faster prepayment speed or a higher discount rate will result in a lower MSA valuation. Because of the significant impact each assumption may have on the overall value of an MSA, it is important that each assumption be carefully considered in determining whether an MSA is appropriately stated.

Hedging

This section is not intended to be a complete discussion of hedge accounting for mortgage banking activities. Rather, it is meant to provide a high-level overview of certain aspects of hedge accounting relevant to mortgage banking.

In order to avoid the complexities of hedge accounting, many banks may elect to account for their MSAs or warehouse loans at fair value under the fair value option. If a bank elects to account for the MSA or warehouse loans at fair value and the hedging instrument is accounted for at fair value, the unrealized gains and losses for both instruments would be included in the income statement (and therefore the amounts would offset each other to the extent the derivative is used to economically hedge the MSAs).

Many banks hedge their MSAs by electing fair value on the MSA and using derivatives or cash instruments that are not considered hedges per ASC 815. If a bank elects to account for the MSAs using the amortization method or account for the warehouse at LOCOM, and designates the derivatives as "hedges" per ASC 815, the accounting must comply with the requirements of ASC 815. Given the difficulty associated with finding instruments that would meet the requirements of ASC 815, many institutions use macro hedges, which do not get accounting hedge treatment. Because of the complexity of hedging activities and the specific requirements of ASC 815, banks should have detailed policies and procedures, transaction-specific documentation, and rigorous processes for effectiveness testing. They should also have sufficient MIS to effectively manage hedge accounting activities. Hedge accounting requires specific expertise in finance, accounting, and statistics, as well as strong internal controls and management reporting. Accordingly, examiners should ensure that institutions that undertake a macro hedge or other accounting program have the requisite skills on their staff.

Banks typically economically hedge various components of their mortgage banking business, including loan commitments, loans held for sale, and MSAs. Many banks use derivative financial instruments (e.g., forwards and options) and investment securities to accomplish their hedging objectives. Examiners should refer to ASC 815 for complete guidance in accounting for derivative instruments and hedging activities.

ASC 815 requires institutions to account for derivative instruments at fair value and to adjust earnings for changes in the instruments' fair values. To better match related gains and losses from hedging activities, however, ASC 815 allows companies to apply special hedge accounting rules to transactions that meet specified criteria. Under hedge accounting, companies can either adjust the carrying amount of a hedged asset, liability, or firm commitment to reflect changes in its fair value attributable to the hedged risk (for fair value hedges) or delay recognition of the change in fair value of a hedging derivative until the hedged projected cash flow affects earnings (for cash flow hedges).

For example, institutions may account for loans that are held for sale (warehouse loans) at LOCOM. Banks typically hedge their warehouse loans using forward sales commitments that meet the definition of a derivative instrument under ASC 815 and, therefore, must be accounted for at fair value. If the fair value of the warehouse loans increases above their cost, the value of the forward sales commitments that hedge the warehouse loans would likely decrease. Without the special hedge accounting treatment permitted under ASC 815, or use of the fair value option, there might be an accounting mismatch because the bank would recognize the full decline in the fair value of the forward sales commitments but could recognize only the increase in the fair value of the warehouse loans up to their original cost. If the transaction qualifies, the bank may elect to apply fair value hedge accounting under ASC 815. In a fair value hedge, the bank would adjust the warehouse loans to reflect the change in the fair value that is attributable to the hedged risk, even if the resulting carrying amount exceeds the original cost of the warehouse loans.

Under ASC 815, a derivative instrument cannot be the hedged item in a hedge accounting relationship. Therefore, because loan commitments related to loans that will be held for sale (the pipeline) are considered derivative instruments, hedge accounting cannot be applied in a hedge of the pipeline, and a bank is required to account for both the pipeline and the hedging instruments (e.g., forward sales commitments) at fair value. While this "economic hedge" does not qualify for hedge accounting, marking both the forward sales commitment and the loan commitment to fair value, in theory, will achieve results similar to a fair value hedge.

Banks that apply fair value hedge accounting to their MSA hedges typically aggregate individual MSAs into designated hedged portfolios for ease of administration. ASC 815 allows groups of similar items to be aggregated as hedged items. The individual items, however, must share the risk exposure for which they are designated as being hedged. In other words, the change in fair value attributable to the hedged risk for individual items must be generally proportionate to the overall change in the fair value attributable to the hedged risk of the portfolio of items. This is often referred to as the "similar asset test." As noted above, banks have the option to account for their MSAs at fair value, which then allows the bank to achieve the desired reporting without having to apply fair value hedge accounting. Once fair value is elected for the MSAs, and the derivative being used to economically hedge is also reported at fair value under ASC 815, the unrealized gains and losses would offset in the income statement. The effect would be similar to that of hedge accounting under ASC 815.

ASC 815 requires that a single, defined method of assessing hedge effectiveness be used consistently throughout the hedge period. In applying fair value hedge accounting, at the inception of a hedge a bank must specify and document the method it will use to assess the hedge's effectiveness. In doing so, the designated hedge period must coincide with the rebalancing of the hedge portfolio (e.g., a one-month hedge period for an MSA stratum would not be appropriate if the stratum is rebalanced on a weekly basis).

Each period, banks must demonstrate that the change in fair value of the hedging instrument was highly effective (e.g., between 80 percent and 125 percent when using the dollar value offset method) in offsetting the change in the fair value attributable to the hedged risk of the hedged MSA portion. Note that the strata used for hedging purposes do not have to be the same strata that are required in the ASC 860 impairment test. Therefore, banks may choose to aggregate their MSAs into different strata for assessing impairment and for evaluating hedge effectiveness.

Applying hedge accounting for MSAs is one of the most difficult and complex areas of accounting for mortgage banking activities. The complexity is primarily in meeting the "highly effective" criteria that is specified in ASC 815. Banks that use statistical techniques (e.g., regression analyses) to assess hedge effectiveness must understand such techniques and consider the statistical validity and relevant outputs of the analyses. To properly assess hedges, banks may need to use specialists to document hedge relationships and to evaluate the statistical techniques that measure hedge effectiveness. Accordingly, examiners should carefully evaluate a bank's hedge accounting approach for MSAs to ensure that it is consistent with GAAP and is effective in managing the specified risk.

For additional guidance on hedging, examiners should seek technical assistance from the OCC's Risk Analysis Division or the Chief Accountant's Office, as appropriate.

Fair Value

ASC 820 defines fair value as the price that would be received for selling an asset or the price paid for transferring a liability in an orderly transaction between market participants at the measurement date. The ASC 820 definition of fair value is based on an exit price (for an asset, the price at which it would be sold) rather than an entry price (for an asset, the price at which it would be bought), regardless of whether the entity plans to hold or sell the asset. Moreover, the ASC 820 definition of fair value is market based rather than entity specific; thus, fair values must rest on assumptions that market participants would use in pricing an asset or liability. Market participants are buyers and sellers in the principal market (or most advantageous market) for the asset or liability; the principal market is the market with the greatest volume and level of activity for the asset or liability; the most advantageous market is the market where the entity receives the highest selling price for an asset or pays the lowest price to transfer the liability after considering transaction costs. The price from the most advantageous market should be used only when there is no principal market.

ASC 820 uses a three-level hierarchy to rank the quality and reliability of information used to determine fair values. Level 1, the most reliable valuation inputs, are quoted market prices for identical assets or liabilities in active markets. Level 2 inputs are market-based inputs, other than Level 1 quoted prices that are observable directly or indirectly. Level 3 inputs are unobservable inputs not corroborated by observable market data. In determining fair value, ASC 820 requires that valuation techniques should maximize, when available, the use of observable inputs. In some cases, inputs for valuation techniques that are used to measure fair value might fall within different levels of the fair value hierarchy. The lowest level of significant input determines the placement of a fair value measure in the hierarchy.

Appendix D: Common Mortgage Banking Structures

The mortgage banking industry continues to consolidate. The large resulting operations have reached sizes and efficiency levels that make it difficult for small and midsize operations to compete directly with them. The largest producers are able to negotiate reduced guarantee fees with GSEs and often securitize loans into MBSs themselves. Integrated computer systems help reduce the cost to produce and service loans. This allows these more efficient competitors to offer lower rates to borrowers that smaller operations may not be able to match. The economies of scale of these large mortgage bankers also affect many other aspects of the mortgage banking industry. The size of their hedging positions can sometimes affect the market prices or availability of certain products (e.g., a few large producers may fill all of the available commitments from an FHLB Mortgage Partnership Finance program).

The following examples illustrate some typical mortgage banking operations and risks. The issues listed for each succeeding type are intended to build on the prior types. This section is intended to help examiners understand some of the prominent risks in mortgage banking, but it should not be used as a template for the examination.

Small, Community-Based Bank That Sells All of One Category of Loan Production

Management of a small, community-based bank originates certain loans that it does not intend to keep in portfolio. Management may structure the operation to act as a loan broker that receives fee income on these sold loans. Alternatively, it may structure the operation to act as a correspondent producer for a larger mortgage banking operation, whereby it might underwrite loans to this investor's standards and sell them on a best efforts or flow basis. In this case, the bank may also receive a servicing release premium (SRP). Management incurs no hedging costs, and the investors that purchase the loans set the interest rates.

When reviewing these types of operations, a key first question is, "At what point do loan sales constitute a mortgage banking operation?" Management at some banks will sell all long-term, fixed-rate loans to limit interest rate risk exposure, or the bank may sell certain ARMs because it lacks the expertise or system capabilities to service the loans properly. If this activity represents only periodic sales to the same investors, there is minimal risk or supervisory concern. As sales volume increases, the activity may expose the bank to greater risk and may warrant further review.

This type of operation generally relies on permanent staff to handle the production volume. A common strategy is to try to better utilize current staff to generate additional fee income by producing extra loans. Note that if management elects to add staff during high volume times, the additions should be temporary rather than permanent.

In this type of operation, the bank (or some designated part of its staff) may act as a loan broker, correspondent, or agent for an investor. Each role has different associated risks, income, and expenses. An agent for an investor, the simplest of these three roles, acts on a particular investor's behalf and is usually paid a set fee for each loan generated.

If the bank acts as a broker, it may deal with a number of investors and receive commissions. The fees earned on each loan may escalate with increasing volume or for consistent loan quality. The fee arrangement may compensate the broker for extra fees, points, and higher rates that the broker can negotiate with the borrower over the investor's quoted rate. One advantage of acting as a loan broker is that operating costs are limited, because the investor underwrites the loans. For the same reason, loan brokers have little or no recourse risk.

A bank acting as a correspondent operation closes the loan in the name of the bank and then sells the loan to the investor. In this type of operation, the bank's production staff underwrites the loan to the investor's standards. Correspondents often sell loans on a flow basis, whereby a commitment from an investor to buy the loan is obtained at the same time a binding loan commitment is issued to the borrower. If the loan does not close, the correspondent does not have to deliver a loan and does not pay a fee (contrary to if there was a forward sale agreement). If the loan closes, the correspondent is expected to deliver the appropriately documented loan to the investor within a set period. The correspondent may receive some of the loan fees, but the main source of income is from SRPs. If a loan with more profitable terms can be delivered, the correspondent can enjoy most of the additional gains.

Even small producers acting as correspondents have underwriting departments capable of handling a range of production volumes, and thus higher general and administrative expenses when compared with institutions without this activity. To improve efficiencies, many larger correspondent operations have begun using AUSs that approve or deny prospective borrowers based on set standards. Depending on the user's systems and process integration, this higher-end technology may contribute to higher operating costs, or it may lead to overall cost reduction. While AUSs often reduce the underwriting burden, approval is contingent on the delivery of certain documentation. There are often cases where the investor may ultimately reject the loan after closing because delivered documentation did not meet the investor's standards. While these rejections typically come within a few months of origination, in peak periods the investor may reject the loan well into the loan term.

Even with the limited nature of this type of mortgage banking activity, management should

- **understand the total costs to produce loans:** Management should estimate the break-even level of production and be able to determine when loan sales are made at net gains or losses. Even a small bank should not have difficulty calculating a reasonable estimate of the costs associated with producing each loan. Regardless of the sophistication of these estimates, they should be revisited as production volumes vary. Estimates should include computer time and MIS, additional staff time needed, and other costs incurred with the production and delivery of the loan.
- **monitor EPD and early payoff (EPO) exposure:** Sales agreements between banks and investors may contain credit enhancement clauses. These clauses can increase capital requirements even if loans have not been repurchased and can possibly limit the bank's ability to fund more production. If any loans have been repurchased, or indemnifications granted, the costs associated with this activity will reduce profitability via actual losses taken or provisioning for potential losses.

Community-Based Bank With Several Loan Production Offices

Management of a community-based bank with several loan production offices (LPO) may produce and sell high loan volumes. These operations typically sell production on a best efforts or flow basis. Investors' rate quotes are used to set loan prices, and there are low or no hedging costs. Achieving higher levels of production generally requires the operation to compete more intensely with similar and larger-size mortgage bankers. Competition may drive down fee income, so SRPs tend to be the primary source for the operation's earnings. Management teams with this style of operation should separate income and expenses between their portfolio-lending and for-sale production activities. At this level, management should capture and report this information at a loan-level basis. This operation requires a more complex monitoring system than the type of operation discussed previously.

Typically, with multiple LPOs management has purposely built a structure to generate higher levels of fee income via increased loan production volumes and sales. The LPOs and a growing network of agents, brokers, and correspondents facilitate this strategy. These additional production sources add other layers of risks and costs. As these wholesale production vehicles become more prevalent, many operations are trying to increase the amount of variable cost components in their earnings streams. If management expands production levels through use of more fixed-cost operations, examiners should carefully evaluate the appropriateness of this expense profile and the resulting effect on the bank's overall risk level.

A best practice standard for this type of operation is for management to separate income and expenses for each of the different production methods. In many cases, one production method will have lower net costs and management should be aware of the differences. Only by separation and stratification will management be able to gather information such as production level and costs, timeliness of loan delivery, and general loan quality data. As production falls or profitability drops, this information allows management to make informed decisions about how to reduce costs.

Most banks operating within this scenario function as correspondents. They may sell loans to other banks or institutions, national mortgage banking firms, or GSEs. Most sales are on a best efforts or flow basis to the investors (e.g., conventional conforming fixed-rate loans), but they also may periodically sell more unique products loan-by-loan (e.g., government-insured loans or unique ARMs). The GSEs and major investors, as well as some individual institutions, have developed AUSs to speed up the loan underwriting and approval process and to help ensure consistent loan quality. Each GSE has an AUS product available for its regular customers to use. Other larger investors may have proprietary systems, but using proprietary systems requires a relatively firm relationship between the loan producer and investor. In most cases, the investor supplying the AUS guarantees that it will purchase all loans underwritten and approved by the system. These automated systems are becoming more widespread in the mortgage banking industry.

With this style of operation, it is common for management to offer rates slightly lower than the investor's quoted rates in order to generate additional volume. For instance, the investor may quote 6 percent and 1.0 point, but the production staff may make the loan at 6 percent and zero points. In this case, management is forgoing some of the fee income it would have received at the investor's quoted rate in order to generate the SRP. Frequently, management's goal is that the increased volume will reduce production costs to a point where the SRP alone generates an acceptable return. Management may also do this in the short term to maintain a certain level of production so it does not have to cut staff.

As the operation gets more complex, the depth of the review should expand. Additional issues to consider in a review of a small bank with several LPOs include the following:

Are adequate information systems in place? Does management monitor EPD or EPO and adjust staff and systems as production levels dictate?

Are loans priced to generate volumes regardless of costs? Some operations have higher fixed costs, so they try to maintain a certain volume to cover these costs. As market rates rise and overall production falls, this operation will have to offer lower loan prices to maintain higher production volumes. This strategy only works if management closely monitors the marginal cost of added volume and is able to maintain profitability.

Is management treating the employees of LPOs or other wholesale production vehicles like permanent branch staff? Some managers are not willing to cut staff in these areas when production falls. The small margins in this area make the need to control costs very important. If management does not reduce costs and staff during production downturns, earnings will decline or the bank may experience losses.

Do originators meet AUS documentation requirements? The AUS may base approvals on specific criteria, such as an acceptable appraisal or income verification. If management does not retain the required documentation, the loan may be subject to a repurchase request.

Does the bank have access to sufficient funding for the operation's needs? Management must ensure that the bank maintains the capital base and borrowing ability to handle its funding needs. In many cases, loan production volumes can exceed fund availability from the existing deposit base. Management must rely on borrowed funds to meet these additional requirements. Management's liquidity plan should address how to deal with changing funding requirements. If there is inadequate liquidity planning, profitability can suffer. In extreme cases, funding shortfalls can be detrimental to a bank's reputation, because it may not be possible for the bank to fulfill its outstanding loan commitments. Alternatively, if longer-term funding arrangements are used, the operation could end up with costly, unused funds when production volumes and warehouse portfolios decline.

Community-Based Bank With a Small, Full-Line Mortgage Banking Operation

A bank with a small, full-line mortgage banking operation must be knowledgeable about loan production, hedged secondary market sales, loan servicing, and MSR valuation requirements. Typically, these banks have annual new loan production of about 100 percent to 500 percent of total assets. Many operations retain the servicing rights on conventional, conforming fixed-rate loans, but sell other products on a servicing-released basis. Managers for this operation may select desirable loans from the mortgage banking operation's loan production to retain for the bank's portfolio. A bank sells most conventional production to the GSEs or other secondary market investors using forward sales, while selling ARMs, jumbos, and other small-volume loan types on a best efforts or flow basis to a different pool of investors.

Management should report and monitor the mortgage banking operation separately from the rest of the bank's operations, using some form of business-line profitability reporting system. The mortgage banking operation may be a service corporation, an operating subsidiary, or a department of the bank. Regardless of the structure, reporting systems should generate separate operating statements and performance metrics for the mortgage banking operation and its component operations. The measurement system should report on a rate/volume basis as well as on an income-and-expense-per-loan basis. Management and the board should compare their internal performance measurements to appropriate industry standards.

This type of operation has more risk exposure and, consequently, should generate higher returns. This risk-reward trade-off is sometimes referred to as moving up the pricing ladder. This bank typically has a full-time secondary marketing employee or department and sets loan prices internally, rather than from other investors' quotes. The mortgage banking operation has more interest rate risk exposure in its pipeline and warehouse than an operation that sells production on a flow basis. The bank must prudently and cost-effectively hedge this risk.

A full-line mortgage banking operation has loan production volumes that require management to know the full costs of the different production methods. Retail production can be relatively costly, but management has better control over the quality of loans produced. Wholesale loan production sources provide a desirable variable cost structure, but they also require systems to monitor loan quality. Loan brokers cost less than correspondents but necessitate additional internal underwriting capacity. Brokers are frequently less reliable in delivering loans than other wholesale sources and thus create a higher fallout component, which raises hedging costs. Correspondents are more expensive than brokers because they generally receive an SRP that is a substantial portion of the MSR's value.

While this operation typically hedges with forward sales agreements, management has numerous options for loan delivery. Management can deliver the loans into the forward sale agreement. Alternatively, it may sell the loans into the agencies' cash programs and pair off the hedge. Management also may deliver the loans and the forward sale agreement to an investor using an assignment of trade. Note that these activities can increase the holding time of warehoused loans significantly more than other types of operations. The secondary marketing department should be delivering the loans to the investor as quickly as possible in order to protect the value generated by the origination department.

While awaiting delivery in the closed-loan warehouse, the bank still owns the loans and earns the spread interest income they generate. When fixed-rate loans are funded with short-term, wholesale monies, the net interest spread may be higher than that earned in the bank's loan portfolio. While this higher spread may be tempting to management, it increases interest rate risk exposure. The secondary marketing operation's goal should be to deliver the loans as quickly and efficiently as possible to the appropriate investor.

As management engages in complex activities, it may elect to rely on external expertise. Any contracts with third parties for products or services should comply with OCC policies. Some of the types of services external companies provide the industry include QC and compliance reviews, secondary marketing and hedging, Internet platforms and hosting, and subservicing arrangements. Examiners reviewing this area should evaluate the costs and benefits for each of these services.

Ideally, this bank should have information systems that differentiate costs between internal loan servicing operations and loan servicing for other investors. Given this type of information, management can determine whether it would like to keep the servicing function in-house or hire a sub-servicer. It is acceptable for management to keep the servicing in-house, even at a higher cost than available through a sub-servicing agreement. This allows management to maintain quality customer service or develop cross-selling opportunities. Regardless, management and the board should have the information to make an informed decision. Similarly, if management elects to retain the MSR in lieu of receiving the SRP, it should periodically reassess the costs and benefits of that decision.

One factor to consider when retaining MSR is that management must have a reasonable system to calculate and record periodic MSR valuations. This process often requires additional systems and staff to track and record the values properly. MSR value must be recorded as required by GAAP.

Increasing complexity of the mortgage banking operation warrants more detailed review. The issues that should be considered in this area include the following:

Does management price loans to meet the demands of the secondary market? The secondary marketing department should set the loan pricing and product selection based on market factors. If pricing is set to maximize production without consideration for investor demand, profitability will suffer.

Does management hold loans to generate extra spread income? Sometimes management may keep loans in the warehouse longer than necessary to earn additional spread interest income. Other than with best efforts or flow basis delivery commitments, management has latitude to choose which loans are delivered into forward sales commitments. As such, it has the option to shift the delivery of a loan into a later commitment or to roll the entire commitment into a later position, leaving the affected loans in the warehouse longer. The market is generally very efficient, so management should support any decision to deviate from the first possible delivery date. Depending on the size of the portfolio of "retained" loans, this decision could create a significant risk warranting corrective action.

Does management consider the secondary marketing department a profit center? Significant profits or losses in this area are generally the result of over- or under-hedging the pipeline, the warehouse, or both. If management is risking more than the expected gain on sale from producing the loans, the activity is a supervisory concern. Some secondary marketers may allow some or all of the warehouse loans to be unhedged in order to create higher earnings. Depending on the size of the unhedged warehouse portfolio, this decision can be a prudent economic choice or it can lead to a major risk exposure that is a significant supervisory concern warranting immediate corrective actions.

Do information systems allow for adequate separation of LSFO from internal loan servicing? MIS must be able to separate the two types of servicing for proper income and expense allocation. Without separate allocations, management cannot evaluate alternatives between selling loans servicing retained versus servicing released.

Does the bank have an adequate system to record and value the MSR? The accounting and reporting systems needed to accurately measure MSR value can carry significant costs. Management must have detailed, loan-level reporting. The bank may group the calculations for reporting purposes. See appendix C for additional detail on MSR and its effect on earnings.

Midsize Regional Bank With a Full-Line, Nationwide Mortgage Banking Operation

A midsize regional bank with a full-line, nationwide mortgage banking operation has substantial production volumes, typically using a mix of retail and wholesale production. Production levels are large enough that the secondary marketing operation may securitize loans into agency MBSs and deliver the loans into forward sales contracts. Management sells all loans servicing retained, but it may sell certain MSR pools for different reasons. The operation has reached a size where management may elect to specialize in one part of the mortgage banking business. The bank may have a large network of brokers and correspondents from which it acquires loans. The operation may be a large servicer of government, conventional, or subprime loans, and management may buy and sell servicing pools to facilitate this operation.

This operation has reached a size where management is in a better position to negotiate a reduced guarantee fee with the GSEs, allowing it to better compete on a national scale. The bank should report the mortgage banking operation separately from the rest of its operations, using a business-line profitability reporting system. The reporting system should also be able to separate operations geographically and by operating function.

While QC is always an important issue, this type of operation has reached a scale where a small deterioration in loan quality can have a large impact on earnings. As such, the higher production levels require a full-time QC department, whether staffed in-house or outsourced.

Banks where most assets are related to the mortgage banking operation also fit into this category. The majority of loans on the balance sheet are those held in the warehouse. The MSR value may comprise a significant amount of the bank's capital. The pipeline and warehouse's exposure determines the bank's interest rate risk, in addition to any sensitivity from the unhedged MSR's rate-shocked value fluctuations. Management bases funding requirements and sources on loan originations, purchases, and sales. Fee income and gain-on-sale income are major components of the bank's overall earnings. Noninterest expenses will also be very high, especially compared with comparably sized traditional FSA operations.

Interest income comes from the longer-term assets while the funding cost is generally short-term. This type of mortgage banking operation takes very little credit risk, so the bank's net interest margin (NIM) is based predominately on the shape of the yield curve. If the yield curve is flat, normal, or steep, NIM should be low, reasonable, or high, respectively.

This type of operation may benefit financially from its size. Production volumes may reach a point where management needs to decide whether new systems are necessary to add more volume. Production costs generally have started to fall but have likely not yet reached an optimum point. The bank now has sufficient production to allow internal securitizations of loan production or bulk whole-loan sales. These additional sales avenues offer more options to improve earnings.

A midsize bank with a full-line, nationwide mortgage banking operation has several complexities that examiners must review carefully. The following additional issues in this area should be considered:

Has the bank experienced large changes in its income? If most or all operations are related to mortgage banking, the bank may be susceptible to large variations in its income from gain on sale, fees, and NIM.

Have changes in the MSR affected shorter-term profitability or capital levels? The MSR value will increase or decrease as interest rates fluctuate, and this shift can have a substantial impact on earnings. If the bank has a major loan production operation, there will be a timing difference between an MSR writedown (or impairment) and the gain-on-sale income from new production.

Full-line, Nationwide Mortgage Banking Business Operating as Separate Business Line From the Bank

A full-line, nationwide mortgage banking operation requires the most in-depth examiner review. The secondary marketing operation sells loans through multiple channels, including private label and agency MBSs. This type of operation often runs on a functional rather than a legal-entity basis. Management's measurement and reporting systems should be based on that functional nature, but the systems should be able to deal with legal-entity basis where necessary and appropriate.

When the MSR is large enough relative to capital, changes in its market value can materially affect the bank's capital and earnings. Management may choose from a variety of instruments to hedge the MSR values to stabilize those value fluctuations. The size of this operation should allow for proportionally lower production and servicing costs as compared with smaller and regional operations. The secondary marketing staff takes advantage of all of the hedging and delivery options the capital markets offer it. Management may purchase and sell MSR, and it may hedge the (anticipatory) MSR value of the loans in the pipeline or warehouse before the actual accounting recognition of that MSR takes place.

A full-line, nationwide mortgage banking operation that is part of a financial institution but runs independently of it has several unique areas that examiners should consider in their reviews:

Does the information system provide management with all necessary information in a timely manner? The size and complexity of this operation require detailed, complex reporting systems. These systems must provide management with critical metrics in a timely manner.

Is management hedging the MSR? Hedging of MSR should factor into profitability analysis for the MSR and for the mortgage banking operation.

Appendix E: Standards for Handling Files With Imminent Foreclosure Sale

Purpose	The following establishes **minimum** standards for the handling and prioritization of borrower files that are subject to imminent (within 60 days) scheduled foreclosure sales. **The purpose of these guidelines is to ensure that borrowers will not lose their homes without their files receiving pre-foreclosure sale reviews conducted under the standards listed in this appendix, which also help ensure loan modifications are considered as appropriate.**
	Bank servicers of residential mortgages should use these review and validation standards to determine whether a scheduled foreclosure sale should be postponed, suspended, or cancelled because of critical foreclosure defects in the borrower's file. These minimum review criteria are intended to ensure a level of consistency across servicers, not to supplant review and validation procedures that go beyond these minimums. Servicers that currently apply more than these minimum standards as part of their own pre-foreclosure sale review and validation procedures are expected to continue to do so.
	These standards are not intended to incorporate the final rules amending Regulation X and Regulation Z, issued by the CFPB on January 17, 2013, and effective on January 10, 2014, which govern mortgage servicers' loss mitigation and foreclosure-processing functions. The OCC expects that all servicers will undertake appropriate action in a timely manner to ensure their practices will be compliant with the new rules by the effective date.
Overview	Bank servicers of residential mortgages should monitor all borrower files in the foreclosure process at least weekly to determine whether foreclosure sales are scheduled within the next 60 days. The servicer should implement procedures to perform and document a timely pre-foreclosure sale review according to the criteria set out in this guidance and appropriately postpone, suspend, or cancel the scheduled foreclosure sale when warranted.
	The servicer will promptly determine whether the borrower is currently in an active loss mitigation program or is being actively considered for or has requested consideration under the Home Affordable Modification Program (HAMP) or other modification or loss mitigation program as further defined in **standard number 9 below**, and whether further foreclosure proceedings or the scheduled foreclosure sale should be postponed, suspended, or cancelled as required by program standards as applicable.
	The following standards are a nonexhaustive list of criteria for which an exception would warrant postponement, suspension, or cancellation of a foreclosure sale until the Minimum Pre-Foreclosure Sale Review Standards are satisfied. As noted above, individual servicers may apply additional standards/criteria to postpone, suspend, or cancel a foreclosure sale.
	Any negative response to these minimum standards is considered a critical defect (except for standard number 7, where a positive response is a defect) and cause to postpone, suspend, or cancel a scheduled foreclosure sale.
	Independent control functions (such as audit, compliance, and risk management) should confirm and document servicer adherence to their own servicing standards/criteria and the standards described in this document through a program of monitoring, sampling, and testing of scheduled and completed foreclosure sales.

Minimum Pre-Foreclosure Sale Review Standards	Date of the scheduled foreclosure sale: _____ Once the date of foreclosure is established, the servicer needs to confirm the following information before foreclosing: 1. Is the loan's default status accurate? 2. Does the servicer have and can the servicer demonstrate the appropriate legal authority to foreclose (documented assignments, note endorsements, and other necessary legal documentation, as applicable)? 3. Have required foreclosure notices or other required communications to the borrower or others, as applicable, been provided in a timely manner? 4. Has the servicer taken all steps necessary to confirm whether the borrower, co-borrower, and all obligors on the mortgage, trust deed, or other security in the nature of a mortgage are entitled to protections under the SCRA, including running queries through the Department of Defense database? If the borrower, co-borrower, or other obligor is subject to SCRA protections, has the servicer complied with all applicable legal requirements to foreclose? 5. Determine whether the borrower is in an active bankruptcy. If so, does the servicer have documented legal authority to foreclose? 6. Determine whether the loan is currently under loss mitigation or other retention review or whether the borrower has requested such a review as part of the foreclosure process. If so, did the servicer notify the borrower that all conditions necessary to effect the loss mitigation or retention action have not been met, what is needed to meet those conditions, and the date necessary to cure the deficiencies to avoid further foreclosure action? If a borrower submitted a complete loan modification application after the foreclosure referral, did the servicer comply with any applicable dual track restrictions? 7. Is the borrower currently in an active trial loss mitigation plan? 8. Determine whether the servicer accepted any payment from the borrower in the preceding 60 days (that is, were borrower payments, including interest, principal, fees, and escrow payments, applied to the borrower's account or retained in a suspense account). If so, did the servicer clearly communicate to the borrower that he or she is neither in nor being considered for a loss mitigation program, and that the bank's acceptance of the payment in no way affected the status of the foreclosure that is proceeding? 9. As applicable, was the borrower solicited for and offered a loss mitigation option, such as those required by HAMP, a GSE, the FHA, the VA, state-level government programs under the Treasury Department, another third-party investor, or the servicer's loss mitigation and modification programs? To the extent applicable, has the servicer complied with its loss mitigation obligations detailed in the National Mortgage Settlement? Have any borrower complaints, appeals, or escalations been considered and addressed? 10. Was the fully executed loan modification application submitted by the borrower, as defined by the applicable modification program, reviewed by the servicer as required, including any timeline or notice requirements? 11. Was the modification decision correct and validated as required by the applicable modification program (to include, as applicable, compliance with program requirements and accuracy of calculations and application of the NPV test) along with appropriate resolution and communication of any borrower complaint, appeal, or escalation?

	12. Was the borrower or the borrower's representative (housing counselor or attorney) notified of the loan modification decision and rationale as required by program or policy guidelines? 13. If required by a GSE or other investor, has the servicer certified to the attorney conducting the foreclosure that all delinquency management requirements have been met, including that there is neither an approved payment plan arrangement nor a foreclosure alternative offer pending or accepted?

Appendix F: Risk Assessment Factors

Quantity of Risk

Low	Moderate	High
The amount of capital allocated to mortgage banking in relation to total capital is low.	A substantial amount of capital is allocated to mortgage banking but is still not high relative to total capital.	The amount of capital allocated to the mortgage banking operation is substantial and significant in relation to total capital.
Mortgage banking revenue or profit is insignificant to the bank's overall revenue or profit.	Mortgage banking revenue or profit is an important contributor to the bank's total revenue or profit.	Mortgage banking revenue or profit is a substantial contributor to the bank's total revenue or operating profit.
Mortgage banking origination channels are mostly noncomplex and highly manageable (i.e., retail originations).	Mortgage banking origination channels are somewhat complex and manageable (i.e., broker accounts).	A significant number of mortgage banking origination sources are complex and large in terms of total volume delivered.
Mortgage banking products and servicing are relatively noncomplex and highly liquid.	Mortgage banking products and servicing are somewhat complex and liquid.	Mortgage banking products are complex, varied by location, and potentially illiquid.
Mortgage banking origination and servicing volumes are low and stable. New product volume is low.	Mortgage banking origination and servicing volume is significant and generally meets or exceeds management expectations. New product volume is high.	Mortgage banking or servicing volume growth is significantly above management expectations. New product volume is significant, complex, and potentially illiquid.
Mortgage banking transaction volume is not significant to operational capacities, and the probability of loss from errors, disruptions, or fraud is minimal.	Mortgage banking transaction volume is substantial, but the probability of loss associated with loss from errors, disruptions, or fraud is acceptable and clearly understood.	Mortgage banking transaction volume is substantial, and the probability of significant loss from errors, disruptions, or fraud is high.
The legal environment for products and activities is noncomplex, subject to stable regulation or law, and involves a large number of jurisdictions with similar legal and compliance requirements.	The legal environment for products and activities is moderately complex, subject to slow-developing and readily anticipated changes in regulation or law, and involves a limited number of jurisdictions or the jurisdictions have generally similar legal and compliance requirements.	The legal environment for products and activities is complex, unstable, and involves multiple jurisdictions that have differing legal and compliance requirements.
The turnover rate of mortgage banking staff is minimal.	The turnover rate of mortgage banking staff is moderate, and the associated reasons are understood and temporary.	The turnover rate of mortgage banking staff is significant or for undefined reasons.

Low	Moderate	High
The number of consumer complaints received is minimal when compared with the volumes originated or serviced. The complaint resolution is timely, complete, and in conjunction with appropriate federal and state laws.	The number of consumer complaints received is moderate when compared with volumes serviced or originated. The complaint resolution is timely, complete, and in conjunction with appropriate federal and state laws.	The likelihood of continued compliance violations is high because a corrective action program does not exist, or extended time is needed to implement such a program.
Technology systems are important to core business processes, but systems operate with limited integration and interdependencies. Alternative or replacement solutions are readily available and can be easily and rapidly implemented. Capacity utilization and scalability are sufficient for significant growth with little operational or financial impact. Functionality exceeds business requirements, or vendor support for purchase solutions is robust.	Technology systems are important to core business processes, but the level of integration and interdependencies does not preclude rapid implementation of alternative or replacement solutions. Technology utilization can support normal growth, and system scalability can be accomplished with modest operational or financial impact. Functionality meets business requirements and can be upgraded; vendor support for purchased solutions is adequate.	Technology systems are essential to all core and noncore business processes. The technology environment is tightly integrated, creates significant interdependencies across multiple critical business processes, and is highly complex. Technology system utilization is at or near capacity, and there is little scalability. IT systems have outmoded or inadequate functionality, vendor support for purchased solutions is inadequate, and upgrade or replacement would be highly disruptive.
Business critical operational processes have low vulnerability to disruption from internal events, the threat frequency is low and stable, and the financial impact would be minor. Contingency plans are robust, rigorously tested, and have demonstrated ability to meet minimum business requirements.	Business critical operational processes have moderate vulnerability to disruption from internal or external events, the threat frequency is moderate and stable, and the impact of disruption would not have material financial impact. Contingency plan testing demonstrates an ability to meet minimum business requirements.	Business critical operational processes are highly vulnerable to disruption from internal or external threats, the threat frequency is high, and disruption would have material consequences. Contingency planning is inadequate to provide the resiliency needed to meet minimum business requirements.

Quality of Risk Management

Strong	Satisfactory	Weak
There is a clear, sound mortgage banking culture. Board and management's appetite for risk is well communicated and fully understood.	The mortgage banking culture is generally sound, but the culture may not be uniform and risk appetite may not be clearly communicated throughout the bank.	A sound mortgage banking culture is absent or is materially flawed. Risk appetite may not be well understood.
Strategic or business plans are consistent with a conservative risk appetite and promote an appropriate balance between risk taking and growth and earnings objectives. New loan products/initiatives are well researched, tested, and approved before implementation.	Strategic and business plans are consistent with a moderate risk appetite. Anxiety for income may lead to some higher-risk transactions. Generally, there is an appropriate balance between risk taking and growth and earnings objectives. New loan products/initiatives may be launched without sufficient testing, but risks are usually understood.	Strategic or business plans encourage taking on liberal levels of risk. Anxiety for income dominates planning activities. The bank engages in new loan products/initiatives without conducting sufficient due diligence testing.
Management is effective. Management and personnel possess sufficient expertise to effectively administer the risk assumed. Responsibilities and accountability are clear, and appropriate remedial or corrective action is taken when they are breached.	Management is adequate to administer assumed risk, but improvements may be needed in one or more areas. Management and personnel generally possess the expertise required to effectively administer assumed risks, but additional expertise may be required in one or more areas. Responsibilities and accountability may require some clarification. Generally, appropriate remedial or corrective action is taken when they are breached.	Management is deficient. Loan management and personnel may not possess sufficient expertise or experience, or otherwise may demonstrate an unwillingness to effectively administer the risk assumed. Responsibilities and accountability may not be clear. Remedial or corrective actions are insufficient to address root causes of problems.
Diversification management is active and effective. Concentration limits are set at reasonable levels. The bank identifies and reports concentrated exposures and initiates actions to limit, reduce, or otherwise mitigate their risk. Management identifies and understands correlated exposures.	Diversification management may need improvement but is adequate. Concentrated exposures are identified and reported, but limits or other action/exception triggers may be absent. Management may initiate actions to limit or mitigate concentrations at the individual loan level, but portfolio level actions may be inadequate. Correlated exposures may not be identified.	Diversification management is passive or otherwise deficient. The bank may not identify concentrated exposures, or it identifies them but takes little or no actions to limit, reduce, or mitigate risk. Management does not understand exposure correlations. Concentration limits, if any, may be exceeded or are raised frequently.
Management and personnel compensation structures provide appropriate balance between loan/revenue production, loan quality, and portfolio administration, including risk identification, and comply with federal and state requirements.	Management and personnel compensation structures provide reasonable balance between loan/revenue production, loan quality, and portfolio administration, and comply with federal requirements.	Loan management and personnel compensation structures are skewed to loan/revenue production. There is little evidence of substantive incentives or accountability for loan quality and portfolio administration.

Strong	Satisfactory	Weak
Staffing levels and expertise are appropriate for the size and complexity of the origination and servicing volume. Staff turnover is reasonable and allows for the orderly transfer of responsibilities. Training programs facilitate ongoing staff development.	Staffing levels and expertise are generally adequate for the size and complexity of the origination and servicing volume. Staff turnover is moderate and may create some gaps in portfolio management. Training initiatives may be inconsistent.	Staffing levels are inadequate in numbers or skill level. Turnover is high. Bank does not provide sufficient resources for staff training.
Policies effectively establish and communicate delivery objectives, risk limits, and loan underwriting and risk-selection standards.	Policies are fundamentally adequate. Enhancements can be achieved in one or more areas but are generally not critical. Specificity of risk limits or underwriting and risk-selection standards may need improvement to fully communicate policy requirements.	Policies are deficient in one or more ways and require significant improvement in one or more areas. They may not be sufficiently clear or are too general to adequately communicate portfolio objectives, risk limits, and loan underwriting and risk-selection standards.
Bank effectively identifies, approves, tracks, and reports significant policy, underwriting, and risk-selection exceptions individually and in aggregate.	Bank identifies, approves, and reports significant policy, underwriting, and risk-selection exceptions on a loan-by-loan basis, including risk exposures associated with off-balance-sheet activities. Little aggregation or trend analysis, however, is conducted to determine the effect on portfolio quality.	Bank approves significant policy exceptions but does not report them individually or in aggregate or does not analyze their effect on portfolio quality. Risk exposures associated with off-balance-sheet activities may not be considered. Policy exceptions may not receive appropriate approval.
Credit analysis is thorough and timely both at underwriting and pre-funding.	Credit analysis appropriately identifies key risks and is conducted within reasonable time frames. Analysis after underwriting may need some strengthening.	Credit analysis is deficient. Analysis is superficial, and key risks are overlooked. Credit data are not reviewed in a timely manner.
Internal or outsourced risk rating and problem loan review and identification systems are accurate and timely. Systems effectively stratify credit risk in both problem and pass-rated credits. They serve as an effective early warning tool and support risk-based pricing, ALLL, and capital allocation processes.	Internal or outsourced risk rating and problem loan review and identification systems are adequate. Although improvement can be achieved in one or more areas, systems adequately identify problem and emerging problem credits. The graduation of pass ratings may need to be expanded to facilitate early warning, risk-based pricing, or capital allocation.	Internal or outsourced risk rating and problem loan review and identification systems are deficient and require improvement. Problem credits may not be identified accurately or in a timely manner; as a result, portfolio risk is likely misstated. The graduation of pass ratings is insufficient to stratify risk in pass credits for early warning or other purposes (loan pricing, ALLL, capital allocation).
Special mention ratings do not indicate any management problems administering the loan portfolio.	Special mention ratings generally do not indicate management problems administering the loan portfolio.	Special mention ratings indicate management is not properly administering the loan portfolio.

Strong	Satisfactory	Weak
MIS provides accurate, timely, and complete portfolio information. Management and the board receive appropriate reports to analyze and understand the bank's credit risk profile, including off-balance-sheet activities. MIS facilitates exception reporting, and MIS infrastructure can support ad hoc queries in a timely manner.	MIS may require modest improvement in one or more areas, but management and the board generally receive appropriate reports to analyze and understand the bank's credit risk profile. MIS facilitates exception reporting, and MIS infrastructure can support ad hoc queries in a timely manner.	MIS has deficiencies requiring attention. The accuracy or timeliness of information may be affected in a material way. Portfolio risk information may be incomplete. As a result, management and the board may not be receiving appropriate or sufficient information to analyze and understand the bank's credit risk profile. Exception reporting requires improvement, and MIS infrastructure may not support ad hoc queries in a timely manner.
The audit program for mortgage banking is strong, comprehensive in scope, adequately staffed, and sufficiently frequent. Identified issues are clearly reported, tracked, and rapidly resolved. Audit activities are based on a comprehensive risk assessment.	The audit program for mortgage banking is satisfactory. There are isolated and manageable weaknesses in scope, staffing, or frequency. Audit reports do not always clearly identify issues, issues are not always closely tracked, or issue resolution may be prolonged. The risk assessment process for developing the audit program has minor weaknesses.	The audit program for mortgage banking is weak. There are significant identified weaknesses in scope, staffing, or frequency that remain unaddressed. Audit reports fail to identify issues, issues are not tracked for resolution, and remediation efforts take excessive time to complete. The risk assessment process is flawed, resulting in inadequate audit activities.
IT infrastructure planning and implementation are well managed to meet current and future business requirements. Sound IT management is in place, including governance, oversight, and reporting.	Infrastructure planning and implementation exhibit minor weaknesses in strategy, project management, or factors involving managing change. IT risk management governance, oversight, and reporting meet fundamental requirements but need improvements or exhibit minor gaps. Issues are identified, and remediation is planned or under way.	IT infrastructure strategic planning and processes for managing implementation and change are inadequate for current or future business needs. Weaknesses in IT management are material and detract from an ability to oversee or manage IT risks. Management is unaware of the material deficiencies or has failed to address them.
Operations are well managed, with appropriate governance structures and oversight. Vendor management programs closely monitor critical third-party service providers for service level performance and compliance with laws and regulations. Operational metrics are comprehensive, effective for decision making and risk management, and appropriately reported.	Operations for critical activities or critical outsourcing relationships are adequately managed, but oversight is not proactive. Noncritical activities or third-party relationships receive insufficient oversight and management. Oversight processes do not ensure that internal or third-party service level performance does not consistently meet business standards. Risk management metrics and MIS support reactive, but not proactive, risk management.	Oversight of internal and outsource operations are materially deficient for critical business processes or systems, or a wide range of noncritical processes or systems, such that there are systemic concerns. Internal and third-party operational performance is below business standards for service level agreements. Metrics are inadequate to manage risk, and MIS distribution fails to support timely decision making.

Strong	Satisfactory	Weak
Compliance with applicable law is consistent and thorough, while the potential for noncompliance is minimal. Identified violations are quickly and effectively corrected. Customer complaints are actively monitored, analyzed, and used as a basis for improving operations and profitability and mitigating compliance risks.	Compliance with applicable law is satisfactory but can be improved. Identified violations are normally corrected in a satisfactory manner. Customer complaints are captured, but analysis is not used robustly to enhance operations and mitigate compliance risk exposure.	Compliance with applicable law is unsatisfactory, and the potential for additional noncompliance is high. Identified violations are not corrected in a timely and effective manner. Customer complaints are not captured, or if captured they are not utilized.

Appendix G: Glossary

A- or A-minus loan: See Alternative A loan (Alt-A).

A-quality credit: The best credit rating, held by borrowers who typically receive the lowest prices that lenders offer.

Accelerated amortization: An accounting technique in which the larger portion of the asset's book value is written off in the early years of the asset's expected life.

Accelerated remittance cycle: An option whereby an entity selling mortgages to or servicing mortgages for Freddie Mac reduces the guarantee fee it pays by making principal and interest payments early and shortening the monthly remittance delay. Remittance requirements are a component of servicing-asset valuation due to their impact on assumptions of float profitability.

Accident and health premium: A payment by a borrower to ensure that mortgage payments continue to be paid if the borrower becomes disabled or ill.

Acquisition cost: In an FHA transaction, the price the borrower pays for the property plus any closing, repair, and financing costs (except discounts in other than a refinancing transaction). Acquisition costs do not include prepaid discounts in a purchase transaction, mortgage insurance premiums, or similar add-on costs.

Adjustable rate mortgage (ARM), also known as **variable rate mortgage:** A mortgage loan that allows a lender to periodically adjust the interest rate in accordance with a specified index agreed to at the inception of the loan.

Alternative A loan (Alt-A): A term used by the industry to denote loans that do not satisfy the regular criteria for conforming or jumbo loan programs but are first-lien loans to prime quality borrowers. Typically these loans have an LTV ratio above 80 percent but lack private mortgage insurance. These loans may be extended to a temporary resident alien or secured by non-owner-occupied property, have no verification of borrower income or assets, or lack requirements that specify minimum income relative to expenses.

Amortization: The process of paying off a loan by gradually reducing the balance through a series of installment payments. Also, the process of writing off MSAs over the expected remaining economic life of the asset.

Annual mortgage statement: A report prepared by the lender or servicing agent for a mortgagor, as required by RESPA, stating the amount of taxes, insurance, and interest paid during the year, as well as the outstanding principal balance.

Automated underwriting system (AUS): A system into which a loan originator enters a borrower's application information, which is subject to verification. The system typically accesses the borrower's credit reports to determine the likelihood that the loan will be repaid as agreed. The assessment is based on the performance of similar mortgages with comparable borrower, property, and loan characteristics. The AUS makes preliminary recommendations regarding the loan (e.g., approve, refer, or caution). Some systems also make pricing recommendations.

Automated valuation model (AVM): Online database that matches similar properties using historical sales prices to derive a range of comparable sales prices. The model considers limited factual data, such as square footage, number of rooms, property age, and lot size. Some AVMs use historical information derived from county records, while others collect information from appraisal reports, in which properties' physical characteristics have been verified.

Balloon mortgage: A mortgage for which the periodic installments of principal and interest do not fully amortize the loan. The balance of the mortgage is due in a lump sum (balloon payment) at the end of the term.

Best efforts commitment, also known as **optional delivery commitment:** An agreement that requires an investor to buy mortgages at an agreed price. The seller, however, is not required to sell or deliver a specified number of mortgages to the investor.

Broker: A person or firm that specializes in loan originations, receiving a commission to bring together a borrower and a lender. The broker performs some or most of the loan processing functions but does not underwrite the mortgage, fund the mortgage at settlement, or service the mortgage. Typically, the loan is closed in the name of the lender that commissioned the broker's services. In some cases, the loan is closed in the broker's name through a table-funded arrangement. See **table funding**.

Bulk acquisition: Purchase of the servicing rights associated with a group of mortgages. Ownership of the underlying mortgages is not affected by the transaction.

Buy-down guarantee: See **guarantee fee buy-down**.

Buy-down mortgage: A mortgage in which a lender accepts a below-market interest rate in return for an interest rate subsidy paid as additional discount points by the builder, seller, or buyer.

Buy-up guarantee: See **guarantee fee buy-up**.

Cap (interest rate): In an ARM, a limit on the amount the interest rate may increase per period or over the life of the loan. See also **floor**.

Capitalize: The act of converting a series of anticipated cash flows into present value by discounting them at an established rate of return.

Capitalized value: The net present value of a set of future cash flows.

Certificate of reasonable value: A document issued by the VA that establishes a maximum value and loan amount for a VA-guaranteed mortgage.

Closing: Consummation of a mortgage transaction during which the note and other legal documents are signed and the loan proceeds are disbursed. If a loan is rescindable, per Regulation Z, proceeds are not immediately disbursed.

Closing costs: Fees paid to effect the closing of a mortgage. Common closing costs include origination fees, discount points, title insurance fees, survey fees, appraisal fees, and attorneys' fees.

Closing statement: A financial disclosure giving an account of all funds received and expected at closing, including escrow deposits for taxes, hazard insurance, and mortgage insurance. All federally insured or guaranteed loans and most conventionally financed loans use a uniform closing statement known as HUD-1, as required by RESPA for residential mortgage transactions.

Commitment (lender/borrower): An agreement, often in writing, between a lender and a borrower to lend money at a future date or for a specified time period subject to specified conditions.

Commitment (seller/investor): A written agreement between a seller of loans and an investor to sell and buy mortgages under specified terms for a specified period of time.

Commitment fee (lender/borrower): A fee paid by a potential borrower to a potential lender for the lender's promise to lend money at a specified date in the future, or for a specified period of time and under specified terms. The timing of income recognition for these fees should follow GAAP using the specified contractual terms.

Commitment fee (seller/investor): A fee paid by a loan seller to an investor in return for the investor's promise to purchase a loan or a package of loans at an agreed price at a future date.

Computerized loan origination system (CLO): An electronic system that provides subscribers current data on available loan programs at various lending institutions. Some CLOs offer mortgage information services and can prequalify borrowers, process loan applications, underwrite loans, and make a commitment of funds.

Conditional prepayment rate (CPR): A standard of measurement of the projected annual rate of prepayment for a seasoned mortgage loan or pool of loans. Although the standard CPR is 6 percent per year, it can be quoted at any percentage. For example, a 10.5 percent CPR assumes that 10.5 percent of the outstanding balance of a mortgage pool will be prepaid each year. See also **Public Securities Administration prepayment model** and **single monthly mortality**.

Conforming mortgage: A mortgage loan that meets all requirements (loan type, amount, and age) for purchase by Fannie Mae or Freddie Mac.

Conventional mortgage: A mortgage loan that is not government-guaranteed or government-insured. There are two types of conventional loans, conforming and nonconforming. See also **conforming mortgage** and **nonconforming mortgage**.

Convertible mortgage: An ARM that may be converted to a fixed-rate mortgage at one or more specified times over its term.

Correspondent: A mortgage bank that originates loans that are sold to other lenders. The correspondent performs some or all of the loan processing functions, as well as underwriting and funding the mortgage at settlement. Typically, the mortgage is closed in the correspondent's name.

Direct endorsement: A HUD program that enables an eligible lender to process and close single-family applications for FHA-insured loans without HUD's prior review.

Discount rate: Used to calculate the present value of future cash flow streams generated by MSR. In more general terms, it is the rate at which future dollars are converted into present value. The time value of money can be interpreted as the rate at which individuals are willing to trade present for future consumption, or as the opportunity cost of capital.

Down payment assistance program: A product developed to assist home buyers who can qualify for a mortgage loan except for the required down payment and closing costs.

Early pool buyouts: An agency-approved loan servicing option of buying eligible delinquent loans from Ginnie Mae pools to eliminate exposure to principal and interest payment pass-through requirements.

Escrow: The portion of the borrower's monthly payments held by the servicer to pay taxes, insurance, mortgage insurance (if required), and other related expenses as they become due. In some parts of the United States, escrows are also known as impounds or reserves.

Escrow analysis: The periodic review of escrow accounts to determine whether current monthly deposits will provide sufficient funds to pay taxes, insurance, and related expenses when due.

Excess yield: The interest rate spread between the weighted average coupon rate (WAC) of a mortgage loan pool and the pass-through interest rate after deducting the servicing fee and guarantee fee. For example, when the WAC is 9 percent for the pool, the pass-through rate is 8.50 percent, the servicing fee is 0.25 percent, and the guarantee fee is 0.21 percent, then the excess yield is 0.04 percent.

Fallout: Loans in the origination pipeline that do not close, or close under terms different from initial expectations (e.g., a rate-locked loan is allowed to close at lower rate to retain the customer). The historical fallout ratio is used to estimate the desired coverage for expected loan closings (pull-through) subject to price risk in the secondary market. Volatile rate changes can significantly affect expected fallout and make pipeline hedging more difficult.

Federal Home Loan Banks (FHLB): Privately capitalized GSEs designed to help finance the country's housing and community development needs. Certain FHLBs purchase single-family mortgages from their member financial institutions. These mortgages must meet the same requirements as mortgages that Fannie Mae and Freddie Mac are permitted to purchase (i.e., one- to four-family conforming loans within the size limit established by Congress).

Federal Home Loan Mortgage Corporation (Freddie Mac): A stockholder-owned corporation created by Congress under the Emergency Home Finance Act of 1970. Freddie Mac operates mortgage purchase and securitization programs to support the secondary market in mortgages on residential property.

Federal Housing Administration (FHA): A federal agency within HUD, established in 1934 under the National Housing Act. The FHA supports the secondary market in mortgages on residential property by providing mortgage insurance for certain residential mortgages.

Federal National Mortgage Association (Fannie Mae): A stockholder-owned corporation (formerly the Federal National Mortgage Bank) created by Congress in a 1968 amendment to the National Housing Act. Fannie Mae operates mortgage purchase and securitization programs to support the secondary market in mortgages on residential property.

FHA loan: A loan insured by the FHA and made through an approved lender.

FHA value: The value established by the FHA as the basis for determining the maximum mortgage amount that may be insured for a particular property. The FHA value is the sum of the appraised value plus the FHA estimate of closing costs.

Fixed-rate mortgage: An amortizing mortgage for which the interest rate and payments remain the same over the life of the loan.

Float: In mortgage servicing, the period between receipt of a borrower's loan payment and remittance of funds to investors.

Floor (interest rate): An investor safeguard on an ARM that limits the amount the interest rate may decline per period or over the life of the loan. See also **cap**.

Forbearance: In mortgage banking, the act of refraining from taking legal action when a mortgage is delinquent. Forbearance usually is granted only if a borrower has made satisfactory arrangements to pay the amount owed at a future date.

Foreclosure: The process by which a party who has loaned money secured by a mortgage or deed of trust on real property (or has an unpaid judgment) requires sale of the real property to recover the money due and unpaid interest, plus the costs of foreclosure, when the debtor fails to make payment. After the payments on the promissory note (which is evidence of the loan) have become delinquent for several months (time varies from state to state), the lender can have a notice of default served on the debtor (borrower) stating the amount due and the amount necessary to "cure" the default. If the delinquency and costs of foreclosure are not paid within a specified period, then the lender (or the trustee in states using deeds of trust) will set a foreclosure date, after which the property may be sold at public sale. Up to the time of foreclosure (or even afterward in some states), the defaulting borrower can pay all delinquencies and costs (which are then greater due to foreclosure costs) and "redeem" the property. Upon sale of the property, the amount due is paid to the creditor (lender or owner of the judgment), and the remainder of the money received from the sale, if any, is paid to the lender.

Ginnie Mae buybacks: See **early pool buyouts**.

Ginnie Mae I: A mortgage-backed security program in which individual mortgage lenders issue securities backed by the "full faith and credit of the United States government." The mortgages comprising the security are government-insured or government-guaranteed. The issuer is responsible for passing principal and interest payments directly to the securities holders, whether or not the homeowner makes the monthly payment on the mortgage. All mortgages in a Ginnie Mae I pool must have the same note rate.

Ginnie Mae II: Under the Ginnie Mae II program, monthly payments are made to the security holders through a paying agent. Multiple issuer pools may be formed through the aggregation of loan packages of more than one Ginnie Mae issuer. Under this option, packages submitted by various Ginnie Mae issuers for a particular issue date and pass-through rate are aggregated into a single pool backing a single issue of Ginnie Mae II certificates. Each security issued under a multiple issuer pool is backed by a proportionate interest in the entire pool rather than solely by the loan package contributed by any one Ginnie Mae issuer. Single-issuer pools also may be formed. Mortgages underlying a particular Ginnie Mae II certificate may have annual interest rates that vary from one another by established thresholds.

Government National Mortgage Association (Ginnie Mae): A federal government corporation created as part of HUD in 1968 by an amendment to the National Housing Act. Ginnie Mae guarantees mortgage-backed securities that are insured by the FHA or guaranteed by the VA and backed by the full faith and credit of the U.S. government.

Government-sponsored enterprise (GSE): A private organization with a government charter and backing. Freddie Mac and Fannie Mae are GSEs.

Graduated-payment mortgage (GPM): A flexible-payment mortgage in which the payments increase for a specified period and then level off. GPMs usually result in negative amortization during the early years of the mortgage's life.

Growing equity mortgage: A graduated-payment mortgage in which increases in the borrower's mortgage payments are used to accelerate reduction of principal on the loan. These mortgages do not involve negative amortization.

Guarantee fee: The fee paid to a federal agency or private entity in return for its agreement to accept a portion of the loss exposure on a loan. Currently, typical guarantee fees required by Fannie Mae and Freddie Mac for loan sales without recourse range from 0.16 percent to 0.25 percent of the pool balance annually. The Ginnie Mae guarantee fee on pools of federally insured or guaranteed loans is lower, 0.06 percent annually.

Guarantee fee buy-down: An arrangement in which the seller of mortgages pays a lower guarantee fee in return for less cash when the loans are sold. Guarantee fee buy-downs allow a bank to collect a higher excess servicing fee over the life of the serviced loans. See also **guarantee fee**.

Guarantee fee buy-up: An up-front fee paid to a loan seller in exchange for a higher guarantee fee. Guarantee fee buy-ups increase the cash received for mortgages when they are sold and reduce the excess servicing fee to be collected over the life of the underlying serviced loans. See also **guarantee fee**.

Hazard insurance: Insurance coverage that protects the insured in case of property loss or damage.

High-LTV residential real estate loan: Any loan, line of credit, or combination of credits secured by liens on or interests in owner-occupied one- to four-family residential property that equals or exceeds 90 percent of the property's appraised value, unless the loan has appropriate credit support. Appropriate credit support may include mortgage insurance, readily marketable collateral, or other acceptable collateral that reduces the LTV ratio below 90 percent.

Interest-only loan (IO loan): A loan on which the borrower is required to pay only interest for a specified number of years (e.g., three or five years). IO loans can be fixed-rate, hybrid, or ARMs. ARMs make up a large portion of IO loans.

Interest-only security (IO security): A security that pays only the interest distributions from a pool of underlying loans. The principal cash flows from the underlying loans are paid to a separate principal-only security. The cash flows from the underlying loans are thus "stripped" into two separate securities. Because the IO security holder receives only interest distributions, the value of the IO security decreases when prepayments on the underlying loans increase, because a fixed amount of cash flow is received for a shorter period than the investor expected. Servicing rights have cash flow risks similar to those of IO securities.

Interest-only strip: A contractual right to receive some or all of the interest due on a bond, mortgage loan, CMO, or other interest-bearing financial asset. The interest-only strip or "excess yield" consists of forward-looking estimates of interest earned on the underlying assets, less the servicing fee paid to the servicer, administration and trustee fees, the coupon paid to investors, and credit losses. Interest-only strips may or may not be in the form of a security.

Investor: A person or institution that buys mortgage loans or securities or has a financial interest in these instruments.

Investor advances: In mortgage banking, funds advanced and costs incurred by the servicer on behalf of a delinquent mortgagor.

Jumbo loan: A mortgage in an amount larger than the statutory limit on loans that may be purchased or securitized by Fannie Mae or Freddie Mac.

Loan guarantee certificate: A VA document that certifies the dollar amount of a mortgage loan that is guaranteed.

Loan-to-value ratio (LTV): The ratio of the mortgage amount to the appraised value of the underlying property. Most mortgage lenders and secondary marketing participants set a maximum LTV for acceptable loans.

Locking the loan: A borrower's exercise of his or her option to lock in an interest rate and points. A lock can be exercised at the time of application or later.

Mandatory commitment: A bank's obligation to deliver a specific dollar volume of mortgages to an investor. If the bank is unable to deliver the required volume within the specified commitment period, it may be required to either purchase loans from other sources to deliver or pay the investor a pair-off fee.

Margin: In an ARM, the spread between the index rate used and the mortgage interest rate.

Mortgage banker: An individual or firm that originates, purchases, sells, or services loans secured by mortgages on real property.

Mortgage broker: An individual or firm that receives a commission for matching mortgage borrowers with lenders. Mortgage brokers typically do not fund the loans they help originate.

Mortgage insurance (MI): Insurance coverage that protects mortgage lenders or investors in the event the borrower defaults. By absorbing some of the credit risk, MI allows lenders to make loans with lower down payments. The federal government offers MI for FHA loans; private companies offer MI for conventional loans. See also **private mortgage insurance**.

Mortgage pool: A group of mortgage loans with similar characteristics that are combined to form the underlying collateral of an MBS.

Mortgage servicing asset (MSA), also known as **mortgage servicing rights (MSR):** The right of a bank to service a mortgage loan or a portfolio of loans for another bank's account. The cost associated with acquiring these rights may be capitalized under certain circumstances.

Negative amortization: The addition of due but unpaid interest to the principal of a mortgage loan, causing the loan balance to increase rather than decrease. Negative amortization occurs when the periodic installment payments on a loan are insufficient to repay interest due.

Negative carry, also known as **negative spread:** In warehousing, the expense incurred when the interest rate paid for short-term warehouse financing is greater than the interest rate earned on the mortgages held in the warehouse.

Negative convexity: A bond characteristic also referred to as price compression, such that the price appreciation will be less than the price depreciation for a large change in yield of a given number of basis points. For example, a fixed-rate mortgage may lose more value as rates go down because of prepayments than it gains as rates go up for a given change in rates.

Nonconforming mortgage: A mortgage loan that does not meet the standards of eligibility for purchase or securitization by Fannie Mae or Freddie Mac, because the loan amount, the LTV ratio, the term, or some other aspect of the loan does not conform to the agencies' standards.

Nontraditional mortgage product: A type of mortgage that allows borrowers to defer payment of principal and sometimes interest. Examples include interest-only loans and payment-option ARMs.

Normal servicing fee: The rate representative of what an investor pays to the servicer for performing servicing duties for similar loans. The servicing fee rates set by Ginnie Mae and the GSEs are generally considered normal servicing fees. Currently, the normal servicing fee rate is 0.25 percent for fixed-rate mortgages, 0.375 percent for ARMs, and 0.44 percent for federally insured and guaranteed loans. A bank may not use its cost to service loans as the normal servicing fee.

Option-adjusted spread (OAS): A methodology using option pricing techniques to value the embedded options risk component of a bond's total spread. OAS measures the incremental return of a fixed-income security, adjusted for embedded options, compared with the term structure of interest rates. OAS is quoted as a spread expressed in basis points.

Optional delivery commitment: See **best efforts commitment**.

Origination fee: The fee a lender charges to prepare documents, make credit checks, and inspect a property being financed. Origination fees are usually stated as a percentage of the face value of the loan.

Overage pricing: Increasing the price or cost (interest rate, fees, or points) of a mortgage loan above the bank's standard rate and fees/points schedule.

Pair-off arrangement: A method to offset a commitment to sell and deliver mortgages. In this transaction, the seller liquidates its commitment to sell (forward sales contract) by paying the counterparty a fee. The amount of this pair-off fee equals the impact of the market movement on the price of mortgages covered under the commitment.

Pair-off fee: See **pair-off arrangement**.

Participation certificate (PC): A mortgage pass-through security issued by Freddie Mac that is backed by a pool of conventional mortgages purchased from a seller. The seller retains a 5 percent to 10 percent interest in the pool.

Pass-through: An MBS in which principal, interest, and prepayments are passed through to the investors as received. The mortgage collateral is held by a trust in which the investors own an undivided interest.

Pass-through rate: The interest rate paid to investors that purchase mortgage loans or MBSs. Typically, the pass-through rate is less than the coupon rate of the underlying mortgages.

Pipeline: In mortgage lending, loan applications in process that have not closed.

Pledged account mortgage: A graduated-payment loan in which part of the borrower's down payment is deposited into a savings account. Funds drawn from the account supplement the borrower's monthly payments during the early years of the mortgage.

Pool: A collection of mortgage loans with similar characteristics.

Positive carry, also known as **positive spread:** In warehousing, the excess income that results when the interest rate paid for short-term warehouse financing is less than the interest rate earned on the mortgages held in the warehouse.

Prepayment: The payment of all or part of a loan before it is contractually due.

Prepayment speed: The rate at which mortgage prepayments occur or are projected to occur, expressed as a percentage of the outstanding principal balance. See also **conditional prepayment rate**, **Public Securities Administration prepayment model**, and **single monthly mortality**.

Price-level-adjusted mortgage: A mortgage loan in which the interest rate remains fixed but the outstanding balance is periodically adjusted for inflation using an appropriate index such as the consumer price index or cost-of-living index. At the end of each period, the outstanding balance is adjusted for inflation and monthly payments are recomputed based on the new balance.

Primary market: For a mortgage lender, the market in which it originates mortgages and lends funds directly to homeowners.

Principal-only security (PO): A security that pays only the principal distributions from a pool of underlying loans. The interest cash flows from the underlying loans are paid to a separate interest-only (IO) security. The cash flows from the underlying loans are thus "stripped" into two separate securities. Because the PO holder receives only principal distributions, the value of the PO rises when prepayments on the underlying loans increase, because a fixed amount of cash flow is received sooner than expected. As a result, mortgage bankers often use PO to hedge the value of servicing rights, which have cash flow risks similar to those of IO securities.

Private mortgage insurance (PMI): Insurance coverage written by a private company that protects the mortgage lender in the event of default by the borrower. See also **mortgage insurance**.

Production flow: The purchase of mortgage loans in combination with the rights to service those loans. The entity acquiring the mortgage loans then resells the loans but retains the accompanying servicing rights.

Public Securities Administration (PSA) prepayment model: A standard of measurement of the projected annual rate of prepayment for a mortgage loan or pool of loans. A 100 PSA prepayment rate assumes that loans prepay at a 6 percent annual rate after the 30th month of origination. From origination to the 30th month, the annualized prepayment rate increases in a linear manner by 0.2 percent each month (6 percent divided by 30). For example, the annualized prepayment on a pool of mortgages would be 0.2 percent when the loans are one month old, 1 percent when the loans are five months old, 4.8 percent at 24 months, and 6 percent at 30 months and beyond. PSA speeds increase or decrease to reflect faster or slower prepayment projections. To illustrate, 200 PSA after the 30th month equals a 12 percent annual prepayment rate, and 50 PSA equals a 3 percent annual prepayment rate. See also **conditional prepayment rate** and **single monthly mortality**.

Quality control (QC): In mortgage banking, policies and procedures designed to maintain optimal levels of quality, accuracy, and efficiency in producing, selling, and servicing mortgage loans.

Real Estate Settlement Procedures Act (RESPA): The Real Estate Settlement Procedures Act of 1974 (12 USC 2601-17) became effective on June 20, 1975. RESPA requires lenders, mortgage brokers, and servicers of home loans to provide borrowers with pertinent and timely disclosures of the nature and costs of the real estate settlement process. The act also protects borrowers against certain abusive practices, such as kickbacks, and places limitations on the use of escrow accounts.

Regulation AB: Regulation AB, and the related rules governing offerings of asset-backed and mortgage-backed securities, provides a consolidated, comprehensive set of registration, disclosure, and reporting requirements for these securities. The rules, which were adopted by the SEC in December 2004, require extensive additional disclosure in asset-backed security prospectuses, including expanded descriptions and financial disclosure regarding transaction parties, and static pool data for portfolios and prior securitizations. The rules include, among other things, requirements for additional periodic reports and new standards for assessment of servicing compliance and the related accountants' attestation.

Retail production: Mortgage loan production for which the origination and underwriting process was handled exclusively by the bank or a consolidated subsidiary of the bank.

Reverse mortgage: A mortgage loan that lets homeowners over 62 years of age convert a portion of their home equity into cash. Reverse mortgage products are sponsored by FHA/HUD, Fannie Mae, and a small number of private lenders, and are offered by many mortgage banks. Reverse mortgages allow borrowers to access their home equity in several ways, including a lump-sum payment, a line of credit, payments over a specified term, or payments for life. Unlike a traditional mortgage, no repayment is required until the borrower no longer uses the home as a principal residence.

Roll rates: Roll rates measure the movement of accounts and balances from one payment status to another (e.g., percentage of accounts or dollars that were current last month rolling to 30 days past due this month).

Satisfaction, also known as **reconveyance:** Once a mortgage or deed of trust is paid, the holder of the mortgage is required to satisfy the mortgage or deed of trust of record to show that the mortgage or deed of trust is no longer a lien on the property.

Scratch-and-dent mortgage: A mortgage that fails to meet all the underwriting requirements or standard representations and warranties in a sales transaction. These mortgages are typically returned or retained by the bank and sold in separate transactions, in which the deficiencies are acknowledged by the buyer.

Seasoned mortgage portfolio: A mortgage portfolio that has reached its peak delinquency level, generally after 30 to 48 months.

Secondary mortgage market: The market in which lenders and investors buy and sell existing mortgages.

Servicing, also known as **loan administration:** A mortgage banking function that includes document custodianship, receipt of payments, cash management, escrow administration, investor accounting, customer service, loan setup and payoff, collections, and the administration of OREO.

Servicing agreement: A written agreement between an investor and a mortgage servicer stipulating the rights and obligations of each party.

Servicing fee: The contractual fee due to the mortgage servicer for performing various loan servicing duties for investors.

Servicing released: A stipulation in a mortgage sales agreement specifying that the seller is not responsible for servicing the loans.

Servicing retained: A stipulation in a mortgage sales agreement specifying that, in return for a fee, the seller is responsible for servicing the mortgages.

Servicing runoff: Reduction in the principal of a servicing portfolio resulting from monthly payments, mortgage prepayments, and foreclosures. Runoff reduces future servicing fee income and other related cash flows as well as the current market value of the servicing portfolio.

Settlement: The consummation of a transaction. In mortgage lending, the closing of a mortgage loan or the delivery of a loan or security to a buyer. See also **closing**.

Shared appreciation mortgage: A mortgage loan in which the lender offers the borrower a below-market interest rate in exchange for a portion of the profit earned when the property is sold.

Short sale: An arrangement entered into between a loan servicer and a delinquent borrower. The servicer allows the borrower to sell the property to a third party at less than the outstanding balance. This saves the servicer the time and expense involved in a foreclosure action. The servicer must normally obtain the approval of the investor before entering into a short sale agreement. See also **forbearance**.

Single monthly mortality: The conditional prepayment rate expressed on a monthly basis. See also **conditional prepayment rate** and **Public Securities Administration prepayment model**.

Static pool analysis: A measure for assessing the performance of a pool of serviced loans by providing a cumulative default and prepayment history for estimating expected future portfolio cash flows and determining the cash yield on servicing assets. Static pool analysis captures information from a specified population of loans originated or acquired during a specified time frame or from a specific origination source, and tracks scheduled payments, prepayments, and default frequency. The information is used to determine performance behavior for evaluation of portfolio cash flow dynamics. These statistics can identify high-risk segments of the portfolio of serviced assets and allow management to determine why a segment failed to perform as profitably as expected.

Subprime loans, also known as **nonprime:** Generally, loans whose borrowers have weakened or incomplete credit histories or reduced repayment capacity.

Table funding: A method of acquiring mortgage loans from third parties, such as brokers or correspondents. As defined in RESPA, table funding is a settlement at which a loan is funded by a contemporaneous advance of loan funds and an assignment of the loan to the party advancing the funds.

VA: See **Veterans Affairs**.

VA loan: A loan made through an approved lender and partly guaranteed by the U.S. Department of Veterans Affairs.

VA no-bid: An option that allows the VA to pay only the amount of its guarantee on a defaulted mortgage loan, leaving the investor with the title to the foreclosed property. The

VA must exercise this option when it is in the government's best interest. No-bid properties become OREO.

Vantage score: A credit risk score that was developed through the use of information from the three national credit reporting companies. In the past, the agencies had each used their own proprietary formulas to create their own scores. With vantage score, a single methodology is used to create the scores.

Veterans Affairs (VA): The U.S. Department of Veterans Affairs, formerly called the Veterans Administration, now a Cabinet-level agency of the U.S. government. The Servicemen's Readjustment Act of 1944 authorized the VA to offer the Home Loan Guaranty program to veterans. The program encourages mortgage lenders to offer long-term, low-down-payment financing to eligible veterans by partially guaranteeing the lender against loss.

Vintage analysis: A tool for analyzing performance trends that entails review of actual serviced portfolio behavior and its implication for future default, prepayment, and delinquency rates that affect the value of MSAs. This information can be compared with historical changes in underwriting standards, credit-scoring processes, and new product development to ensure that loan pricing is consistent with perceived product risk.

Warehouse (loan): In mortgage lending, loans that are funded and awaiting sale or delivery to an investor.

Warehouse financing: The short-term borrowing of funds by a mortgage banker based on the collateral of warehouse loans. This form of interim financing is used until the warehouse loans are sold to a permanent investor.

Weighted average coupon rate (WAC): The weighted average of the gross interest rates of the mortgages in a mortgage pool. The balance of each mortgage is used as the weighting factor.

Weighted average maturity: The weighted average of the remaining terms to maturity of the mortgages in a mortgage pool as of the security issue date.

Weighted average remaining maturity: The weighted average of the remaining terms to maturity of the mortgages in a mortgage pool subsequent to the security issue date. The difference between the weighted average maturity and the weighted average remaining maturity is known as the weighted average loan age.

Yield spread premium: Payments from lenders to brokers based on the difference between the interest rate at which a broker originates the loan and the par, or market, rate offered by a lender. Yield spread premiums permit homebuyers to pay some or all of up-front settlement costs over the life of the mortgage through a higher interest rate.

Appendix H: Abbreviations

ABA:	affiliated business arrangement
AFS:	available for sale
ALLL:	allowance for loan and lease losses
ARM:	adjustable rate mortgage
ASC:	Accounting Standards Codification
AUS:	automated underwriting system
AVM:	automated valuation model
BSA:	Bank Secrecy Act
CFPB:	Consumer Financial Protection Bureau
CLO:	computerized loan origination system
CLTV:	combined loan to value
CMM:	constant maturity mortgage
CMO:	collateralized mortgage obligation
CPR:	conditional prepayment rate
DTI:	debt to income
EaR:	earnings at risk
ECOA:	Equal Credit Opportunity Act
EIC:	examiner-in-charge
EPD:	early payment default
EPO:	early payoff
E&O:	errors and omissions
Fannie Mae:	Federal National Mortgage Association
FASB:	Federal Accounting Standards Board
FCRA:	Fair Credit Reporting Act
FDIC:	Federal Deposit Insurance Corporation
FFIEC:	Federal Financial Institutions Examination Council
FHA:	Federal Housing Administration
FHLB:	Federal Home Loan Bank
FRA:	forward rate agreement
Freddie Mac:	Federal Home Loan Mortgage Corporation
FSA:	federal savings association
FTC:	Federal Trade Commission
GAAP:	generally accepted accounting principles
Ginnie Mae:	Government National Mortgage Association
GPM:	graduated-payment mortgage
GSE:	government-sponsored enterprise
G&A:	general and administrative
HAMP:	Home Affordable Modification Program
HELOC:	home equity line of credit
HMDA:	Home Mortgage Disclosure Act
HOEPA:	Home Ownership and Equity Protection Act
HPA:	Homeowners Protection Act
HUD:	U.S. Department of Housing and Urban Development
ICQ:	internal control questionnaire

IO:	interest only
IT:	information technology
LIBOR:	London interbank offered rate
LOCOM:	lower of cost or market
LPO:	loan production office
LTV:	loan to value
MBS:	mortgage-backed security
MERS:	Mortgage Electronic Registration Systems
MI:	mortgage insurance
MIS:	management information system
MPF:	Mortgage Partnership Finance Program
MPP:	Mortgage Partnership Program
MRA:	matter requiring attention
MSA:	mortgage servicing asset
MSL:	mortgage servicing liability
MSR:	mortgage servicing rights
NIM:	net interest margin
OAS:	option-adjusted spread
OCC:	Office of the Comptroller of the Currency
OREO:	other real estate owned
OTC:	over the counter
PC:	participation certificate
PMI:	private mortgage insurance
PO:	principal only
PSA:	Public Securities Association
QC:	quality control
QSPE:	qualified special purpose entity
RESPA:	Real Estate Settlement Procedures Act
SCRA:	Servicemembers Civil Relief Act
SMM:	single monthly mortality
SPE:	special purpose entity
SRP:	servicing release premium
TBA:	to be announced
TILA:	Truth in Lending Act
USAP:	Uniform Single Attestation Program
VA:	U.S. Department of Veterans Affairs
VaR:	value at risk
WAC:	weighted average coupon rate

References

Federal Consumer Protection Laws and Implementing Regulations Applicable to Real Estate Lending

Community Reinvestment Act: 12 USC 2901 et seq; 12 CFR 25

Equal Credit Opportunity Act: 15 USC 1691 et seq; 12 CFR 1002 (Regulation B)

Fair Credit Reporting Act: 15 USC 1681 et seq as amended by the Fair and Accurate Credit Transactions Act; 12 CFR 1022 (Regulation V)

Fair Debt Collection Practices Act: 15 USC 1692 et seq; 12 CFR 1006 (Regulation F)

Fair Housing Act: 42 USC 3601 et seq; 24 CFR 100 and 110

Federal Trade Commission Act: 15 USC 45

Flood Disaster Protection Act: 42 USC 4001–4129 12 CFR 22 (NB), 12 CFR 172 (FSA)

Gramm-Leach-Bliley Act: 15 USC 6801 et seq; 12 CFR 1016 (Regulation P)

Home Mortgage Disclosure Act: 12 USC 2801 et seq; 12 CFR 1003 (Regulation C)

Homeowners Protection Act: 12 USC 4901 et seq

Home Ownership and Equity Protection Act: 15 USC 1601 et seq (amended TILA); 12 CFR 1026.32 (Regulation Z)

Protecting Tenants at Foreclosure Act: 12 USC 5220, note

Real Estate Settlement Procedures Act: 12 USC 2601 et seq; 12 CFR 1024 (Regulation X)

Secure and Fair Enforcement for Mortgage Licensing Act: 12 USC 5101 et seq; 12 CFR 1008 (Regulation H)

Truth in Lending Act (TILA): 15 USC 1601 et seq; 12 CFR 1026 (Regulation Z)

Other Laws and Regulations Applicable to Real Estate Lending

National Bank Statutes and Regulations

12 USC 24, "Corporate Powers of Associations"

12 USC 29, "Power to Hold Real Property"

12 USC 371, "Real Estate Loans"

12 USC 484, "Limitation on Visitorial Powers"

12 CFR 3, appendix A, section 3, "Risk-Based Capital: Residential Mortgage Loans Modified Pursuant to the Home Affordable Mortgage Program"

12 CFR 7, "Bank Activities and Operations"

12 CFR 21.11, "Suspicious Activity Report"

12 CFR 27, "Fair Housing Home Loan Data System"

12 CFR 30, "Safety and Soundness Standards"

12 CFR 30, appendix C, "OCC Guidelines Establishing Standards for Residential Mortgage Lending Practices"

12 CFR 34, "Real Estate Lending and Appraisals"

12 CFR 37, "Debt Cancellation Contracts and Debt Suspension Agreements"

FSA Statutes and Regulations

12 USC 1461 et seq, "Home Owners' Loan Act"

12 USC 1464, "Federal Savings Associations"

12 CFR 128, "Nondiscrimination Requirements"
12 CFR 160.30, "General Lending and Investment Powers of Federal Savings Associations"
12 CFR 160, "Lending and Investment"
12 CFR 160.101, "Real Estate Lending Standards"
12 CFR 160.110, "Most Favored Lender Usury Preemption for All Savings Associations"
12 CFR 160.170, "Records for Lending Transactions"
12 CFR 162, "Regulatory Reporting Standards
12 CFR 163.176, "Interest-Rate-Risk-Management Procedures"
12 CFR 163.180, "Suspicious Activity Reports and Other Reports and Statements"
12 CFR 164, "Appraisals"
12 CFR 167.5, "Components of Capital"
12 CFR 167.6, "Risk-Based Capital Credit Risk-Weight Categories"
12 CFR 170, "Safety and Soundness Guidelines and Compliance Procedures"
12 CFR 190.4, "Federally Related Residential Manufactured Housing Loans—Consumer Protection Provisions"

Other Agency Statutes and Regulations

12 USC 1818, "Termination of Status as Insured Depository Institution"
31 USC 5312(a)(2), "Bank Secrecy Act"
17 CFR 229.1100, "Asset-Backed Securities" (Regulation AB)
24 CFR 203, subpart C, "Servicing Responsibilities"
12 CFR 330.7(d), "Accounts Held by Agent, Nominee, Guardian, Custodian, or Conservator"

Comptroller's Handbook

Examination Process

"Bank Supervision Process"
"Community Bank Supervision"
"Federal Branches and Agencies Supervision"
"Large Bank Supervision"
"Sampling Methodologies"

Safety and Soundness, Asset Quality

"Other Real Estate Owned"
"Residential Real Estate Lending" (to be published)
"Retail Lending Examination Procedures"

Safety and Soundness, Liquidity

"Asset Securitization"

Safety and Soundness, Management

"Internal and External Audits"
"Internal Control"

Asset Management
    "Custody Services"

Consumer Compliance
    "Fair Credit Reporting"
    "Fair Lending"
    "Flood Disaster Protection Act"
    "Home Mortgage Disclosure Act"
    "Other Consumer Protection Laws and Regulations"
    "Privacy of Consumer Financial Information"
    "Protecting Tenants at Foreclosure Act"
    "Real Estate Settlement Procedures Act"
    "Servicemembers Civil Relief Act"
    "Truth in Lending Act"

OCC Issuances

Advisory Letter 2000-7, "Abusive Lending Practices" (July 25, 2000)

Advisory Letter 2002-3, "Guidance on Unfair or Deceptive Acts or Practices" (March 22, 2002)

Advisory Letter 2003-2, "Guidelines for National Banks to Guard Against Predatory and Abusive Lending Practices" (February 21, 2003)

Advisory Letter 2003-3, "Avoiding Predatory and Abusive Lending Practices in Brokered and Purchased Loans" (February 21, 2003)

OCC Bulletin 1997-24, "Credit Scoring Models: Examination Guidance" (May 20, 1997)

OCC Bulletin 1999-10, "Interagency Guidance on Subprime Lending" (March 5, 1999)

OCC Bulletin 1999-38, "Interagency Guidelines for Real Estate Lending Policies: Treatment of High LTV Residential Real Estate Loans" (October 13, 1999)

OCC Bulletin 1999-46, "Interagency Guidance on Asset Securitization Activities" (December 13, 1999)

OCC Bulletin 2000-3, "Consumer Credit Reporting Practices: FFIEC Advisory Letter" (February 16, 2000)

OCC Bulletin 2001-6, "Expanded Guidance for Subprime Lending Programs" (January 31, 2001)

OCC Bulletin 2001-37, "Policy Statement on Allowance for Loan and Lease Losses Methodologies and Documentation for Banks and Savings Institutions" (July 20, 2001)

OCC Bulletin 2002-20, "Implicit Recourse in Asset Securitization: Policy Implementation" (May 23, 2002)

OCC Bulletin 2002-22, "Capital Treatment of Recourse, Direct Credit Substitutes, and Residual Interests in Asset Securitizations: Interpretations of Final Rule" (May 23, 2002)

OCC Bulletin 2003-01, "Credit Card Lending: Account Management and Loss Allowance Guidance" (January 8, 2003)

OCC Bulletin 2003-9, "Mortgage Banking: Interagency Advisory on Mortgage Banking" (February 25, 2003)

OCC Bulletin 2003-21, "Application of Recent Corporate Governance Initiatives to Non-Public Banking Organizations: Interagency Statement" (May 29, 2003)

OCC Bulletin 2005-6, "Appraisal Regulations and the Interagency Statement on Independent Appraisal and Evaluation Functions: Frequently Asked Questions" (March 22, 2005)

OCC Bulletin 2005-18, "Interagency Advisory on Accounting and Reporting for Commitments to Originate and Sell Mortgage Loans" (May 3, 2005)

OCC Bulletin 2005-22, "Home Equity Lending: Credit Risk Management Guidance" (May 16, 2005)

OCC Bulletin 2005-27, "Real Estate Settlement Procedures Act: Sham Controlled Business Arrangements" (August 4, 2005)

OCC Bulletin 2006-43, "Home Equity Lending: Addendum to OCC Bulletin 2005-22" (October 4, 2006)

OCC Bulletin 2006-41, "Guidance on Nontraditional Mortgage Product Risks" (October 4, 2006)

OCC Bulletin 2007-14, "Working with Mortgage Borrowers: Interagency Statement" (April 18, 2007)

OCC Bulletin 2007-26, "Statement on Subprime Mortgage Lending" (July 25, 2007)

OCC Bulletin 2007-28, "Nontraditional Mortgage Products: Illustrations of Consumer Information" (August 21, 2007)

OCC Bulletin 2007-38, "Working with Borrowers: Statement on Residential Real Estate Loan Restructurings for Serviced Loans" (October 11, 2007)

OCC Bulletin 2007-40, "Limitations on Terms of Consumer Credit Extended to Military Service Members and Dependents: Department of Defense Final Rule" (October 17, 2007)

OCC Bulletin 2007-47, "Implementation of the Advanced Approaches of the Basel II Capital Accord: Final Rulemaking" (December 7, 2007)

OCC Bulletin 2009-11, "Other-Than-Temporary Impairment Accounting: OCC Advisory on Financial Accounting Standards Board Changes" (April 17, 2009)

OCC Bulletin 2009-23, "Fair Credit Reporting: Accuracy and Integrity of Consumer Report Information and Direct Consumer Dispute Regulations and Guidelines: Final Rules and Guidelines Together With Advance Notice of Proposed Rulemaking" (July 20, 2009)

OCC Bulletin 2010-25, "Property Assessed Clean Energy PACE) Programs: Supervisory Guidance" (July 6, 2010)

OCC Bulletin 2010-42, "Sound Practices for Appraisals and Evaluations: Interagency Appraisal and Evaluation Guidelines" (December 10, 2010)

OCC Bulletin 2011-6, "SAFE Act Mortgage Loan Originator Registration Requirements: Notice of Initial Registration Period" (February 3, 2011)

OCC Bulletin 2011-12, "Sound Practices for Model Risk Management" (April 4, 2011)

OCC Bulletin 2011-16, "Servicemembers Civil Relief Act: Revised Examination Procedures" (May 3, 2011)

OCC Bulletin 2011-15, "Protecting Tenants at Foreclosure Act of 2009: Revised Examination Procedures" (May 3, 2011)

OCC Bulletin 2013-19, "Commercial Real Estate Lending: Comptroller's Handbook Revisions and Recissions" (August 20, 2013)

OCC Bulletin 2013-29, "Third-Party Relationships: Risk Management Guidance" (October 30, 2013)

Other

FFIEC "Instructions for Preparation of Consolidated Reports of Condition and Income" (call report instructions)

FFIEC Information Technology Examination Handbook

FFIEC, "The Detection and Deterrence of Mortgage Fraud Against Financial Institutions: A White Paper" (February 2010)

49317381R00143

Made in the USA
Lexington, KY
01 February 2016